YOUR KNOWLEDGE

- We will publish your bachelor's and master's thesis, essays and papers

- Your own eBook and book - sold worldwide in all relevant shops

- Earn money with each sale

Upload your text at www.GRIN.com and publish for free

Stefanie Merenyi

Consolidated Substances Legislation (CSL)

Band 2

REACH: Regulation (EC) No 1907/2006

Consolidated version (June 2012) with an introduction and future prospects regarding the area of Chemicals legislation

GRIN Verlag

Bibliografische Information der Deutschen Nationalbibliothek:

Die Deutsche Bibliothek verzeichnet diese Publikation in der Deutschen National-
bibliografie; detaillierte bibliografische Daten sind im Internet über http://dnb.d-
nb.de/ abrufbar.

Imprint:

Copyright © 2012 GRIN Verlag GmbH
Druck und Bindung: Books on Demand GmbH, Norderstedt Germany
ISBN: 978-3-656-29438-2

This book at GRIN:

http://www.grin.com/en/e-book/203248/reach-regulation-ec-no-1907-2006

Stefanie Merenyi
Rechtsanwältin
Dipl.-Informationswirtin (Chemie)

Consolidated Substances Legislation

REACH
Regulation 1907/2006
**Consolidated version
June 2012**

For Layla Gabrielle

Preface

Chemicals legislation is quite a dynamic regulatory arena. As is the case in the science of Chemistry there is also no standstill in chemicals legislation. Most of the relevant regulations are subject to permanent revisions.

In order to keep up with the actual legislation beyond the efforts of a loose-leaf-binder the series

CSL: Consolidated Substances Legislation

has been created.

It offers a compact outline regarding the different fields of substances legislation (besides the general substances legislation like REACH also cosmetics legislation, etc.) and provides users with the relevant legislative texts in an actual and **consolidated** manner, i.e. starting from the original regulation all modifications can be found at their respective position within the legal text. Therefore, the need for a detailed compilation of each and any corrigendum, amendment and adaptation to the technical progress can be reduced to a minimum.

The area of substances legislation is both a fascinating and demanding legal field that can hardly be compared to any other, as its regulations create direct effects on everyone.

The **CSL** series offers a new access to its original sources.

Schoeneck, Germany, September 2012

Stefanie Merenyi

Introduction

In June 2007 the **REACH** regulation entered into force. Symbolized by its acronym it created the legal base for the most important mechanisms in chemicals legislation, **r**egistration, **e**valuation, **a**uthorisation and restriction of **ch**emicals. Until mid 2012 these mechanisms led to the following results:

Registration

The **obligation to register** substances has been newly implemented with REACH. Therefore, nearly all substances which are produced in or imported into the European Union have to be registered at the European Chemicals Agency (ECHA), however "step-by-step". Substances which are not registered are **not marketable in Europe**. In addition, for example, German law provides for the possibility to prosecute with a maximum penalty of two years prison, persons who are found responsible for production and distribution of substances unregistered contrary to duty. However, the legal consequences of breaches of the REACH regulation differ widely in different Member States.

Registration means the transmission of data about the effects of a certain substance on **man and environment**. Extent and details of the needed data are defined in the Annexes of the REACH regulation and depend on the production/import volume of a substance.

The **first registration phase** ended 1 December 2010. It referred to substances produced in very high amounts (> 1.000 tonnes per year per manufacturer/importer), with certain adverse effects in the aquatic environment, or which are deemed carcinogenic, mutagenic or toxic to reproduction. Within this first phase about **4.300 substances** have been registered. Further information about the registered substances is published on the Agency's webpage (http://echa.europa.eu/information-on-chemicals/registered-substances).

On **1 June 2013** the **second registration phase** will end. By that time all substances produced in amounts of 100 tonnes or more per year per manufacturer/importer must be registered – independent of their hazard property profile. Substances which have already been identified by industry for their registration in this second phase have been collected in a list which can be reviewed at ECHA's website (http://echa.europa.eu/information-on-chemicals/registered-substances/identified-substances-for-registration-in-2013).

All remaining substances – likewise independent of their hazard profile – will have to be registered within the **third and last registration phase**, ending **1 June 2018**.

Substance evaluation

From the multiplicity of registered substances those substances which give **cause for serious concern** and therefore require a closer examination (substance evaluation) will be selected according to the specifications of the regulation (Art. 44). Such a concern can result from an already known **adverse effect** of a substance. Moreover, the selection will consider to what extent man and environment are exposed to the relevant substance **(exposition)** and also its **amounts of production and use** as very high production amounts can indicate a potential wide ranging risk of a substance.

This selection **(prioritisation)** is made by ECHA in collaboration with the 27 EU Member States. It is established within the so called **CoRAP** (Community Rolling Action Plan). The first CoRAP lists 90 substances. It is published at ECHA's webpage   (http://echa.europa.eu/information-on-chemicals/evaluation/community-rolling-action-plan).

Substances listed in the CoRAP are planned to receive a closer evaluation by the 27 EU Member States within a time frame of three years (2012-2014). This evaluation can result in certain provisions under the authorisation- or restriction scheme.

Besides the substance evaluation, REACH also knows two more regulation mechanisms which are also called "evaluation" (cf. http://echa.europa.eu/regulations/reach/evaluation).

Authorisation

The authorisation mechanism probably is the most powerful weapon of chemicals legislation. It has newly been introduced with REACH. The scope of the authorisation regime will exclusively apply to those substances which show certain extremely problematic effects, e. g. carcinogenic, mutagenic or toxic to reproduction (cf. Art. 57).

In a first step the substances of this class can be declared so called "substances of very high concern" **(SVHCs)**. Substances which are declared SVHCs are then included in **Annex XIV** REACH. Until now 14 substances are listed there. Currently 54 more substances are proposed to potentially become SVHCs (cf. http://echa.europa.eu/proposals-to-identify-substances-of-very-high-concern).

Substances listed in Annex XIV are subject to an "authorisation obligation". This means they are **generally no longer allowed to be marketed and used**. Detailed and narrow exemptions (authorisation) from this general ban may be granted by the European Commission following a complex **application procedure**. This in principle banned SVHC may then also be applied again for very specific uses inside the EU.

The grant of an authorisation however requires the applicant's demonstration that the **risks of using a SVHC are adequately controlled** (1st alternative) or that the **significance of the substance outweighs the risks involved**

(2nd alternative). In the case of the 2nd alternative, the definition of trade-offs within the framework is subject of the Socio Economic Analysis (SEA) procedure. Here, the preconditions for the original aim of the authorisation scheme, the **substitution of SVHCs** by **comparably effective but less harmful** alternatives are also to be examined. In the end all SVHCs should become substituted this way.

Restriction

Restriction in the context of the REACH regulation means "any condition for or prohibition of the **manufacture, use** or **placing on the market**" of a certain substance (Art. 3 Nr. 31). Restrictions under REACH therefore differ from restrictions under the former Chemicals legislation. At that time the restriction directive (76/769/EEC) did not refer to any production but mostly to single specific uses of a substance. Moreover, because of its legal nature as a directive, restrictions based on the former mechanism needed a transformation into the national law of the single Member States. REACH as a **regulation**, on the contrary, is binding in its entirety and directly applicable in all Member States.

Many restrictions derived from the old system were transferred into the new restriction scheme under REACH. Together with the newly established restrictions under REACH they are listed in **Annex XVII**, the most extensive Annex of the regulation.

As distinguished from substances within the authorisation scheme which are generally banned, use and marketing of substances in the REACH restriction scheme stays basically permitted. Only those actions which are explicitly described in Annex XVII are prohibited.

Prospects

REACH is described as one of the most complex and demanding regulation efforts of all time. Many problems were unsolved when it was enacted, many problems are still open now. Some questions became apparent only when the regulation was directly applied. Due to the enormous complexity of this regulation system, answers can only be generated step by step. This is why **REACH** appears as a " **learning system**" to everyone engaged, to manufacturers/importers of substances as well as to the administrative, executive and legislative authorities.

The lawmaker itself provided for a number of **review procedures** of the new system and gave detailed time frames within the text of the regulation **(Art. 138)**. Therefore, **amendments** are to be expected **at all levels** of the regulation.

Improvements within the **legislative text** of the regulation itself are to be expected mainly with regard to its **scope** as this was subject to a broad study examining potential overlaps between REACH and other legislation. The European Commission is expected to suggest corresponding developments soon.

A review of the **Annexes I, II, IV, V, XI, XIII und XVII** is already being discussed and can be followed at the webpage of

- GD enterprise
  (http://ec.europa.eu/enterprise/sectors/chemicals/documents/reach/review-annexes/index_en.htm) and
- GD environment
  (http://ec.europa.eu/environment/chemicals/reach/reviews_en.htm).

Finally, further developments are to be expected at the **guidance level** (documents emanated from the former REACH Implementation Projects = RIPs). Here, the topic of **Substance Identity** probably will remain of high significance.

With regard to this,

the book
„**REACH: About Substances and Mixtures**"
will be shortly published –
a **graphical directory**
leading through the vocabulary of scientific (chemical) and legal concepts, i.e. through the world of the producers and applicants of substances (chemists), on the one hand, and the regulators of substances (lawmakers and lawyers) on the other.

As no details are known so far it remains to be seen how lawmakers intend to handle "nanoscale substances or nanomaterials".

The series **C**onsolidated **S**ubstances **L**egislation (**CSL**) will also be reporting on this theme.

Consolidated version of

**REGULATION (EC) No 1907/2006 OF THE EUROPEAN
PARLIAMENT AND OF THE COUNCIL**

of 18 December 2006

concerning the Registration, Evaluation, Authorisation and Restriction of
Chemicals (REACH),

establishing a European Chemicals Agency, amending Directive 1999/45/EC
and repealing

Council Regulation (EEC) No 793/93 and

Commission Regulation (EC) No 1488/94

as well as Council Directive 76/769/EEC and

Commission Directives 91/155/EEC, 93/67/EEC, 93/105/EC and 2000/21/EC

last amended by

Commission Regulation (EU) No 125/2012 of 14 February 2012

Important Notice:

Consolidation implies the integration of Community legislation,
i.e. their basic instruments, amendments and corrections
in one single, non-official document.

Therefore, this document is only intended as a documentation tool.

As outlined by the European Court of Justice several times,
only European Union legislation
printed in the paper edition of the
Official Journal of the European Union
is deemed authentic.

Therefore, the publishers as well as the author exclude liability
for any errors and omissions with regard to
the integrity and accurateness of the following text.

Table of contents of the consolidated version

Origin of the following reproduced legal text:

This document is meant purely as a documentation tool and the institutions do not assume any liability for its contents

►B   ►C1 REGULATION (EC) No 1907/2006 OF THE EUROPEAN PARLIAMENT AND OF THE COUNCIL

of 18 December 2006

concerning the Registration, Evaluation, Authorisation and Restriction of Chemicals (REACH), establishing a European Chemicals Agency, amending Directive 1999/45/EC and repealing Council Regulation (EEC) No 793/93 and Commission Regulation (EC) No 1488/94 as well as Council Directive 76/769/EEC and Commission Directives 91/155/EEC, 93/67/EEC, 93/105/EC and 2000/21/EC

(Text with EEA relevance) ◄

(OJ L 396, 30.12.2006, p. 1)

Amended by:

		Official Journal		
		No	page	date
►M1	Council Regulation (EC) No 1354/2007 of 15 November 2007	L 304	1	22.11.2007
►M2	Commission Regulation (EC) No 987/2008 of 8 October 2008	L 268	14	9.10.2008
►M3	Regulation (EC) No 1272/2008 of the European Parliament and of the Council of 16 December 2008	L 353	1	31.12.2008
►M4	Commission Regulation (EC) No 134/2009 of 16 February 2009	L 46	3	17.2.2009
►M5	Commission Regulation (EC) No 552/2009 of 22 June 2009	L 164	7	26.6.2009
►M6	Commission Regulation (EU) No 276/2010 of 31 March 2010	L 86	7	1.4.2010
►M7	Commission Regulation (EU) No 453/2010 of 20 May 2010	L 133	1	31.5.2010
►M8	Commission Regulation (EU) No 143/2011 of 17 February 2011	L 44	2	18.2.2011
►M9	Commission Regulation (EU) No 207/2011 of 2 March 2011	L 58	27	3.3.2011
►M10	Commission Regulation (EU) No 252/2011 of 15 March 2011	L 69	3	16.3.2011
►M11	Commission Regulation (EU) No 253/2011 of 15 March 2011	L 69	7	16.3.2011
►M12	Commission Regulation (EU) No 366/2011 of 14 April 2011	L 101	12	15.4.2011
►M13	Commission Regulation (EU) No 494/2011 of 20 May 2011	L 134	2	21.5.2011
►M14	Commission Regulation (EU) No 109/2012 of 9 February 2012	L 37	1	10.2.2012
►M15	Commission Regulation (EU) No 125/2012 of 14 February 2012	L 41	1	15.2.2012

Corrected by:

►C1	Corrigendum, OJ L 136, 29.5.2007, p. 3 (1907/2006)
►C2	Corrigendum, OJ L 141, 31.5.2008, p. 22 (1907/2006)
►C3	Corrigendum, OJ L 36, 5.2.2009, p. 84 (1907/2006)
►C4	Corrigendum, OJ L 49, 24.2.2011, p. 52 (143/2011)
►C5	Corrigendum, OJ L 136, 24.5.2011, p. 105 (494/2011)

▼B
▼C1

REGULATION (EC) No 1907/2006 OF THE EUROPEAN
PARLIAMENT AND OF THE COUNCIL

of 18 December 2006

concerning the Registration, Evaluation, Authorisation and
Restriction of Chemicals (REACH), establishing a European
Chemicals Agency, amending Directive 1999/45/EC and repealing
Council Regulation (EEC) No 793/93 and Commission Regulation
(EC) No 1488/94 as well as Council Directive 76/769/EEC and
Commission Directives 91/155/EEC, 93/67/EEC, 93/105/EC and
2000/21/EC

(Text with EEA relevance)

THE EUROPEAN PARLIAMENT AND THE COUNCIL OF THE
EUROPEAN UNION,

Having regard to the Treaty establishing the European Community, and
in particular Article 95 thereof,

Having regard to the proposal from the Commission,

Having regard to the opinion of the European Economic and Social
Committee (¹),

Having regard to the opinion of the Committee of the Regions (²),

Acting in accordance with the procedure laid down in Article 251 of the
Treaty (³),

Whereas:

(1)   This Regulation should ensure a high level of protection of
       human health and the environment as well as the free
       movement of substances, on their own, in ►M3 mixtures ◄
       and in articles, while enhancing competitiveness and innovation.
       This Regulation should also promote the development of alter-
       native methods for the assessment of hazards of substances.

(2)   The efficient functioning of the internal market for substances can
       be achieved only if requirements for substances do not differ
       significantly from Member State to Member State.

(3)   A high level of human health and environmental protection
       should be ensured in the approximation of legislation on
       substances, with the goal of achieving sustainable development.
       That legislation should be applied in a non-discriminatory manner
       whether substances are traded on the internal market or interna-
       tionally in accordance with the Community's international
       commitments.

(¹) OJ C 112, 30.4.2004, p. 92 and OJ C 294, 25.11.2005, p. 38.
(²) OJ C 164, 5.7.2005, p. 78.
(³) Opinion of the European Parliament of 17 November 2005 (OJ C 280 E,
    18.11.2006, p. 303), Council Common Position of 27 June 2006 (OJ C 276
    E, 14.11.2006, p. 1) and Position of the European Parliament of 13 December
    2006 (not yet published in the Official Journal). Council Decision of
    18 December 2006.

▼C1

(4) Pursuant to the implementation plan adopted on 4 September 2002 at the Johannesburg World Summit on sustainable development, the European Union is aiming to achieve that, by 2020, chemicals are produced and used in ways that lead to the minimisation of significant adverse effects on human health and the environment.

(5) This Regulation should apply without prejudice to Community workplace and environment legislation.

(6) This Regulation should contribute to fulfilment of the Strategic Approach to International Chemical Management (SAICM) adopted on 6 February 2006 in Dubai.

(7) To preserve the integrity of the internal market and to ensure a high level of protection for human health, especially the health of workers, and the environment, it is necessary to ensure that manufacturing of substances in the Community complies with Community law, even if those substances are exported.

(8) Special account should be taken of the potential impact of this Regulation on small- and medium-sized enterprises (SMEs) and the need to avoid any discrimination against them.

(9) The assessment of the operation of the four main legal instruments governing chemicals in the Community, i.e. Council Directive 67/548/EEC of 27 June 1967 on the approximation of the laws, regulations and administrative provisions relating to the classification, packaging and labelling of dangerous substances (¹), Council Directive 76/769/EEC of 27 July 1976 on the approximation of the laws, regulations and administrative provisions of the Member States relating to restrictions on the marketing and use of certain dangerous substances and preparations (²), Directive 1999/45/EC of the European Parliament and of the Council of 31 May 1999 concerning the approximation of the laws, regulations and administrative provisions of the Member States relating to the classification, packaging and labelling of dangerous preparations (³) and Council Regulation (EEC) No 793/93 of 23 March 1993 on the evaluation and control of the risks of existing substances (⁴), identified a number of problems in the functioning of Community legislation on chemicals, resulting in disparities between the laws, regulations and administrative provisions in Member States directly affecting the functioning of the internal market in this field, and the need to do more to protect public health and the environment in accordance with the precautionary principle.

(¹) OJ 196, 16.8.1967, p. 1. Directive as last amended by Commission Directive 2004/73/EC (OJ L 152, 30.4.2004, p. 1). Corrected in OJ L 216, 16.6.2004, p. 3.
(²) OJ L 262, 27.9.1976, p. 201. Directive as last amended by Commission Directive 2006/139/EC (OJ L 384, 29.12.2006, p. 94).
(³) OJ L 200, 30.7.1999, p. 1. Directive as last amended by Commission Directive 2006/8/EC (OJ L 19, 24.1.2006, p. 12).
(⁴) OJ L 84, 5.4.1993, p. 1. Regulation as amended by Regulation (EC) No 1882/2003 of the European Parliament and of the Council (OJ L 284, 31.10.2003, p. 1).

▼C1

(10) Substances under customs supervision which are in temporary storage, in free zones or free warehouses with a view to re-exportation or in transit are not used within the meaning of this Regulation and should therefore be excluded from its scope. The carriage of dangerous substances and of dangerous ►M3 mixtures ◄ by rail, road, inland waterways, sea or air should also be excluded from its scope as specific legislation already applies to such carriage.

(11) To ensure workability and to maintain the incentives for waste recycling and recovery, wastes should not be regarded as substances, ►M3 mixtures ◄ or articles within the meaning of this Regulation.

(12) An important objective of the new system to be established by this Regulation is to encourage and in certain cases to ensure that substances of high concern are eventually replaced by less dangerous substances or technologies where suitable econom-ically and technically viable alternatives are available. This Regu-lation does not affect the application of Directives on worker protection and the environment, especially Directive 2004/37/EC of the European Parliament and of the Council of 29 April 2004 on the protection of workers from the risks related to exposure to carcinogens or mutagens at work (Sixth individual Directive within the meaning of Article 16(1) of Council Directive 89/391/EEC) [1] and Council Directive 98/24/EC of 7 April 1998 on the protection of the health and safety of workers from the risks related to chemical agents at work (four-teenth individual Directive within the meaning of Article 16(1) of Directive 89/391/EEC) [2] under which employers are required to eliminate dangerous substances, wherever technically possible, or to substitute dangerous substances with less dangerous substances.

(13) This Regulation should apply without prejudice to the prohi-bitions and restrictions laid down in Council Directive 76/768/EEC of 27 July 1976 on the approximation of the laws of the Member States relating to cosmetic products [3] in so far as substances are used and marketed as cosmetic ingredients and are within the scope of this Regulation. A phase-out of testing on vertebrate animals for the purpose of protecting human health as specified in Directive 76/768/EEC should take place with regard to the uses of those substances in cosmetics.

[1] OJ L 158, 30.4.2004, p. 50, corrected in OJ L 229, 29.6.2004, p. 23.
[2] OJ L 131, 5.5.1998, p. 11.
[3] OJ L 262, 27.9.1976, p. 169. Directive as last amended by Commission Directive 2007/1/EC (OJ L 25, 1.2.2007, p. 9).

▼C1

(14) This Regulation will generate information on substances and their uses. Available information, including that generated by this Regulation, should be used by the relevant actors in the application and implementation of appropriate Community legislation, for example that covering products, and Community voluntary instruments, such as the eco-labelling scheme. The Commission should consider in the review and development of relevant Community legislation and voluntary instruments how information generated by this Regulation should be used, and examine possibilities for establishing a European quality mark.

(15) There is a need to ensure effective management of the technical, scientific and administrative aspects of this Regulation at Community level. A central entity should therefore be created to fulfil this role. A feasibility study on the resource requirements for this central entity concluded that an independent central entity offered a number of long-term advantages over other options. A European Chemicals Agency (hereinafter referred to as the Agency) should therefore be established.

(16) This Regulation lays down specific duties and obligations on manufacturers, importers and downstream users of substances on their own, in ►M3 mixtures ◄ and in articles. This Regulation is based on the principle that industry should manufacture, import or use substances or place them on the market with such responsibility and care as may be required to ensure that, under reasonably foreseeable conditions, human health and the environment are not adversely affected.

(17) All available and relevant information on substances on their own, in ►M3 mixtures ◄ and in articles should be collected to assist in identifying hazardous properties, and recommendations about risk management measures should systematically be conveyed through supply chains, as reasonably necessary, to prevent adverse effects on human health and the environment. In addition, communication of technical advice to support risk management should be encouraged in the supply chain, where appropriate.

(18) Responsibility for the management of the risks of substances should lie with the natural or legal persons that manufacture, import, place on the market or use these substances. Information on the implementation of this Regulation should be easily accessible, in particular for SMEs.

(19) Therefore, the registration provisions should require manufacturers and importers to generate data on the substances they manufacture or import, to use these data to assess the risks related to these substances and to develop and recommend appropriate risk management measures. To ensure that they actually meet these obligations, as well as for transparency reasons, registration should require them to submit a dossier containing all this information to the Agency. Registered substances should be allowed to circulate on the internal market.

▼C1

(20) The evaluation provisions should provide for follow-up to registration, by allowing for checks on whether registrations are in compliance with the requirements of this Regulation and if necessary by allowing for generation of more information on the properties of substances. If the Agency in cooperation with the Member States considers that there are grounds for considering that a substance constitutes a risk to human health or the environment, the Agency should, after having included the substance in the Community rolling action plan for substance evaluation, relying on the competent authorities of Member States, ensure that this substance is evaluated.

(21) Although the information yielded on substances through evaluation should be used in the first place by manufacturers and importers to manage the risks related to their substances, it may also be used to initiate the authorisation or restrictions procedures under this Regulation or risk management procedures under other Community legislation. Therefore it should be ensured that this information is available to the competent authorities and may be used by them for the purpose of such procedures.

(22) The authorisation provisions should ensure the good functioning of the internal market while assuring that the risks from substances of very high concern are properly controlled. Authorisations for the placing on the market and use should be granted by the Commission only if the risks arising from their use are adequately controlled, where this is possible, or the use can be justified for socio-economic reasons and no suitable alternatives are available, which are economically and technically viable.

(23) The restriction provisions should allow the manufacturing, placing on the market and use of substances presenting risks that need to be addressed, to be made subject to total or partial bans or other restrictions, based on an assessment of those risks.

(24) In preparation for this Regulation, the Commission has launched REACH Implementation Projects (RIPs), involving relevant experts from stakeholder groups. Some of those projects aim at developing draft guidelines and tools which should help the Commission, the Agency, Member States, manufacturers, importers and downstream users of substances to fulfil, in concrete terms, their obligations under this Regulation. This work should enable the Commission and the Agency to make available appropriate technical guidance, in due time, with regard to the deadlines introduced by this Regulation.

▼C1

(25) The responsibility to assess the risks and hazards of substances should be given, in the first place, to the natural or legal persons that manufacture or import substances, but only when they do so in quantities exceeding a certain volume, to enable them to carry the associated burden. Natural or legal persons handling chemicals should take the necessary risk management measures in accordance with the assessment of the risks of substances and pass on relevant recommendations along the supply chain. This should include describing, documenting and notifying in an appropriate and transparent fashion the risks stemming from the production, use and disposal of each substance.

(26) In order to undertake chemical safety assessments of substances effectively, manufacturers and importers of substances should obtain information on these substances, if necessary by performing new tests.

(27) For purposes of enforcement and evaluation and for reasons of transparency, the information on these substances, as well as related information, including on risk management measures, should normally be submitted to authorities.

(28) Scientific research and development normally takes place in quantities below one tonne per year. There is no need to exempt such research and development because substances in those quantities do not have to be registered in any case. However, in order to encourage innovation, product and process oriented research and development should be exempted from the obligation to register for a certain time period where a substance is not yet intended to be placed on the market to an indefinite number of customers because its application in ►M3 mixtures ◄ or articles still requires further research and development performed by the potential registrant himself or in cooperation with a limited number of known customers. In addition, it is appropriate to provide for a similar exemption to downstream users using the substance for the purposes of product and process oriented research and development, provided that the risks to human health and the environment are adequately controlled in accordance with the requirements of legislation for the protection of workers and the environment.

(29) Since producers and importers of articles should be responsible for their articles, it is appropriate to impose a registration requirement on substances which are intended to be released from articles and have not been registered for that use. In the case of substances of very high concern which are present in articles above tonnage and concentration thresholds, where exposure to the substance cannot be excluded and where the substance has not been registered by any person for this use, the Agency should be notified. The Agency should also be empowered to request that a registration be submitted if it has grounds for suspecting that the release of a substance from the article may present a risk to human health or the environment and the substance is present in those articles in quantities totalling over one tonne per producer or importer per year. The Agency should consider the need for a proposal for a restriction where it considers that the use of such substances in articles poses a risk to human health or the environment that is not adequately controlled.

▼C1

(30) The requirements for undertaking chemical safety assessments by manufacturers and importers should be defined in detail in a technical annex to allow them to meet their obligations. To achieve fair burden sharing with their customers, manufacturers and importers should in their chemical safety assessment address not only their own uses and the uses for which they place their substances on the market, but also all uses which their customers ask them to address.

(31) The Commission, in close cooperation with industry, Member States and other relevant stakeholders, should develop guidance to fulfil the requirements under this Regulation related to ►M3 mixtures ◄ (in particular with regard to safety data sheets incorporating exposure scenarios) including assessment of substances incorporated into special ►M3 mixtures ◄ — such as metals incorporated in alloys. In doing so, the Commission should take full account of the work that will have been carried out within the framework of the RIPs and should include the necessary guidance on this matter in the overall REACH guidance package. This guidance should be available before the application of this Regulation.

(32) A chemical safety assessment should not need to be performed for substances in ►M3 mixtures ◄ in certain very small concentrations which are considered as not giving rise to concern. Substances in ►M3 mixtures ◄ in such low concentrations should also be exempt from authorisation. These provisions should apply equally to ►M3 mixtures ◄ that are solid mixtures of substances until a specific shape is given to such a ►M3 mixture ◄ that transforms it into an article.

(33) Joint submission and the sharing of information on substances should be provided for in order to increase the efficiency of the registration system, to reduce costs and to reduce testing on vertebrate animals. One of a group of multiple registrants should submit information on behalf of the others according to rules which ensure that all the required information is submitted, while allowing sharing of the costs burden. A registrant should be able to submit information directly to the Agency in certain specified cases.

(34) Requirements for generation of information on substances should be tiered according to the volumes of manufacture or importation of a substance, because these provide an indication of the potential for exposure of man and the environment to the substances, and should be described in detail. To reduce the possible impact on low volume substances, new toxicological and ecotoxicological information should only be required for priority substances between 1 and 10 tonnes. For other substances in that quantity range there should be incentives to encourage manufacturers and importers to provide this information.

(35) The Member States, the Agency and all interested parties should take full account of the results of the RIPs, in particular with regard to the registration of substances which occur in nature.

▼C1

(36) It is necessary to consider the application of Article 2(7)(a) and (b) and Annex XI to substances derived from mineralogical processes and the review of Annexes IV and V should fully take this into account.

(37) If tests are performed, they should comply with the relevant requirements of protection of laboratory animals, set out in Council Directive 86/609/EEC of 24 November 1986 on the approximation of laws, regulations and administrative provisions of the Member States regarding the protection of animals used for experimental and other scientific purposes (¹), and, in the case of ecotoxicological and toxicological tests, good laboratory practice, set out in Directive 2004/10/EC of the European Parliament and of the Council of 11 February 2004 on the harmonisation of laws, regulations and administrative provisions relating to the application of the principles of good laboratory practice and the verification of their application for tests on chemical substances (²).

(38) The generation of information by alternative means offering equivalence to prescribed tests and test methods should also be allowed, for example when this information comes from valid qualitative or quantitative structure activity models or from structurally related substances. To this end the Agency, in cooperation with Member States and interested parties, should develop appropriate guidance. It should also be possible not to submit certain information if appropriate justification can be provided. Based on experience gained through RIPs, criteria should be developed defining what constitutes such justification.

(39) In order to help companies, and in particular SMEs, to comply with the requirements of this Regulation, Member States, in addition to the operational guidance documents provided by the Agency, should establish national helpdesks.

(40) The Commission, Member States, industry and other stakeholders should continue to contribute to the promotion of alternative test methods on an international and national level including computer supported methodologies, *in vitro* methodologies, as appropriate, those based on toxicogenomics, and other relevant methodologies. The Community's strategy to promote alternative test methods is a priority and the Commission should ensure that within its future Research Framework Programmes and initiatives such as the Community Action Plan on the Protection and Welfare of Animals 2006 to 2010 this remains a priority topic. Participation of stakeholders and initiatives involving all interested parties should be sought.

_____

(¹) OJ L 358, 18.12.1986, p. 1. Directive as amended by Directive 2003/65/EC of the European Parliament and of the Council (OJ L 230, 16.9.2003, p. 32).
(²) OJ L 50, 20.2.2004, p. 44.

▼C1

(41) For reasons of workability and because of their special nature, specific registration requirements should be laid down for intermediates. Polymers should be exempted from registration and evaluation until those that need to be registered due to the risks posed to human health or the environment can be selected in a practicable and cost-efficient way on the basis of sound technical and valid scientific criteria.

(42) To avoid overloading authorities and natural or legal persons with the work arising from the registration of phase-in substances already on the internal market, that registration should be spread over an appropriate period of time, without introducing undue delay. Deadlines for the registration of these substances should therefore be set.

(43) Data for substances already notified in accordance with Directive 67/548/EEC should be eased into the system and should be upgraded when the next tonnage quantity threshold is reached.

(44) In order to provide a harmonised, simple system, all registrations should be submitted to the Agency. To ensure a consistent approach and efficient use of resources, it should perform a completeness check on all registrations and take responsibility for any final rejections of registrations.

(45) The European Inventory of Existing Commercial Chemical Substances (EINECS) included certain complex substances in a single entry. UVCB substances (substances of unknown or variable composition, complex reaction products or biological materials) may be registered as a single substance under this Regulation, despite their variable composition, provided that the hazardous properties do not differ significantly and warrant the same classification.

(46) To ensure that the information gathered through the registration is kept up-to-date, an obligation on registrants to inform the Agency of certain changes to the information should be introduced.

(47) In accordance with Directive 86/609/EEC, it is necessary to replace, reduce or refine testing on vertebrate animals. Implementation of this Regulation should be based on the use of alternative test methods, suitable for the assessment of health and environmental hazards of chemicals, wherever possible. The use of animals should be avoided by recourse to alternative methods validated by the Commission or international bodies, or recognised by the Commission or the Agency as appropriate to meet the information requirements under this Regulation. To this end, the Commission, following consultation with relevant stakeholders, should propose to amend the future Commission Regulation on test methods or this Regulation, where appropriate, to replace, reduce or refine animal testing. The Commission and the Agency should ensure that reduction of animal testing is a key consideration in the development and maintenance of guidance for stakeholders and in the Agency's own procedures.

▼C1

(48) This Regulation should be without prejudice to the full and complete application of the Community competition rules.

(49) In order to avoid duplication of work, and in particular to reduce testing involving vertebrate animals, the provisions concerning preparation and submission of registrations and updates should require sharing of information where this is requested by any registrant. If the information concerns vertebrate animals, the registrant should be obliged to request it.

(50) It is in the public interest to ensure the quickest possible circulation of test results on human health or environmental hazards of certain substances to those natural or legal persons which use them, in order to limit any risks associated with their use. Sharing of information should occur where this is requested by any registrant, in particular in the case of information involving tests on vertebrate animals, under conditions that ensure a fair compensation for the company that has undertaken the tests.

(51) In order to strengthen the competitiveness of Community industry and to ensure that this Regulation is applied as efficiently as possible, it is appropriate to make provision for the sharing of data between registrants on the basis of fair compensation.

(52) In order to respect the legitimate property rights of those generating testing data, the owner of such data should, for a period of 12 years, be able to claim compensation from those registrants who benefit from that data.

(53) In order to allow a potential registrant of a phase-in substance to proceed with his registration, even if he cannot reach agreement with a previous registrant, the Agency, on request, should allow use of any summary or robust study summary of tests already submitted. The registrant who receives these data should be obliged to pay a contribution to the costs to the owner of the data. For non-phase-in substances, the Agency may ask for evidence that a potential registrant has paid the owner of a study before the Agency gives permission for the potential registrant to use that information in his registration.

▼C1

(54) In order to avoid duplication of work, and in particular to avoid duplication of testing, registrants of phase-in substances should pre-register as early as possible with a database managed by the Agency. A system should be established in order to provide for the establishment of Substance Information Exchange Forums (SIEF) to help exchange of information on the substances that have been registered. SIEF participants should include all relevant actors submitting information to the Agency on the same phase-in substance. They should include both potential registrants, who must provide and be supplied with any information relevant to the registration of their substances, and other participants, who may receive financial compensation for studies they hold but are not entitled to request information. In order to ensure the smooth functioning of that system they should fulfil certain obligations. If a member of a SIEF does not fulfil his obligations, he should be penalised accordingly but other members should be enabled to continue preparing their own registration. In cases where a substance has not been pre-registered, measures should be taken to help downstream users find alternative sources of supply.

(55) Manufacturers and importers of a substance on its own or in a ►M3 mixture ◄ should be encouraged to communicate with the downstream users of the substance with regard to whether they intend to register the substance. Such information should be provided to a downstream user sufficiently in advance of the relevant registration deadline if the manufacturer or importer does not intend to register the substance, in order to enable the downstream user to look for alternative sources of supply.

(56) Part of the responsibility of manufacturers or importers for the management of the risks of substances is the communication of information on these substances to other professionals such as downstream users or distributors. In addition, producers or importers of articles should supply information on the safe use of articles to industrial and professional users, and consumers on request. This important responsibility should also apply throughout the supply chain to enable all actors to meet their responsibility in relation to management of risks arising from the use of substances.

(57) As the existing safety data sheet is already being used as a communication tool within the supply chain of substances and ►M3 mixtures ◄, it is appropriate to develop it further and make it an integral part of the system established by this Regulation.

▼C1

(58) In order to have a chain of responsibilities, downstream users should be responsible for assessing the risks arising from their uses of substances if those uses are not covered by a safety data sheet received from their suppliers, unless the downstream user concerned takes more protective measures than those recommended by his supplier or unless his supplier was not required to assess those risks or provide him with information on those risks. For the same reason, downstream users should manage the risks arising from their uses of substances. In addition, it is appropriate that any producer or importer of an article containing a substance of very high concern should provide sufficient information to allow safe use of such an article.

(59) The requirements for undertaking chemical safety assessments by downstream users should also be prescribed in detail to allow them to meet their obligations. These requirements should only apply above a total quantity of one tonne of substance or ►M3 mixture ◄. In any case, however, the downstream users should consider the use and identify and apply appropriate risk management measures. Downstream users should report certain basic information on use to the Agency.

(60) For enforcement and evaluation purposes, downstream users of substances should be required to report to the Agency certain basic information if their use is outside the conditions of the exposure scenario detailed in the safety data sheet communicated by their original manufacturer or importer and to keep such reported information up-to-date.

(61) For reasons of workability and proportionality, it is appropriate to exempt downstream users using low quantities of a substance from such reporting.

(62) Communication up and down the supply chain should be facilitated. The Commission should develop a system categorising brief general descriptions of uses taking into account the outcomes of the RIPs.

(63) It is also necessary to ensure that generation of information is tailored to real information needs. To this end evaluation should require the Agency to decide on the programmes of testing proposed by manufacturers and importers. In cooperation with Member States, the Agency should give priority to certain substances, for instance those which may be of very high concern.

(64) In order to prevent unnecessary animal testing, interested parties should have a period of 45 days during which they may provide scientifically valid information and studies that address the relevant substance and hazard end-point, which is addressed by the testing proposal. The scientifically valid information and studies received by the Agency should be taken into account for decisions on testing proposals.

▼C1

(65) In addition, it is necessary to instil confidence in the general quality of registrations and to ensure that the public at large as well as all stakeholders in the chemicals industry have confidence that natural or legal persons are meeting the obligations placed upon them. Accordingly, it is appropriate to provide for recording which information has been reviewed by an assessor possessing appropriate experience, and for a percentage of registrations to be checked for compliance by the Agency.

(66) The Agency should also be empowered to require further information from manufacturers, importers or downstream users on substances suspected of posing a risk to human health or the environment, including by reason of their presence on the internal market in high volumes, on the basis of evaluations performed. Based on the criteria for prioritising substances developed by the Agency in cooperation with the Member States a Community rolling action plan for substance evaluation should be established, relying on Member State competent authorities to evaluate substances included therein. If a risk equivalent to the level of concern arising from the use of substances subject to authorisation arises from the use of isolated intermediates on site, the competent authorities of the Member States should also be allowed to require further information, when justified.

(67) Collective agreement within the Agency's Member State Committee on its draft decisions should provide the basis for an efficient system that respects the principle of subsidiarity, while maintaining the internal market. If one or more Member States or the Agency do not agree to a draft decision, it should be adopted subject to a centralised procedure. If the Member State Committee fails to reach unanimous agreement, the Commission should adopt a decision in accordance with a Committee procedure.

(68) Evaluation may lead to the conclusion that action should be taken under the restriction or authorisation procedures or that risk management action should be considered in the framework of other appropriate legislation. Information on the progress of evaluation proceedings should therefore be made public.

(69) To ensure a sufficiently high level of protection for human health, including having regard to relevant human population groups and possibly to certain vulnerable sub-populations, and the environment, substances of very high concern should, in accordance with the precautionary principle, be subject to careful attention. Authorisation should be granted where natural or legal persons applying for an authorisation demonstrate to the granting authority that the risks to human health and the environment arising from the use of the substance are adequately controlled. Otherwise, uses may still be authorised if it can be shown that the socio-economic benefits from the use of the substance outweigh the risks connected with its use and there are no suitable alternative substances or technologies that are economically and technically viable. Taking into account the good functioning of the internal market it is appropriate that the Commission should be the granting authority.

▼C1

(70) Adverse effects on human health and the environment from substances of very high concern should be prevented through the application of appropriate risk management measures to ensure that any risks from the uses of a substance are adequately controlled, and with a view to progressively substituting these substances with a suitable safer substance. Risk management measures should be applied to ensure, when substances are manufactured, placed on the market and used, that exposure to these substances including discharges, emissions and losses, throughout the whole life-cycle is below the threshold level beyond which adverse effects may occur. For any substance for which authorisation has been granted, and for any other substance for which it is not possible to establish a safe level of exposure, measures should always be taken to minimise, as far as technically and practically possible, exposure and emissions with a view to minimising the likelihood of adverse effects. Measures to ensure adequate control should be identified in any Chemical Safety Report. These measures should be applied and, where appropriate, recommended to other actors down the supply chain.

(71) Methodologies to establish thresholds for carcinogenic and mutagenic substances may be developed taking into account the outcomes of RIPs. The relevant Annex may be amended on the basis of these methodologies to allow thresholds where appropriate to be used while ensuring a high level of protection of human health and the environment.

(72) To support the aim of eventual replacement of substances of very high concern by suitable alternative substances or technologies, all applicants for authorisation should provide an analysis of alternatives considering their risks and the technical and economic feasibility of substitution, including information on any research and development the applicant is undertaking or intends to undertake. Furthermore, authorisations should be subject to time-limited review whose periods would be determined on a case-by-case basis and normally be subject to conditions, including monitoring.

(73) Substitution of a substance on its own, in a ►M3 mixture ◄ or in an article should be required when manufacture, use or placing on the market of that substance causes an unacceptable risk to human health or to the environment, taking into account the availability of suitable safer alternative substances and technologies, and the socio-economic benefits from the uses of the substance posing an unacceptable risk.

(74) Substitution of a substance of very high concern by suitable safer alternative substances or technologies should be considered by all those applying for authorisations of uses of such substances on their own, in ►M3 mixtures ◄ or for incorporation of substances into articles by making an analysis of alternatives, the risks involved in using any alternative and the technical and economic feasibility of substitution.

▼__C1__

(75) The possibility of introducing restrictions on the manufacturing, placing on the market and use of dangerous substances, ►__M3__ mixtures ◄ and articles applies to all substances falling within the scope of this Regulation, with minor exemptions. Restrictions on the placing on the market and the use of substances which are carcinogenic, mutagenic or toxic to reproduction, category 1 or 2, for their use by consumers on their own or in ►__M3__ mixtures ◄ should continue to be introduced.

(76) Experience at international level shows that substances with characteristics rendering them persistent, liable to bioaccumulate and toxic, or very persistent and very liable to bioaccumulate, present a very high concern, while criteria have been developed allowing the identification of such substances. For certain other substances concerns are sufficiently high to address them in the same way on a case-by-case basis. The criteria in Annex XIII should be reviewed taking into account the current and any new experience in the identification of these substances and if appropriate, be amended with a view to ensuring a high level of protection for human health and the environment.

(77) In view of workability and practicality considerations, both as regards natural or legal persons, who have to prepare application files and take appropriate risk management measures, and as regards the authorities, who have to process authorisation applications, only a limited number of substances should be subjected to the authorisation procedure at the same time and realistic deadlines should be set for applications, while allowing certain uses to be exempted. Substances identified as meeting the criteria for authorisation should be included in a candidate list for eventual inclusion in the authorisation procedure. Within this list, substances on the Agency's work programme should be clearly identified.

(78) The Agency should provide advice on the prioritisation of substances to be made subject to the authorisation procedure, to ensure that decisions reflect the needs of society as well as scientific knowledge and developments.

(79) A total ban on a substance would mean that none of its uses could be authorised. It would therefore be pointless to allow the submission of applications for authorisation. In such cases the substance should be removed from the list of substances for which applications can be submitted and added to the list of restricted substances.

(80) The proper interaction between the provisions on authorisation and restriction should be ensured in order to preserve the efficient functioning of the internal market and the protection of human health, safety and the environment. Restrictions that exist when the substance in question is added to the list of substances for which applications for authorisation can be submitted, should be maintained for that substance. The Agency should consider whether the risk from substances in articles is adequately controlled and, if it is not, prepare a dossier in relation to introduction of further restrictions for substances for which the use requires authorisation.

▼C1

(81) In order to provide a harmonised approach to the authorisation of the uses of particular substances, the Agency should issue opinions on the risks arising from those uses, including whether or not the substance is adequately controlled and on any socio-economic analysis submitted to it by third parties. These opinions should be taken into account by the Commission when considering whether or not to grant an authorisation.

(82) To allow effective monitoring and enforcement of the authorisation requirement, downstream users benefiting from an authorisation granted to their supplier should inform the Agency of their use of the substance.

(83) It is suitable in these circumstances that final decisions granting or refusing authorisations be adopted by the Commission pursuant to a regulatory procedure in order to allow for an examination of their wider implications within the Member States and to associate the latter more closely with the decisions.

(84) In order to accelerate the current system the restriction procedure should be restructured and Directive 76/769/EEC, which has been substantially amended and adapted several times, should be replaced. In the interests of clarity and as a starting point for this new accelerated restriction procedure, all the restrictions developed under that Directive should be incorporated into this Regulation. Where appropriate, the application of Annex XVII of this Regulation should be facilitated by guidance developed by the Commission.

(85) In relation to Annex XVII Member States should be allowed to maintain for a transitional period more stringent restrictions, provided that these restrictions have been notified according to the Treaty. This should concern substances on their own, substances in ►M3 mixtures ◄ and substances in articles, the manufacturing, the placing on the market and the use of which is restricted. The Commission should compile and publish an inventory of these restrictions. This would provide an opportunity for the Commission to review the measures concerned with a view to possible harmonisation.

(86) It should be the responsibility of the manufacturer, importer and downstream user to identify the appropriate risk management measures needed to ensure a high level of protection for human health and the environment from the manufacturing, placing on the market or use of a substance on its own, in a ►M3 mixture ◄ or in an article. However, where this is considered to be insufficient and where Community legislation is justified, appropriate restrictions should be laid down.

▼C1

(87) In order to protect human health and the environment, restrictions on the manufacture, placing on the market or use of a substance on its own, in a ►M3 mixture ◄ or in an article may include any condition for, or prohibition of, the manufacture, placing on the market or use. Therefore it is necessary to list such restrictions and any amendments thereto.

(88) In order to prepare a restrictions proposal and in order for such legislation to operate effectively, there should be good cooperation, coordination and information between the Member States, the Agency, other bodies of the Community, the Commission and the interested parties.

(89) In order to give Member States the opportunity to submit proposals to address a specific risk for human health and the environment, they should prepare a dossier in conformity with detailed requirements. The dossier should set out the justification for Community-wide action.

(90) In order to provide a harmonised approach to restrictions, the Agency should fulfil a role as coordinator of this procedure, for example by appointing the relevant rapporteurs and verifying conformity with the requirements of the relevant Annexes. The Agency should maintain a list of substances for which a restriction dossier is being prepared.

(91) In order to give the Commission the opportunity to address a specific risk for human health and the environment that needs to be addressed Community wide, it should be able to entrust the Agency with the preparation of a restriction dossier.

(92) For reasons of transparency, the Agency should publish the relevant dossier including the suggested restrictions while requesting comments.

(93) In order to finalise the procedure in due time, the Agency should submit its opinions on the suggested action and its impact on the basis of a draft opinion prepared by a rapporteur.

(94) In order to speed up the procedure for restrictions, the Commission should prepare its draft amendment within a specific time limit of receiving the Agency's opinions.

(95) The Agency should be central to ensuring that chemicals legislation and the decision-making processes and scientific basis underlying it have credibility with all stakeholders and the public. The Agency should also play a pivotal role in coordinating communication around this Regulation and in its implementation. The confidence in the Agency of the Community institutions, the Member States, the general public and interested parties is therefore essential. For this reason, it is vital to ensure its independence, high scientific, technical and regulatory capacities, as well as transparency and efficiency.

▼<u>C1</u>

(96)   The structure of the Agency should be suitable for the tasks that it should fulfil. Experience with similar Community agencies provides some guidance in this respect but the structure should be adapted to meet the specific needs of this Regulation.

(97)   The effective communication of information on chemical risks and how they can be managed is an essential part of the system established by this Regulation. Best practice from the chemicals and other sectors should be considered in the preparation of guidance by the Agency to all stakeholders.

(98)   In the interests of efficiency, the staff of the Agency Secretariat should perform essentially technical-administrative and scientific tasks without calling on the scientific and technical resources of the Member States. The Executive Director should ensure the efficient execution of the Agency's tasks in an independent manner. To ensure that the Agency fulfils its role, the composition of the Management Board should be designed to represent each Member State, the Commission and other interested parties appointed by the Commission in order to ensure the involvement of stakeholders, and the European Parliament and to secure the highest standard of competence and a broad range of relevant expertise in chemicals safety or the regulation of chemicals, whilst ensuring that there is relevant expertise in the field of general financial and legal matters.

(99)   The Agency should have the means to perform all the tasks required to carry out its role.

(100) A Commission Regulation should specify the structure and amounts of fees, including specifying the circumstances under which a proportion of the fees will be transferred to the relevant Member State competent authority.

(101) The Management Board of the Agency should have the necessary powers to establish the budget, check its implementation, draw up internal rules, adopt financial regulations and appoint the Executive Director.

(102) Through a Committee for Risk Assessment and a Committee for Socio-economic Analysis, the Agency should take over the role of the Scientific Committees attached to the Commission in issuing scientific opinions in its field of competence.

(103) Through a Member State Committee, the Agency should aim to reach agreement amongst Member States' authorities on specific issues which require a harmonised approach.

▼C1

(104) It is necessary to ensure close cooperation between the Agency and the competent authorities working within the Member States so that the scientific opinions of the Committee for Risk Assessment and the Committee for Socio-economic Analysis are based on the broadest possible scientific and technical expertise appropriate which is available within the Community. To the same end, these Committees should be able to rely on additional particular expertise.

(105) In the light of the increased responsibility of natural or legal persons for ensuring safe use of chemicals, enforcement needs to be strengthened. The Agency should therefore provide a Forum for Member States to exchange information on and to coordinate their activities related to the enforcement of chemicals legislation. The currently informal cooperation between Member States in this respect would benefit from a more formal framework.

(106) A Board of Appeal should be set up within the Agency to guarantee processing of appeals for any natural or legal person affected by decisions taken by the Agency.

(107) The Agency should be financed partly by fees paid by natural or legal persons and partly by the general budget of the European Communities. The Community budgetary procedure should remain applicable as far as any subsidies chargeable to the general budget of the European Communities are concerned. Moreover, the auditing of accounts should be undertaken by the Court of Auditors in accordance with Article 91 of Commission Regulation (EC, Euratom) No 2343/2002 of 23 December 2002 on the framework Financial Regulation for the bodies referred to in Article 185 of Council Regulation (EC, Euratom) No 1605/2002 on the Financial Regulation applicable to the general budget of the European Communities (¹).

(108) Where the Commission and Agency consider it appropriate, it should be possible for representatives of third countries to participate in the work of the Agency.

(109) The Agency should contribute, through cooperation with organisations having interests in the harmonisation of international regulations, to the role of the Community and the Member States in such harmonisation activities. To promote broad international consensus the Agency should take account of existing and emerging international standards in the regulation of chemicals such as the Globally Harmonised System (GHS) of classification and labelling of chemicals.

(110) The Agency should provide the infrastructure needed for natural or legal persons to meet their obligations under the data-sharing provisions.

_____
(¹) OJ L 357, 31.12.2002, p. 72.

▼C1

(111) It is important to avoid confusion between the mission of the Agency and the respective missions of the European Medicines Agency (EMEA) established by Regulation (EC) No 726/2004 of the European Parliament and of the Council of 31 March 2004 laying down Community procedures for the authorisation and supervision of medicinal products for human and veterinary use and establishing a European Medicines Agency (¹), the European Food Safety Authority (EFSA) established by Regulation (EC) No 178/2002 of the European Parliament and of the Council of 28 January 2002 laying down the general principles and requirements of food law, establishing the European Food Safety Authority and laying down procedures in matters of food safety (²) and the Advisory Committee on Safety, Hygiene and Health Protection at Work set up by the Council Decision of 22 July 2003 (³). Consequently, the Agency should establish rules of procedure where cooperation with the EFSA or the Advisory Committee on Safety, Hygiene and Health Protection at Work is necessary. This Regulation should otherwise be without prejudice to the competence conferred on the EMEA, the EFSA and the Advisory Committee on Safety, Hygiene and Health Protection at Work by Community legislation.

(112) In order to achieve the functioning of the internal market for substances on their own or in ►M3 mixtures ◄, while at the same time ensuring a high level of protection for human health and the environment, rules should be established for a classification and labelling inventory.

(113) The classification and labelling for any substance either subject to registration or covered by Article 1 of Directive 67/548/EEC and placed on the market should therefore be notified to the Agency to be included in the inventory.

(114) To ensure a harmonised protection for the general public, and, in particular, for persons who come into contact with certain substances, and the proper functioning of other Community legislation relying on the classification and labelling, an inventory should record the classification in accordance with Directive 67/548/EEC and Directive 1999/45/EC agreed by manufacturers and importers of the same substance, if possible, as well as decisions taken at Community level to harmonise the classification and labelling of some substances. This should take full account of the work and experience accumulated in connection with the activities under Directive 67/548/EEC, including the classification and labelling of specific substances or groups of substances listed in Annex I of Directive 67/548/EEC.

(¹) OJ L 136, 30.4.2004, p. 1. Regulation as amended by Regulation (EC) No 1901/2006 (OJ L 378, 27.12.2006, p. 1).
(²) OJ L 31, 1.2.2002, p. 1. Regulation as last amended by Commission Regulation (EC) No 575/2006 (OJ L 100, 8.4.2006, p. 3).
(³) OJ C 218, 13.9.2003, p. 1.

▼C1

(115) Resources should be focused on substances of the highest concern. A substance should therefore be added to Annex I of Directive 67/548/EEC if it meets the criteria for classification as carcinogenic, mutagenic or toxic for reproduction categories 1, 2 or 3, as a respiratory sensitiser, or in respect of other effects on a case-by-case basis. Provision should be made to enable competent authorities to submit proposals to the Agency. The Agency should give its opinion on the proposal while interested parties should have an opportunity to comment. The Commission should take a decision subsequently.

(116) Regular reports by the Member States and the Agency on the operation of this Regulation will be an indispensable means of monitoring the implementation of this Regulation as well as trends in this field. Conclusions drawn from findings in the reports will be useful and practical tools for reviewing this Regulation and, where necessary, for formulating proposals for amendments.

(117) EU citizens should have access to information about chemicals to which they may be exposed, in order to allow them to make informed decisions about their use of chemicals. A transparent means of achieving this is to grant them free and easy access to basic data held in the Agency's database, including brief profiles of hazardous properties, labelling requirements and relevant Community legislation including authorised uses and risk management measures. The Agency and Member States should allow access to information in accordance with Directive 2003/4/EC of the European Parliament and of the Council of 28 January 2003 on public access to environmental information (¹), Regulation (EC) No 1049/2001 of the European Parliament and of the Council of 30 May 2001 regarding public access to European Parliament, Council and Commission documents (²) and with the UNECE Convention on Access to Information, Public Participation in Decision-Making and Access to Justice in Environmental Matters, to which the European Community is a party.

(118) Disclosure of information under this Regulation is subject to the specific requirements of Regulation (EC) No 1049/2001. That Regulation sets binding deadlines for the release of information as well as procedural guarantees, including the right of appeal. The Management Board should adopt the practical arrangements for application of those requirements to the Agency.

(¹) OJ L 41, 14.2.2003, p. 26.
(²) OJ L 145, 31.5.2001, p. 43.

▼C1

(119) Apart from their participation in the implementation of Community legislation, Member State competent authorities should, because of their closeness to stakeholders in the Member States, play a role in the exchange of information on risks of substances and on the obligations of natural or legal persons under chemicals legislation. At the same time, close co-operation between the Agency, the Commission and the competent authorities of the Member States is necessary to ensure the coherence and efficiency of the global communication process.

(120) In order for the system established by this Regulation to operate effectively, there should be good cooperation, coordination and exchange of information between the Member States, the Agency and the Commission regarding enforcement.

(121) In order to ensure compliance with this Regulation, Member States should put in place effective monitoring and control measures. The necessary inspections should be planned, carried out and their results should be reported.

(122) In order to ensure transparency, impartiality and consistency in the level of enforcement activities by Member States, it is necessary for Member States to set up an appropriate framework for penalties with a view to imposing effective, proportionate and dissuasive penalties for non-compliance, as non-compliance can result in damage to human health and the environment.

(123) The measures necessary for the implementation of this Regulation and certain amendments to it should be adopted in accordance with Council Decision 1999/468/EC of 28 June 1999 laying down the procedures for the exercise of implementing powers conferred on the Commission (¹).

(124) In particular, power should be conferred on the Commission to amend the Annexes in certain cases, to set rules on test methods, to vary the percentage of dossiers selected for compliance checking and to modify the criteria for their selection, and to set the criteria defining what constitutes adequate justification that testing is technically not possible. Since these measures are of general scope and are designed to amend non-essential elements of this Regulation or supplement this Regulation by adding new non-essential elements thereto, they should be adopted in accordance with the regulatory procedure with scrutiny provided for in Article 5a of Decision 1999/468/EC.

(125) It is essential that chemicals be regulated in an effective and timely manner during the transition to full applicability of the provisions of this Regulation and, in particular, during the start-up period of the Agency. Provision should therefore be made for the Commission to provide the necessary support towards the setting up of the Agency, including the conclusion of contracts and the appointment of an Executive Director *ad interim* until the Agency's Management Board can appoint an Executive Director itself.

(¹) OJ L 184, 17.7.1999, p. 23. Decision as amended by Decision 2006/512/EC (OJ L 200, 22.7.2006, p. 11).

▼C1

(126) To take full advantage of the work performed under Regulation (EEC) No 793/93 as well as under Directive 76/769/EEC and to avoid such work being lost, the Commission should be empowered during the start-up period to initiate restrictions based on that work without following the full restrictions procedure laid down in this Regulation. All those elements should be used, as soon as this Regulation enters into force, to support risk reduction measures.

(127) It is appropriate for the provisions of this Regulation to enter into force in a staggered way to smooth the transition to the new system. Moreover, a gradual entry into force of the provisions should allow all parties involved, authorities, natural or legal persons as well as stakeholders, to focus resources in the preparation for new duties at the right times.

(128) This Regulation replaces Directive 76/769/EEC, Commission Directive 91/155/EEC (¹), Commission Directive 93/67/EEC (²), Commission Directive 93/105/EC (³), Commission Directive 2000/21/EC (⁴), Regulation (EEC) No 793/93 and Commission Regulation (EC) No 1488/94 (⁵). These Directives and Regulations should therefore be repealed.

(129) For the sake of consistency, Directive 1999/45/EC which already addresses matters covered by this Regulation should be amended.

(130) Since the objectives of this Regulation, namely laying down rules for substances and establishing a European Chemicals Agency, cannot be sufficiently achieved by the Member States and can therefore be better achieved at Community level, the Community may adopt measures, in accordance with the principle of subsidiarity as set out in Article 5 of the Treaty. In accordance with the principle of proportionality, as set out in that Article, this Regulation does not go beyond what is necessary in order to achieve those objectives.

_____

(¹) Commission Directive 91/155/EEC of 5 March 1991 defining and laying down the detailed arrangements for the system of specific information relating to dangerous ►M3 mixtures ◄ in implementation of Article 10 of Directive 88/379/EEC (OJ L 76, 22.3.1991, p. 35). Directive as last amended by Directive 2001/58/EC (OJ L 212, 7.8.2001, p. 24).

(²) Commission Directive 93/67/EEC of 20 July 1993 laying down the principles for assessment of risks to man and the environment of substances notified in accordance with Council Directive 67/548/EEC (OJ L 227, 8.9.1993, p. 9).

(³) Commission Directive 93/105/EC of 25 November 1993 laying down Annex VII D, containing information required for the technical dossier referred to in Article 12 of the seventh amendment of Council Directive 67/548/EEC (OJ L 294, 30.11.1993, p. 21).

(⁴) Commission Directive 2000/21/EC of 25 April 2000 concerning the list of Community legislation referred to in the fifth indent of Article 13(1) of Council Directive 67/548/EEC (OJ L 103, 28.4.2000, p. 70).

(⁵) Commission Regulation (EC) No 1488/94 of 28 June 1994 laying down the principles for the assessment of risks to man and the environment of existing substances in accordance with Council Regulation (EEC) No 793/93 (OJ L 161, 29.6.1994, p. 3).

▼C1

(131) The Regulation observes the fundamental rights and principles which are acknowledged in particular in the Charter of Fundamental Rights of the European Union (¹). In particular, it seeks to ensure full compliance with the principles of environmental protection and sustainable development guaranteed by Article 37 of that Charter,

HAVE ADOPTED THIS REGULATION:

_____
(¹) OJ C 364, 18.12.2000, p. 1.

▼<u>C1</u>

TABLE OF CONTENTS

▼C1

ANNEX I	GENERAL PROVISIONS FOR ASSESSING SUBSTANCES AND PREPARING CHEMICAL SAFETY REPORTS
ANNEX II	GUIDE TO THE COMPILATION OF SAFETY DATA SHEETS
ANNEX III	CRITERIA FOR SUBSTANCES REGISTERED IN QUANTITIES BETWEEN 1 AND 10 TONNES
ANNEX IV	EXEMPTIONS FROM THE OBLIGATION TO REGISTER IN ACCORDANCE WITH ARTICLE 2(7)(a)
ANNEX V	EXEMPTIONS FROM THE OBLIGATION TO REGISTER IN ACCORDANCE WITH ARTICLE 2(7)(b)
ANNEX VI	INFORMATION REQUIREMENTS REFERRED TO IN ARTICLE 10
ANNEX VII	STANDARD INFORMATION REQUIREMENTS FOR SUBSTANCES MANUFACTURED OR IMPORTED IN QUANTITIES OF ONE TONNE OR MORE
ANNEX VIII	STANDARD INFORMATION REQUIREMENTS FOR SUBSTANCES MANUFACTURED OR IMPORTED IN QUANTITIES OF 10 TONNES OR MORE
ANNEX IX	STANDARD INFORMATION REQUIREMENTS FOR SUBSTANCES MANUFACTURED OR IMPORTED IN QUANTITIES OF 100 TONNES OR MORE
ANNEX X	STANDARD INFORMATION REQUIREMENTS FOR SUBSTANCES MANUFACTURED OR IMPORTED IN QUANTITIES OF 1 000 TONNES OR MORE
ANNEX XI	GENERAL RULES FOR ADAPTATION OF THE STANDARD TESTING REGIME SET OUT IN ANNEXES VII TO X
ANNEX XII	GENERAL PROVISIONS FOR DOWNSTREAM USERS TO ASSESS SUBSTANCES AND PREPARE CHEMICAL SAFETY REPORTS
ANNEX XIII	CRITERIA FOR THE IDENTIFICATION OF PERSISTENT, BIOACCUMULATIVE AND TOXIC SUBSTANCES, AND VERY PERSISTENT AND VERY BIOACCUMULATIVE SUBSTANCES
ANNEX XIV	LIST OF SUBSTANCES SUBJECT TO AUTHORIS-ATION
ANNEX XV	DOSSIERS
ANNEX XVI	SOCIO-ECONOMIC ANALYSIS
ANNEX XVII	RESTRICTIONS ON THE MANUFACTURE, PLACING ON THE MARKET AND USE OF CERTAIN DANGEROUS SUBSTANCES, MIXTURES AND ARTICLES

▼C1

TITLE I

GENERAL ISSUES

CHAPTER 1

Aim, scope and application

Article 1

Aim and scope

1. The purpose of this Regulation is to ensure a high level of protection of human health and the environment, including the promotion of alternative methods for assessment of hazards of substances, as well as the free circulation of substances on the internal market while enhancing competitiveness and innovation.

2. This Regulation lays down provisions on substances and ►M3 mixtures ◄ within the meaning of Article 3. These provisions shall apply to the manufacture, placing on the market or use of such substances on their own, in ►M3 mixtures ◄ or in articles and to the placing on the market of ►M3 mixtures ◄.

3. This Regulation is based on the principle that it is for manufacturers, importers and downstream users to ensure that they manufacture, place on the market or use such substances that do not adversely affect human health or the environment. Its provisions are underpinned by the precautionary principle.

Article 2

Application

1. This Regulation shall not apply to:

(a) radioactive substances within the scope of Council Directive 96/29/Euratom of 13 May 1996 laying down basic safety standards for the protection of the health of workers and the general public against the dangers arising from ionising radiation ([1]);

(b) substances, on their own, in a ►M3 mixture ◄ or in an article, which are subject to customs supervision, provided that they do not undergo any treatment or processing, and which are in temporary storage, or in a free zone or free warehouse with a view to re-exportation, or in transit;

(c) non-isolated intermediates;

(d) the carriage of dangerous substances and dangerous substances in dangerous ►M3 mixtures ◄ by rail, road, inland waterway, sea or air.

2. Waste as defined in Directive 2006/12/EC of the European Parliament and of the Council ([2]) is not a substance, ►M3 mixture ◄ or article within the meaning of Article 3 of this Regulation.

([1]) OJ L 159, 29.6.1996, p. 1.
([2]) OJ L 114, 27.4.2006, p. 9.

▼C1

3. Member States may allow for exemptions from this Regulation in specific cases for certain substances, on their own, in a ►M3 mixture ◄ or in an article, where necessary in the interests of defence.

4. This Regulation shall apply without prejudice to:

(a) Community workplace and environmental legislation, including Council Directive 89/391/EEC of 12 June 1989 on the introduction of measures to encourage improvements in the safety and health of workers at work (^{1}), Council Directive 96/61/EC of 24 September 1996 concerning integrated pollution prevention and control (^{2}); Directive 98/24/EC, Directive 2000/60/EC of the European Parliament and of the Council of 23 October 2000 establishing a framework for Community action in the field of water policy (^{3}) and Directive 2004/37/EC;

(b) Directive 76/768/EEC as regards testing involving vertebrate animals within the scope of that Directive.

5. The provisions of Titles II, V, VI and VII shall not apply to the extent that a substance is used:

(a) in medicinal products for human or veterinary use within the scope of Regulation (EC) No 726/2004, Directive 2001/82/EC of the European Parliament and of the Council of 6 November 2001 on the Community code relating to veterinary medicinal products (^{4}) and Directive 2001/83/EC of the European Parliament and of the Council of 6 November 2001 on the Community code relating to medicinal products for human use (^{5});

(b) in food or feedingstuffs in accordance with Regulation (EC) No 178/2002 including use:

(i) as a food additive in foodstuffs within the scope of Council Directive 89/107/EEC of 21 December 1988 on the approximation of the laws of the Member States concerning food additives authorised for use in foodstuffs intended for human consumption (^{6});

(^{1}) OJ L 183, 29.6.1989, p. 1. Directive as amended by Regulation (EC) No 1882/2003.
(^{2}) OJ L 257, 10.10.1996, p. 26. Directive as last amended by Regulation (EC) No 166/2006 of the European Parliament and of the Council (OJ L 33, 4.2.2006, p. 1).
(^{3}) OJ L 327, 22.12.2000, p. 1. Directive as amended by Decision No 2455/2001/EC (OJ L 331, 15.12.2001, p. 1).
(^{4}) OJ L 311, 28.11.2001, p. 1. Directive as last amended by Directive 2004/28/EC (OJ L 136, 30.4.2004, p. 58).
(^{5}) OJ L 311, 28.11.2001, p. 67. Directive as last amended by Regulation (EC) No 1901/2006.
(^{6}) OJ L 40, 11.2.1989, p. 27. Directive as last amended by Regulation (EC) No 1882/2003.

▼C1

(ii) as a flavouring in foodstuffs within the scope of Council Directive 88/388/EEC of 22 June 1988 on the approximation of the laws of the Member States relating to flavourings for use in foodstuffs and to source materials for their production (¹) and Commission Decision 1999/217/EC of 23 February 1999 adopting a register of flavouring substances used in or on foodstuffs drawn up in application of Regulation (EC) No 2232/96 of the European Parliament and of the Council (²);

(iii) as an additive in feedingstuffs within the scope of Regulation (EC) No 1831/2003 of the European Parliament and of the Council of 22 September 2003 on additives for use in animal nutrition (³);

(iv) in animal nutrition within the scope of Council Directive 82/471/EEC of 30 June 1982 concerning certain products used in animal nutrition (⁴).

6.   The provisions of Title IV shall not apply to the following ►M3 mixtures ◄ in the finished state, intended for the final user:

(a) medicinal products for human or veterinary use, within the scope of Regulation (EC) No 726/2004 and Directive 2001/82/EC and as defined in Directive 2001/83/EC;

(b) cosmetic products as defined in Directive 76/768/EEC;

(c) medical devices which are invasive or used in direct physical contact with the human body in so far as Community measures lay down provisions for the classification and labelling of dangerous substances and ►M3 mixtures ◄ which ensure the same level of information provision and protection as Directive 1999/45/EC;

(d) food or feedingstuffs in accordance with Regulation (EC) No 178/2002 including use:

(i) as a food additive in foodstuffs within the scope of Directive 89/107/EEC;

(ii) as a flavouring in foodstuffs within the scope of Directive 88/388/EEC and Decision 1999/217/EC;

(iii) as an additive in feedingstuffs within the scope of Regulation (EC) No 1831/2003;

(iv) in animal nutrition within the scope of Directive 82/471/EEC.

(¹) OJ L 184, 15.7.1988, p. 61. Directive as last amended by Regulation (EC) No 1882/2003.
(²) OJ L 84, 27.3.1999, p. 1. Decision as last amended by Decision 2006/253/EC (OJ L 91, 29.3.2006, p. 48).
(³) OJ L 268, 18.10.2003, p. 29. Regulation as amended by Commission Regulation (EC) No 378/2005 (OJ L 59, 5.3.2005, p. 8).
(⁴) OJ L 213, 21.7.1982, p. 8. Directive as last amended by Commission Directive 2004/116/EC (OJ L 379, 24.12.2004, p. 81).

▼C1

7. The following shall be exempted from Titles II, V and VI:

(a) substances included in Annex IV, as sufficient information is known about these substances that they are considered to cause minimum risk because of their intrinsic properties;

(b) substances covered by Annex V, as registration is deemed inappropriate or unnecessary for these substances and their exemption from these Titles does not prejudice the objectives of this Regulation;

(c) substances on their own or in ►M3 mixtures ◄, registered in accordance with Title II, exported from the Community by an actor in the supply chain and re-imported into the Community by the same or another actor in the same supply chain who shows that:

(i) the substance being re-imported is the same as the exported substance;

(ii) he has been provided with the information in accordance with Articles 31 or 32 relating to the exported substance;

(d) substances, on their own, in ►M3 mixtures ◄ or in articles, which have been registered in accordance with Title II and which are recovered in the Community if:

(i) the substance that results from the recovery process is the same as the substance that has been registered in accordance with Title II; and

(ii) the information required by Articles 31 or 32 relating to the substance that has been registered in accordance with Title II is available to the establishment undertaking the recovery.

8. On-site isolated intermediates and transported isolated intermediates shall be exempted from:

(a) Chapter 1 of Title II, with the exception of Articles 8 and 9; and

(b) Title VII.

9. The provisions of Titles II and VI shall not apply to polymers.

CHAPTER 2

Definitions and general provision

Article 3

Definitions

For the purposes of this Regulation:

1. substance: means a chemical element and its compounds in the natural state or obtained by any manufacturing process, including any additive necessary to preserve its stability and any impurity deriving from the process used, but excluding any solvent which may be separated without affecting the stability of the substance or changing its composition;

2. ►M3 mixture ◄: means a mixture or solution composed of two or more substances;

▼C1

3. article: means an object which during production is given a special shape, surface or design which determines its function to a greater degree than does its chemical composition;

4. producer of an article: means any natural or legal person who makes or assembles an article within the Community;

5. polymer: means a substance consisting of molecules characterised by the sequence of one or more types of monomer units. Such molecules must be distributed over a range of molecular weights wherein differences in the molecular weight are primarily attributable to differences in the number of monomer units. A polymer comprises the following:

(a) a simple weight majority of molecules containing at least three monomer units which are covalently bound to at least one other monomer unit or other reactant;

(b) less than a simple weight majority of molecules of the same molecular weight.

In the context of this definition a 'monomer unit' means the reacted form of a monomer substance in a polymer;

6. monomer: means a substance which is capable of forming covalent bonds with a sequence of additional like or unlike molecules under the conditions of the relevant polymer-forming reaction used for the particular process;

7. registrant: means the manufacturer or the importer of a substance or the producer or importer of an article submitting a registration for a substance;

8. manufacturing: means production or extraction of substances in the natural state;

9. manufacturer: means any natural or legal person established within the Community who manufactures a substance within the Community;

10. import: means the physical introduction into the customs territory of the Community;

11. importer: means any natural or legal person established within the Community who is responsible for import;

12. placing on the market: means supplying or making available, whether in return for payment or free of charge, to a third party. Import shall be deemed to be placing on the market;

13. downstream user: means any natural or legal person established within the Community, other than the manufacturer or the importer, who uses a substance, either on its own or in a ►M3 mixture ◄, in the course of his industrial or professional activities. A distributor or a consumer is not a downstream user. A re-importer exempted pursuant to Article 2(7)(c) shall be regarded as a downstream user;

14. distributor: means any natural or legal person established within the Community, including a retailer, who only stores and places on the market a substance, on its own or in a ►M3 mixture ◄, for third parties;

▼C1

15. intermediate: means a substance that is manufactured for and consumed in or used for chemical processing in order to be transformed into another substance (hereinafter referred to as synthesis):

(a) non-isolated intermediate: means an intermediate that during synthesis is not intentionally removed (except for sampling) from the equipment in which the synthesis takes place. Such equipment includes the reaction vessel, its ancillary equipment, and any equipment through which the substance(s) pass(es) during a continuous flow or batch process as well as the pipework for transfer from one vessel to another for the purpose of the next reaction step, but it excludes tanks or other vessels in which the substance(s) are stored after the manufacture;

(b) on-site isolated intermediate: means an intermediate not meeting the criteria of a non-isolated intermediate and where the manufacture of the intermediate and the synthesis of (an)other substance(s) from that intermediate take place on the same site, operated by one or more legal entities;

(c) transported isolated intermediate: means an intermediate not meeting the criteria of a non-isolated intermediate and transported between or supplied to other sites;

16. site: means a single location, in which, if there is more than one manufacturer of (a) substance(s), certain infrastructure and facilities are shared;

17. actors in the supply chain: means all manufacturers and/or importers and/or downstream users in a supply chain;

18. Agency: means the European Chemicals Agency as established by this Regulation;

19. competent authority: means the authority or authorities or bodies established by the Member States to carry out the obligations arising from this Regulation;

20. phase-in substance: means a substance which meets at least one of the following criteria:

(a) it is listed in the European Inventory of Existing Commercial Chemical Substances (EINECS);

▼M1

(b) it was manufactured in the Community, or in the countries acceding to the European Union on 1 January 1995, on 1 May 2004 or on 1 January 2007, but not placed on the market by the manufacturer or importer, at least once in the 15 years before the entry into force of this Regulation, provided the manufacturer or importer has documentary evidence of this;

▼C3

(c) it was placed on the market in the Community, or in the countries acceding to the European Union on 1 January 1995, on 1 May 2004 or on 1 January 2007, by the manufacturer or importer before the entry into force of this Regulation and it was considered as having been notified in accordance with the first indent of Article 8(1) of Directive 67/548/EEC in the version of Article 8(1) resulting from the amendment effected by Directive 79/831/EEC, but it does not meet the definition of a polymer as set out in this Regulation, provided the manufacturer or importer has documentary evidence of this, including proof that the substance was placed on the market by any manufacturer or importer between 18 September 1981 and 31 October 1993 inclusive;

▼C1

21. notified substance: means a substance for which a notification has been submitted and which could be placed on the market in accordance with Directive 67/548/EEC;

22. product and process orientated research and development: means any scientific development related to product development or the further development of a substance, on its own, in ►M3 mixtures ◄ or in articles in the course of which pilot plant or production trials are used to develop the production process and/or to test the fields of application of the substance;

23. scientific research and development: means any scientific experimentation, analysis or chemical research carried out under controlled conditions in a volume less than one tonne per year;

24. use: means any processing, formulation, consumption, storage, keeping, treatment, filling into containers, transfer from one container to another, mixing, production of an article or any other utilisation;

25. registrant's own use: means an industrial or professional use by the registrant;

26. identified use: means a use of a substance on its own or in a ►M3 mixture ◄, or a use of a ►M3 mixture ◄, that is intended by an actor in the supply chain, including his own use, or that is made known to him in writing by an immediate downstream user;

27. full study report: means a complete and comprehensive description of the activity performed to generate the information. This covers the complete scientific paper as published in the literature describing the study performed or the full report prepared by the test house describing the study performed;

28. robust study summary: means a detailed summary of the objectives, methods, results and conclusions of a full study report providing sufficient information to make an independent assessment of the study minimising the need to consult the full study report;

29. study summary: means a summary of the objectives, methods, results and conclusions of a full study report providing sufficient information to make an assessment of the relevance of the study;

▼C1

30. per year: means per calendar year, unless stated otherwise, for phase-in substances that have been imported or manufactured for at least three consecutive years, quantities per year shall be calculated on the basis of the average production or import volumes for the three preceding calendar years;

31. restriction: means any condition for or prohibition of the manufacture, use or placing on the market;

32. supplier of a substance or a ►M3 mixture ◄: means any manufacturer, importer, downstream user or distributor placing on the market a substance, on its own or in a ►M3 mixture ◄, or a ►M3 mixture ◄;

33. supplier of an article: means any producer or importer of an article, distributor or other actor in the supply chain placing an article on the market;

34. recipient of a substance or a ►M3 mixture ◄: means a downstream user or a distributor being supplied with a substance or a ►M3 mixture ◄;

35. recipient of an article: means an industrial or professional user, or a distributor, being supplied with an article but does not include consumers;

36. SME: means small and medium-sized enterprises as defined in the Commission Recommendation of 6 May 2003 concerning the definition of micro, small and medium-sized enterprises (¹);

37. exposure scenario: means the set of conditions, including operational conditions and risk management measures, that describe how the substance is manufactured or used during its life-cycle and how the manufacturer or importer controls, or recommends downstream users to control, exposures of humans and the environment. These exposure scenarios may cover one specific process or use or several processes or uses as appropriate;

38. use and exposure category: means an exposure scenario covering a wide range of processes or uses, where the processes or uses are communicated, as a minimum, in terms of the brief general description of use;

39. substances which occur in nature: means a naturally occurring substance as such, unprocessed or processed only by manual, mechanical or gravitational means, by dissolution in water, by flotation, by extraction with water, by steam distillation or by heating solely to remove water, or which is extracted from air by any means;

40. not chemically modified substance: means a substance whose chemical structure remains unchanged, even if it has undergone a chemical process or treatment, or a physical mineralogical transformation, for instance to remove impurities;

_____
(¹) OJ L 124, 20.5.2003, p. 36.

▼C1

41. alloy: means a metallic material, homogenous on a macroscopic scale, consisting of two or more elements so combined that they cannot be readily separated by mechanical means.

Article 4

General provision

Any manufacturer, importer, or where relevant downstream user, may, whilst retaining full responsibility for complying with his obligations under this Regulation, appoint a third party representative for all proceedings under Article 11, Article 19, Title III and Article 53 involving discussions with other manufacturers, importers, or where relevant downstream users. In these cases, the identity of a manufacturer or importer or downstream user who has appointed a representative shall not normally be disclosed by the Agency to other manufacturers, importers, or, where relevant, downstream users.

TITLE II

REGISTRATION OF SUBSTANCES

CHAPTER 1

General obligation to register and information requirements

Article 5

No data, no market

Subject to Articles 6, 7, 21 and 23, substances on their own, in ►M3 mixtures ◄ or in articles shall not be manufactured in the Community or placed on the market unless they have been registered in accordance with the relevant provisions of this Title where this is required.

Article 6

General obligation to register substances on their own or in ►M3 mixtures ◄

1. Save where this Regulation provides otherwise, any manufacturer or importer of a substance, either on its own or in one or more ►M3 mixture ◄(s), in quantities of one tonne or more per year shall submit a registration to the Agency.

2. For monomers that are used as on-site isolated intermediates or transported isolated intermediates, Articles 17 and 18 shall not apply.

3. Any manufacturer or importer of a polymer shall submit a registration to the Agency for the monomer substance(s) or any other substance(s), that have not already been registered by an actor up the supply chain, if both the following conditions are met:

(a) the polymer consists of 2 % weight by weight (w/w) or more of such monomer substance(s) or other substance(s) in the form of monomeric units and chemically bound substance(s);

▼C1

(b) the total quantity of such monomer substance(s) or other substance(s) makes up one tonne or more per year.

4.   A submission for registration shall be accompanied by the fee required in accordance with Title IX.

Article 7

Registration and notification of substances in articles

1.   Any producer or importer of articles shall submit a registration to the Agency for any substance contained in those articles, if both the following conditions are met:

(a) the substance is present in those articles in quantities totalling over one tonne per producer or importer per year;

(b) the substance is intended to be released under normal or reasonably foreseeable conditions of use.

A submission for registration shall be accompanied by the fee required in accordance with Title IX.

2.   Any producer or importer of articles shall notify the Agency, in accordance with paragraph 4 of this Article, if a substance meets the criteria in Article 57 and is identified in accordance with Article 59(1), if both the following conditions are met:

(a) the substance is present in those articles in quantities totalling over one tonne per producer or importer per year;

(b) the substance is present in those articles above a concentration of 0,1 % weight by weight (w/w).

3.   Paragraph 2 shall not apply where the producer or importer can exclude exposure to humans or the environment during normal or reasonably foreseeable conditions of use including disposal. In such cases, the producer or importer shall supply appropriate instructions to the recipient of the article.

4.   The information to be notified shall include the following:

(a) the identity and contact details of the producer or importer as specified in section 1 of Annex VI, with the exception of their own use sites;

(b) the registration number(s) referred to in Article 20(1), if available;

(c) the identity of the substance as specified in sections 2.1 to 2.3.4 of Annex VI;

(d) the classification of the substance(s) as specified in sections 4.1 and 4.2 of Annex VI;

(e) a brief description of the use(s) of the substance(s) in the article as specified in section 3.5 of Annex VI and of the uses of the article(s);

(f) the tonnage range of the substance(s), such as 1 to 10 tonnes, 10 to 100 tonnes and so on.

▼C1

5. The Agency may take decisions requiring producers or importers of articles to submit a registration, in accordance with this Title, for any substance in those articles, if all the following conditions are met:

(a) the substance is present in those articles in quantities totalling over one tonne per producer or importer per year;

(b) the Agency has grounds for suspecting that:

(i) the substance is released from the articles, and

(ii) the release of the substance from the articles presents a risk to human health or the environment;

(c) the substance is not subject to paragraph 1.

A submission for registration shall be accompanied by the fee required in accordance with Title IX.

6. Paragraphs 1 to 5 shall not apply to substances that have already been registered for that use.

7. From 1 June 2011 paragraphs 2, 3 and 4 of this Article shall apply six months after a substance is identified in accordance with Article 59(1).

8. Any measures for the implementation of paragraphs 1 to 7 shall be adopted in accordance with the procedure referred to in Article 133(3).

Article 8

Only representative of a non-Community manufacturer

1. A natural or legal person established outside the Community who manufactures a substance on its own, in ►**M3** mixtures ◄ or in articles, formulates a ►**M3** mixture ◄ or produces an article that is imported into the Community may by mutual agreement appoint a natural or legal person established in the Community to fulfil, as his only representative, the obligations on importers under this Title.

2. The representative shall also comply with all other obligations of importers under this Regulation. To this end, he shall have a sufficient background in the practical handling of substances and the information related to them and, without prejudice to Article 36, shall keep available and up-to-date information on quantities imported and customers sold to, as well as information on the supply of the latest update of the safety data sheet referred to in Article 31.

3. If a representative is appointed in accordance with paragraphs 1 and 2, the non-Community manufacturer shall inform the importer(s) within the same supply chain of the appointment. These importers shall be regarded as downstream users for the purposes of this Regulation.

▼C1

Article 9

Exemption from the general obligation to register for product and process orientated research and development (PPORD)

1.   Articles 5, 6, 7, 17, 18 and 21 shall not apply for a period of five years to a substance manufactured in the Community or imported for the purposes of product and process orientated research and development by a manufacturer or importer or producer of articles, by himself or in cooperation with listed customers and in a quantity which is limited to the purpose of product and process orientated research and development.

2.   For the purpose of paragraph 1, the manufacturer or importer or producer of articles shall notify the Agency of the following information:

(a) the identity of the manufacturer or importer or producer of articles as specified in section 1 of Annex VI;

(b) the identity of the substance, as specified in section 2 of Annex VI;

(c) the classification of the substance as specified in section 4 of Annex VI, if any;

(d) the estimated quantity as specified in section 3.1 of Annex VI;

(e) the list of customers referred to in paragraph 1, including their names and addresses.

The notification shall be accompanied by the fee required in accordance with Title IX.

The period set out in paragraph 1 shall begin at receipt of the notification at the Agency.

3.   The Agency shall check the completeness of the information supplied by the notifier and Article 20(2) shall apply adapted as necessary. The Agency shall assign a number to the notification and a notification date, which shall be the date of receipt of the notification at the Agency, and shall forthwith communicate that number and date to the manufacturer, or importer, or producer of articles concerned. The Agency shall also communicate this information to the competent authority of the Member State(s) concerned.

4.   The Agency may decide to impose conditions with the aim of ensuring that the substance or the ▶M3 mixture ◀ or article in which the substance is incorporated will be handled only by staff of listed customers as referred to in paragraph 2(e) in reasonably controlled conditions, in accordance with the requirements of legislation for the protection of workers and the environment, and will not be made available to the general public at any time either on its own or in a ▶M3 mixture ◀ or article and that remaining quantities will be re-collected for disposal after the exemption period.

In such cases, the Agency may ask the notifier to provide additional necessary information.

5.   In the absence of any indication to the contrary, the manufacturer or importer of the substance or the producer or importer of articles may manufacture or import the substance or produce or import the articles not earlier than two weeks after the notification.

▼C1

6. The manufacturer or importer or producer of articles shall comply with any conditions imposed by the Agency in accordance with paragraph 4.

7. The Agency may decide to extend the five-year exemption period by a further maximum of five years or, in the case of substances to be used exclusively in the development of medicinal products for human or veterinary use, or for substances that are not placed on the market, for a further maximum of ten years, upon request if the manufacturer or importer or producer of articles can demonstrate that such an extension is justified by the research and development programme.

8. The Agency shall forthwith communicate any draft decisions to the competent authorities of each Member State in which the manufacture, import, production or product and process orientated research takes place.

When taking decisions as provided for in paragraphs 4 and 7, the Agency shall take into account any comments made by such competent authorities.

9. The Agency and the competent authorities of the Member States concerned shall always keep confidential the information submitted in accordance with paragraphs 1 to 8.

10. An appeal may be brought, in accordance with Articles 91, 92 and 93, against Agency decisions under paragraphs 4 and 7 of this Article.

Article 10

Information to be submitted for general registration purposes

A registration required by Article 6 or by Article 7(1) or (5) shall include all the following information:

(a) a technical dossier including:

   (i) the identity of the manufacturer(s) or importer(s) as specified in section 1 of Annex VI;

   (ii) the identity of the substance as specified in section 2 of Annex VI;

   (iii) information on the manufacture and use(s) of the substance as specified in section 3 of Annex VI; this information shall represent all the registrant's identified use(s). This information may include, if the registrant deems appropriate, the relevant use and exposure categories;

   (iv) the classification and labelling of the substance as specified in section 4 of Annex VI;

   (v) guidance on safe use of the substance as specified in Section 5 of Annex VI;

   (vi) study summaries of the information derived from the application of Annexes VII to XI;

   (vii) robust study summaries of the information derived from the application of Annexes VII to XI, if required under Annex I;

▼C1

(viii) an indication as to which of the information submitted under (iii), (iv), (vi), (vii) or subparagraph (b) has been reviewed by an assessor chosen by the manufacturer or importer and having appropriate experience;

(ix) proposals for testing where listed in Annexes IX and X;

(x) for substances in quantities of 1 to 10 tonnes, exposure information as specified in section 6 of Annex VI;

(xi) a request as to which of the information in Article 119(2) the manufacturer or importer considers should not be made available on the Internet in accordance with Article 77(2)(e), including a justification as to why publication could be harmful for his or any other concerned party's commercial interests.

Except in cases covered under Article 25(3), Article 27(6) or Article 30(3), the registrant shall be in legitimate possession of or have permission to refer to the full study report summarised under (vi) and (vii) for the purpose of registration;

(b) a chemical safety report when required under Article 14, in the format specified in Annex I. The relevant sections of this report may include, if the registrant considers appropriate, the relevant use and exposure categories.

Article 11

Joint submission of data by multiple registrants

1. When a substance is intended to be manufactured in the Community by one or more manufacturers and/or imported by one or more importers, and/or is subject to registration under Article 7, the following shall apply.

Subject to paragraph 3, the information specified in Article 10(a)(iv), (vi), (vii) and (ix), and any relevant indication under Article 10(a)(viii) shall first be submitted by the one registrant acting with the agreement of the other assenting registrant(s) (hereinafter referred to as the lead registrant).

Each registrant shall subsequently submit separately the information specified in Article 10(a)(i), (ii), (iii) and (x), and any relevant indication under Article 10(a)(viii).

The registrants may decide themselves whether to submit the information specified in Article 10(a)(v) and (b) and any relevant indication under Article 10(a)(viii) separately or whether one registrant is to submit this information on behalf of the others.

2. Each registrant need only comply with paragraph 1 for items of information specified in Article 10(a)(iv), (vi), (vii) and (ix) that are required for the purposes of registration within his tonnage band in accordance with Article 12.

▼C1

3.   A registrant may submit the information referred to in Article 10(a)(iv), (vi), (vii) or (ix) separately if:

(a) it would be disproportionately costly for him to submit this information jointly; or

(b) submitting the information jointly would lead to disclosure of information which he considers to be commercially sensitive and is likely to cause him substantial commercial detriment; or

(c) he disagrees with the lead registrant on the selection of this information.

If points (a), (b) or (c) apply, the registrant shall submit, along with the dossier, an explanation as to why the costs would be disproportionate, why disclosure of information was likely to lead to substantial commercial detriment or the nature of the disagreement, as the case may be.

4.   A submission for registration shall be accompanied by the fee required in accordance with Title IX.

Article 12

Information to be submitted depending on tonnage

1.   The technical dossier referred to in Article 10(a) shall include under points (vi) and (vii) of that provision all physicochemical, toxicological and ecotoxicological information that is relevant and available to the registrant and as a minimum the following:

(a) the information specified in Annex VII for non-phase-in substances, and for phase-in substances meeting one or both of the criteria specified in Annex III, manufactured or imported in quantities of one tonne or more per year per manufacturer or importer;

(b) the information on physicochemical properties specified in Annex VII, section 7 for phase-in substances manufactured or imported in quantities of one tonne or more per year per manufacturer or importer which do not meet either of the criteria specified in Annex III;

(c) the information specified in Annexes VII and VIII for substances manufactured or imported in quantities of 10 tonnes or more per year per manufacturer or importer;

(d) the information specified in Annexes VII and VIII and testing proposals for the provision of the information specified in Annex IX for substances manufactured or imported in quantities of 100 tonnes or more per year per manufacturer or importer;

(e) the information specified in Annexes VII and VIII and testing proposals for the provision of the information specified in Annexes IX and X for substances manufactured or imported in quantities of 1 000 tonnes or more per year per manufacturer or importer.

2.   As soon as the quantity of a substance per manufacturer or importer that has already been registered reaches the next tonnage threshold, the manufacturer or importer shall inform the Agency immediately of the additional information he would require under paragraph 1. Article 26(3) and (4) shall apply adapted as necessary.

▼C1

3.   This Article shall apply to producers of articles adapted as necessary.

Article 13

General requirements for generation of information on intrinsic properties of substances

1.   Information on intrinsic properties of substances may be generated by means other than tests, provided that the conditions set out in Annex XI are met. In particular for human toxicity, information shall be generated whenever possible by means other than vertebrate animal tests, through the use of alternative methods, for example, *in vitro* methods or qualitative or quantitative structure-activity relationship models or from information from structurally related substances (grouping or read-across). Testing in accordance with Annex VIII, Sections 8.6 and 8.7, Annex IX and Annex X may be omitted where justified by information on exposure and implemented risk management measures as specified in Annex XI, section 3.

2.   These methods shall be regularly reviewed and improved with a view to reducing testing on vertebrate animals and the number of animals involved. The Commission, following consultation with relevant stakeholders, shall, as soon as possible, make a proposal, if appropriate, to amend the Commission Regulation on test methods adopted in accordance with the procedure referred to in Article 133(4), and the Annexes of this Regulation, if relevant, so as to replace, reduce or refine animal testing. Amendments to that Commission Regulation shall be adopted in accordance with the procedure specified in paragraph 3 and amendments to the Annexes of this Regulation shall be adopted in accordance with the procedure referred to in Article 131.

3.   Where tests on substances are required to generate information on intrinsic properties of substances, they shall be conducted in accordance with the test methods laid down in a Commission Regulation or in accordance with other international test methods recognised by the Commission or the Agency as being appropriate. The Commission shall adopt that Regulation, designed to amend the non-essential elements of this Regulation by supplementing it, in accordance with the procedure referred to in Article 133(4).

Information on intrinsic properties of substances may be generated in accordance with other test methods provided that the conditions set out in Annex XI are met.

4.   Ecotoxicological and toxicological tests and analyses shall be carried out in compliance with the principles of good laboratory practice provided for in Directive 2004/10/EC or other international standards recognised as being equivalent by the Commission or the Agency and with the provisions of Directive 86/609/EEC, if applicable.

5.   If a substance has already been registered, a new registrant shall be entitled to refer to the study summaries or robust study summaries, for the same substance submitted earlier, provided that he can show that the substance that he is now registering is the same as the one previously registered, including the degree of purity and the nature of impurities, and that the previous registrant(s) have given permission to refer to the full study reports for the purpose of registration.

▼C1

A new registrant shall not refer to such studies in order to provide the information required in Section 2 of Annex VI.

Article 14

Chemical safety report and duty to apply and recommend risk reduction measures

1. Without prejudice to Article 4 of Directive 98/24/EC, a chemical safety assessment shall be performed and a chemical safety report completed for all substances subject to registration in accordance with this Chapter in quantities of 10 tonnes or more per year per registrant.

The chemical safety report shall document the chemical safety assessment which shall be conducted in accordance with paragraphs 2 to 7 and with Annex I for either each substance on its own or in a ►M3 mixture ◄ or in an article or a group of substances.

2. A chemical safety assessment in accordance with paragraph 1 need not be performed for a substance which is present in a ►M3 mixture ◄ if the concentration of the substance in the ►M3 mixture ◄ is less than the lowest of any of the following:

(a) the applicable concentrations defined in the table of Article 3(3) of Directive 1999/45/EC;

▼M3

(b) the specific concentration limits that have been set in Part 3 of Annex VI to Regulation (EC) No 1272/2008 of the European Parliament and of the Council of 16 December 2008 on classification, labelling and packaging of substances and mixtures (¹);

(ba) for substances classified as hazardous to the aquatic environment, if a multiplying factor (hereinafter referred to as 'M-factor') has been set in Part 3 of Annex VI to Regulation (EC) No 1272/2008, the cut-off value in Table 1.1 of Annex I to that Regulation adjusted using the calculation set out in section 4.1 of Annex I to that Regulation;

▼C1

(c) the concentration limits given in Part B of Annex II to Directive 1999/45/EC;

(d) the concentration limits given in Part B of Annex III to Directive 1999/45/EC;

▼M3

(e) the specific concentration limits given in an agreed entry in the classification and labelling inventory referred to in Article 42 of Regulation (EC) No 1272/2008;

(ea) for substances classified as hazardous to the aquatic environment, if an M-factor has been set in an agreed entry in the classification and labelling inventory referred to in Article 42 of Regulation (EC) No 1272/2008, the cut-off value in Table 1.1 of Annex I to that Regulation adjusted using the calculation set out in section 4.1 of Annex I to that Regulation;

(¹) OJ L 353, 31.12.2008, p. 1;

▼C1

(f) 0,1 % weight by weight (w/w), if the substance meets the criteria in Annex XIII of this Regulation.

3. A chemical safety assessment of a substance shall include the following steps:

(a) human health hazard assessment;

(b) physicochemical hazard assessment;

(c) environmental hazard assessment;

(d) persistent, bioaccumulative and toxic (PBT) and very persistent and very bioaccumulative (vPvB) assessment.

▼M3

4. If, as a result of carrying out steps (a) to (d) of paragraph 3, the registrant concludes that the substance fulfils the criteria for any of the following hazard classes or categories set out in Annex I to Regulation (EC) No 1272/2008:

(a) hazard classes 2.1 to 2.4, 2.6 and 2.7, 2.8 types A and B, 2.9, 2.10, 2.12, 2.13 categories 1 and 2, 2.14 categories 1 and 2, 2.15 types A to F;

(b) hazard classes 3.1 to 3.6, 3.7 adverse effects on sexual function and fertility or on development, 3.8 effects other than narcotic effects, 3.9 and 3.10;

(c) hazard class 4.1;

(d) hazard class 5.1,

or is assessed to be a PBT or vPvB, the chemical safety assessment shall include the following additional steps:

▼C1

(a) exposure assessment including the generation of exposure scenario(s) (or the identification of relevant use and exposure categories if appropriate) and exposure estimation;

(b) risk characterisation.

The exposure scenarios (where appropriate the use and exposure categories), exposure assessment and risk characterisation shall address all identified uses of the registrant.

5. The chemical safety report need not include consideration of the risks to human health from the following end uses:

▼C1

(a) in food contact materials within the scope of Regulation (EC) No 1935/2004 of the European Parliament and of the Council of 27 October 2004 on materials and articles intended to come into contact with food ([1]);

(b) in cosmetic products within the scope of Directive 76/768/EEC.

6.   Any registrant shall identify and apply the appropriate measures to adequately control the risks identified in the chemical safety assessment, and where suitable, recommend them in the safety data sheets which he supplies in accordance with Article 31.

7.   Any registrant required to conduct a chemical safety assessment shall keep his chemical safety report available and up to date.

CHAPTER 2

Substances regarded as being registered

Article 15

Substances in plant protection and biocidal products

1.   Active substances and co-formulants manufactured or imported for use in plant protection products only and included either in Annex I to Council Directive 91/414/EEC ([2]) or in Commission Regulation (EEC) No 3600/92 ([3]), Commission Regulation (EC) No 703/2001 ([4]), Commission Regulation (EC) No 1490/2002 ([5]), or Commission Decision 2003/565/EC ([6]) and for any substance for which a Commission Decision on the completeness of the dossier has been taken pursuant to Article 6 of Directive 91/414/EEC shall be regarded as being registered and the registration as completed for manufacture or import for the use as a plant protection product and therefore as fulfilling the requirements of Chapters 1 and 5 of this Title.

([1]) OJ L 338, 13.11.2004, p. 4.

([2]) Council Directive 91/414/EEC of 15 July 1991 concerning the placing of plant protection products on the market (OJ L 230, 19.8.1991, p. 1). Directive as last amended by Commission Directive 2006/136/EC (OJ L 349, 12.12.2006, p. 42).

([3]) Commission Regulation (EEC) No 3600/92 of 11 December 1992 laying down the detailed rules for the implementation of the first stage of the programme of work referred to in Article 8(2) of Council Directive 91/414/EEC concerning the placing of plant protection products on the market (OJ L 366, 15.12.1992, p. 10). Regulation as last amended by Regulation (EC) No 2266/2000 (OJ L 259, 13.10.2000, p. 27).

([4]) Commission Regulation (EC) No 703/2001 of 6 April 2001 laying down the active substances of plant protection products to be assessed in the second stage of the work programme referred to in Article 8(2) of Council Directive 91/414/EEC and revising the list of Member States designated as rapporteurs for those substances (OJ L 98, 7.4.2001, p. 6).

([5]) Commission Regulation (EC) No 1490/2002 of 14 August 2002 laying down further detailed rules for the implementation of the third stage of the programme of work referred to in Article 8(2) of Council Directive 91/414/EEC (OJ L 224, 21.8.2002, p. 23). Regulation as last amended by Regulation (EC) No 1744/2004 (OJ L 311, 8.10.2004, p. 23).

([6]) Commission Decision 2003/565/EC of 25 July 2003 extending the time period provided for in Article 8(2) of Council Directive 91/414/EEC (OJ L 192, 31.7.2003, p. 40).

▼C1

2.   Active substances manufactured or imported for use in biocidal products only and included either in Annexes I, IA or IB to Directive 98/8/EC of the European Parliament and of the Council of 16 February 1998 concerning the placing of biocidal products on the market [1] or in Commission Regulation (EC) No 2032/2003 [2] on the second phase of the 10-year work programme referred to in Article 16(2) of Directive 98/8/EC, until the date of the decision referred to in the second sub-paragraph of Article 16(2) of Directive 98/8/EC, shall be regarded as being registered and the registration as completed for manufacture or import for the use in a biocidal product and therefore as fulfilling the requirements of Chapters 1 and 5 of this Title.

Article 16

Duties of the Commission, the Agency and registrants of substances regarded as being registered

1.   The Commission or the relevant Community body shall make information equivalent to that required by Article 10 available to the Agency for substances regarded as registered according to Article 15. The Agency shall include this information or a reference thereto in its databases and notify the competent authorities thereof by 1 December 2008.

2.   Articles 21, 22 and 25 to 28 shall not apply to uses of substances regarded as registered according to Article 15.

CHAPTER 3

Obligation to register and information requirements for certain types of isolated intermediates

Article 17

Registration of on-site isolated intermediates

1.   Any manufacturer of an on-site isolated intermediate in quantities of one tonne or more per year shall submit a registration to the Agency for the on-site isolated intermediate.

2.   A registration for an on-site isolated intermediate shall include all the following information, to the extent that the manufacturer is able to submit it without any additional testing:

(a) the identity of the manufacturer as specified in Section 1 of Annex VI;

(b) the identity of the intermediate as specified in Sections 2.1 to 2.3.4 of Annex VI;

(c) the classification of the intermediate as specified in Section 4 of Annex VI;

---

[1] OJ L 123, 24.4.1998, p. 1. Directive as last amended by Commission Directive 2006/140/EC (OJ L 414, 30.12.2006, p. 78).

[2] OJ L 307, 24.11.2003, p. 1. Regulation as last amended by Regulation (EC) No 1849/2006 (OJ L 355, 15.12.2006, p. 63).

▼C1

(d) any available existing information on physicochemical, human health or environmental properties of the intermediate. Where a full study report is available, a study summary shall be submitted;

(e) a brief general description of the use, as specified in Section 3.5 of Annex VI;

(f) details of the risk management measures applied.

Except in cases covered under Article 25(3), Article 27(6) or Article 30(3), the registrant shall be in legitimate possession of or have permission to refer to the full study report summarised under (d) for the purpose of registration.

The registration shall be accompanied by the fee required in accordance with Title IX.

3.   Paragraph 2 shall apply only to on-site isolated intermediates if the manufacturer confirms that the substance is only manufactured and used under strictly controlled conditions in that it is rigorously contained by technical means during its whole lifecycle. Control and procedural technologies shall be used to minimise emission and any resulting exposure.

If these conditions are not fulfilled, the registration shall include the information specified in Article 10.

Article 18

Registration of transported isolated intermediates

1.   Any manufacturer or importer of a transported isolated intermediate in quantities of one tonne or more per year shall submit a registration to the Agency for the transported isolated intermediate.

2.   A registration for a transported isolated intermediate shall include all the following information:

(a) the identity of the manufacturer or importer as specified in Section 1 of Annex VI;

(b) the identity of the intermediate as specified in Sections 2.1 to 2.3.4 of Annex VI;

(c) the classification of the intermediate as specified in Section 4 of Annex VI;

(d) any available existing information on physicochemical, human health or environmental properties of the intermediate. Where a full study report is available, a study summary shall be submitted;

(e) a brief general description of the use, as specified in Section 3.5 of Annex VI;

(f) information on risk management measures applied and recommended to the user in accordance with paragraph 4.

▼C1

Except in cases covered under Article 25(3), Article 27(6) or Article 30(3), the registrant shall be in legitimate possession of or have permission to refer to the full study report summarised under (d) for the purpose of registration.

The registration shall be accompanied by the fee required in accordance with Title IX.

3. A registration for a transported isolated intermediate in quantities of more than 1 000 tonnes per year per manufacturer or importer shall include the information specified in Annex VII in addition to the information required under paragraph 2.

For the generation of this information, Article 13 shall apply.

4. Paragraphs 2 and 3 shall apply only to transported isolated intermediates if the manufacturer or importer confirms himself or states that he has received confirmation from the user that the synthesis of (an)other substance(s) from that intermediate takes place on other sites under the following strictly controlled conditions:

(a) the substance is rigorously contained by technical means during its whole lifecycle including manufacture, purification, cleaning and maintenance of equipment, sampling, analysis, loading and unloading of equipment or vessels, waste disposal or purification and storage;

(b) procedural and control technologies shall be used that minimise emission and any resulting exposure;

(c) only properly trained and authorised personnel handle the substance;

(d) in the case of cleaning and maintenance works, special procedures such as purging and washing are applied before the system is opened and entered;

(e) in cases of accident and where waste is generated, procedural and/or control technologies are used to minimise emissions and the resulting exposure during purification or cleaning and maintenance procedures;

(f) substance-handling procedures are well documented and strictly supervised by the site operator.

If the conditions listed in the first subparagraph are not fulfilled, the registration shall include the information specified in Article 10.

Article 19

Joint submission of data on isolated intermediates by multiple registrants

1. When an on-site isolated intermediate or transported isolated intermediate is intended to be manufactured in the Community by one or more manufacturers and/or imported by one or more importers, the following shall apply.

▼C1

Subject to paragraph 2 of this Article, the information specified in Article 17(2)(c) and (d) and Article 18(2)(c) and (d) shall first be submitted by one manufacturer or importer acting with the agreement of the other assenting manufacturer(s) or importer(s) (hereinafter referred to as 'the lead registrant').

Each registrant shall subsequently submit separately the information specified in Article 17(2)(a), (b), (e) and (f) and Article 18(2)(a),(b), (e) and (f).

2. A manufacturer or importer may submit the information referred to in Article 17(2)(c) or (d) and Article 18(2)(c) or (d) separately if:

(a) it would be disproportionately costly for him to submit this jointly; or

(b) submitting the information jointly would lead to disclosure of information which he considers to be commercially sensitive and is likely to cause him substantial commercial detriment; or

(c) he disagrees with the lead registrant on the selection of this information.

If points (a), (b) or (c) apply, the manufacturer or importer shall submit, along with the dossier, an explanation as to why the costs would be disproportionate, why disclosure of information was likely to lead to substantial commercial detriment, or the nature of the disagreement, as the case may be.

3. A submission for registration shall be accompanied by the fee required in accordance with Title IX.

CHAPTER 4

Common provisions for all registrations

Article 20

Duties of the Agency

1. The Agency shall assign a submission number to each registration, which is to be used for all correspondence regarding the registration until the registration is deemed to be complete, and a submission date, which shall be the date of receipt of the registration at the Agency.

2. The Agency shall undertake a completeness check of each registration in order to ascertain that all the elements required under Articles 10 and 12 or under Articles 17 or 18, as well as the registration fee referred to in Article 6(4), Article 7(1) and (5), Article 17(2) or Article 18(2), have been provided. The completeness check shall not include an assessment of the quality or the adequacy of any data or justifications submitted.

The Agency shall undertake the completeness check within three weeks of the submission date, or within three months of the relevant deadline of Article 23, as regards registrations of phase-in substances submitted in the course of the two-month period immediately preceding that deadline.

▼C1

If a registration is incomplete, the Agency shall inform the registrant, before expiry of the three-week or three-month period referred to in the second subparagraph, as to what further information is required in order for the registration to be complete, while setting a reasonable deadline for this. The registrant shall complete his registration and submit it to the Agency within the deadline set. The Agency shall confirm the submission date of the further information to the registrant. The Agency shall perform a further completeness check, considering the further information submitted.

The Agency shall reject the registration if the registrant fails to complete his registration within the deadline set. The registration fee shall not be reimbursed in such cases.

3.   Once the registration is complete, the Agency shall assign a registration number to the substance concerned and a registration date, which shall be the same as the submission date. The Agency shall without delay communicate the registration number and registration date to the registrant concerned. The registration number shall be used for all subsequent correspondence regarding registration.

4.   The Agency shall notify the competent authority of the relevant Member State within 30 days of the submission date, that the following information is available in the Agency database:

(a) the registration dossier together with the submission or registration number;

(b) the submission or registration date;

(c) the result of the completeness check; and

(d) any request for further information and deadline set in accordance with the third subparagraph of paragraph 2.

The relevant Member State shall be the Member State within which the manufacture takes place or the importer is established.

If the manufacturer has production sites in more than one Member State, the relevant Member State shall be the one in which the head office of the manufacturer is established. The other Member States where the production sites are established shall also be notified.

The Agency shall forthwith notify the competent authority of the relevant Member State(s) when any further information submitted by the registrant is available on the Agency database.

5.   An appeal may be brought, in accordance with Articles 91, 92 and 93, against Agency decisions under paragraph 2 of this Article.

6.   Where additional information for a particular substance is submitted to the Agency by a new registrant, the Agency shall notify the existing registrants that this information is available on the database for the purposes of Article 22.

▼C1

Article 21

Manufacturing and import of substances

1.   A registrant may start or continue the manufacture or import of a substance or production or import of an article, if there is no indication to the contrary from the Agency in accordance with Article 20(2) within the three weeks after the submission date, without prejudice to Article 27(8).

In the case of registrations of phase-in substances, such a registrant may continue the manufacture or import of the substance or production or import of an article, if there is no indication to the contrary from the Agency in accordance with Article 20(2) within the three weeks after the submission date or, if submitted within the two-month period before the relevant deadline of Article 23, if there is no indication to the contrary from the Agency in accordance with Article 20(2) within the three months from that deadline, without prejudice to Article 27(8).

In the case of an update of a registration according to Article 22 a registrant may continue the manufacture or import of the substance, or the production or import of the article, if there is no indication to the contrary from the Agency in accordance with Article 20(2) within the three weeks after the update date, without prejudice to Article 27(8).

2.   If the Agency has informed the registrant that he is to submit further information in accordance with the third subparagraph of Article 20(2), the registrant may start the manufacture or import of a substance or production or import of an article if there is no indication to the contrary from the Agency within the three weeks after receipt by the Agency of the further information necessary to complete his registration, without prejudice to Article 27(8).

3.   If a lead registrant submits parts of the registration on behalf of one or more other registrants, as provided for in Articles 11 or 19, any of the other registrants may manufacture or import the substance or produce or import the articles only after the expiry of the time-limit laid down in paragraph 1 or 2 of this Article and provided that there is no indication to the contrary from the Agency in respect of the registration of the lead registrant acting on behalf of the others and his own registration.

Article 22

Further duties of registrants

1.   Following registration, a registrant shall be responsible on his own initiative for updating his registration without undue delay with relevant new information and submitting it to the Agency in the following cases:

(a) any change in his status, such as being a manufacturer, an importer or a producer of articles, or in his identity, such as his name or address;

(b) any change in the composition of the substance as given in Section 2 of Annex VI;

▼C1

(c) changes in the annual or total quantities manufactured or imported by him or in the quantities of substances present in articles produced or imported by him if these result in a change of tonnage band, including cessation of manufacture or import;

(d) new identified uses and new uses advised against as in Section 3.7 of Annex VI for which the substance is manufactured or imported;

(e) new knowledge of the risks of the substance to human health and/or the environment of which he may reasonably be expected to have become aware which leads to changes in the safety data sheet or the chemical safety report;

(f) any change in the classification and labelling of the substance;

(g) any update or amendment of the chemical safety report or Section 5 of Annex VI;

(h) the registrant identifies the need to perform a test listed in Annex IX or Annex X, in which cases a testing proposal shall be developed;

(i) any change in the access granted to information in the registration.

The Agency shall communicate this information to the competent authority of the relevant Member State.

2. A registrant shall submit to the Agency an update of the registration containing the information required by the decision made in accordance with Articles 40, 41 or 46 or take into account a decision made in accordance with Articles 60 and 73, within the deadline specified in that decision. The Agency shall notify the competent authority of the relevant Member State that the information is available on its database.

3. The Agency shall undertake a completeness check according to Article 20(2) first and second subparagraphs of each updated registration. In cases where the update is in accordance with Article 12(2) and with paragraph 1(c) of this Article then the Agency shall check the completeness of the information supplied by the registrant and Article 20(2) shall apply adapted as necessary.

4. In cases covered by Articles 11 or 19, each registrant shall submit separately the information specified in paragraph 1(c) of this Article.

5. An update shall be accompanied by the relevant part of the fee required in accordance with Title IX.

▼C1

CHAPTER 5

Transitional provisions applicable to phase-in substances and notified substances

Article 23

Specific provisions for phase-in substances

1. Article 5, Article 6, Article 7(1), Article 17, Article 18 and Article 21 shall not apply until 1 December 2010 to the following substances:

(a) phase-in substances classified as carcinogenic, mutagenic or toxic to reproduction, category 1 or 2, in accordance with Directive 67/548/EEC and manufactured in the Community or imported, in quantities reaching one tonne or more per year per manufacturer or per importer, at least once after 1 June 2007;

(b) phase-in substances classified as very toxic to aquatic organisms which may cause long-term adverse effects in the aquatic environment (R50/53) in accordance with Directive 67/548/EEC, and manufactured in the Community or imported in quantities reaching 100 tonnes or more per year per manufacturer or per importer, at least once after 1 June 2007;

(c) phase-in substances manufactured in the Community or imported, in quantities reaching 1 000 tonnes or more per year per manufacturer or per importer, at least once after 1 June 2007.

2. Article 5, Article 6, Article 7(1), Article 17, Article 18 and Article 21 shall not apply until 1 June 2013 to phase-in substances manufactured in the Community or imported, in quantities reaching 100 tonnes or more per year per manufacturer or per importer, at least once after 1 June 2007.

3. Article 5, Article 6, Article 7(1), Article 17, Article 18 and Article 21 shall not apply until 1 June 2018 to phase-in substances manufactured in the Community or imported, in quantities reaching one tonne or more per year per manufacturer or per importer, at least once after 1 June 2007.

4. Without prejudice to paragraphs 1 to 3, a registration can be submitted at any time before the relevant deadline.

5. This Article shall also apply to substances registered under Article 7 adapted as necessary.

Article 24

Notified substances

1. A notification in accordance with Directive 67/548/EEC shall be regarded as a registration for the purposes of this Title and the Agency shall assign a registration number by 1 December 2008.

▼C1

2.   If the quantity of a notified substance manufactured or imported per manufacturer or importer reaches the next tonnage threshold under Article 12, the additional required information corresponding to that tonnage threshold, as well as to all the lower tonnage thresholds, shall be submitted in accordance with Articles 10 and 12, unless it has already been submitted in accordance with those Articles.

TITLE III

DATA SHARING AND AVOIDANCE OF UNNECESSARY TESTING

CHAPTER 1

Objectives and general rules

Article 25

Objectives and general rules

1.   In order to avoid animal testing, testing on vertebrate animals for the purposes of this Regulation shall be undertaken only as a last resort. It is also necessary to take measures limiting duplication of other tests.

2.   The sharing and joint submission of information in accordance with this Regulation shall concern technical data and in particular information related to the intrinsic properties of substances. Registrants shall refrain from exchanging information concerning their market behaviour, in particular as regards production capacities, production or sales volumes, import volumes or market shares.

3.   Any study summaries or robust study summaries of studies submitted in the framework of a registration under this Regulation at least 12 years previously can be used for the purposes of registration by another manufacturer or importer.

CHAPTER 2

Rules for non-phase-in substances and registrants of phase-in substances who have not pre-registered

Article 26

Duty to inquire prior to registration

1.   Every potential registrant of a non-phase-in substance, or potential registrant of a phase-in substance who has not pre-registered in accordance with Article 28, shall inquire from the Agency whether a registration has already been submitted for the same substance. He shall submit all the following information to the Agency with the inquiry:

(a) his identity as specified in Section 1 of Annex VI, with the exception of the use sites;

▼C1

(b) the identity of the substance, as specified in Section 2 of Annex VI;

(c) which information requirements would require new studies involving vertebrate animals to be carried out by him;

(d) which information requirements would require other new studies to be carried out by him.

2.   If the same substance has previously not been registered, the Agency shall inform the potential registrant accordingly.

3.   If the same substance has previously been registered less than 12 years earlier, the Agency shall inform the potential registrant without delay of the names and addresses of the previous registrant(s) and of the relevant summaries or robust study summaries, as the case may be, already submitted by them.

Studies involving vertebrate animals shall not be repeated.

The Agency shall simultaneously inform the previous registrants of the name and address of the potential registrant. The available studies shall be shared with the potential registrant in accordance with Article 27.

4.   If several potential registrants have made an inquiry in respect of the same substance, the Agency shall inform all potential registrants without delay of the name and address of the other potential registrants.

Article 27

Sharing of existing data in the case of registered substances

1.   Where a substance has previously been registered less than 12 years earlier as referred to in Article 26(3), the potential registrant:

(a) shall, in the case of information involving tests on vertebrate animals; and

(b) may, in the case of information not involving tests on vertebrate animals,

request from the previous registrant(s) the information he requires with respect to Article 10(a)(vi) and (vii) in order to register.

2.   When a request for information has been made according to paragraph 1, the potential and the previous registrant(s) as referred to in paragraph 1 shall make every effort to reach an agreement on the sharing of the information requested by the potential registrant(s) with respect to Article 10(a)(vi) and (vii). Such an agreement may be replaced by submission of the matter to an arbitration board and acceptance of the arbitration order.

▼C1

3. The previous registrant and potential registrant(s) shall make every effort to ensure that the costs of sharing the information are determined in a fair, transparent and non-discriminatory way. This may be facilitated by following cost sharing guidance based on those principles which is adopted by the Agency in accordance with Article 77(2)(g). Registrants are only required to share in the costs of information that they are required to submit to satisfy their registration requirements.

4. On agreement on the sharing of the information, the previous registrant shall make available to the new registrant the agreed information and shall give the new registrant the permission to refer to the previous registrant's full study report.

5. If there is failure to reach such an agreement, the potential registrant(s) shall inform the Agency and the previous registrant(s) thereof at the earliest one month after receipt, from the Agency, of the name and address of the previous registrant(s).

6. Within one month from the receipt of the information referred to in paragraph 5, the Agency shall give the potential registrant permission to refer to the information requested by him in his registration dossier, subject to the potential registrant providing, upon request by the Agency, proof that he has paid the previous registrant(s) for that information a share of cost incurred. The previous registrant(s) shall have a claim on the potential registrant for a proportionate share of the cost incurred by him. Calculation of the proportionate share may be facilitated by the guidance adopted by the Agency in accordance with Article 77(2)(g). Provided he makes the full study report available to the potential registrant, the previous registrant(s) shall have a claim on the potential registrant for an equal share of the cost incurred by him, which shall be enforceable in the national courts.

7. An appeal may be brought, in accordance with Articles 91, 92 and 93, against Agency decisions under paragraph 6 of this Article.

8. The registration waiting period in accordance with Article 21(1) for the new registrant shall be extended by a period of four months, if the previous registrant so requests.

CHAPTER 3

Rules for phase-in-substances

Article 28

Duty to pre-register for phase-in substances

1. In order to benefit from the transitional regime provided for in Article 23 each potential registrant of a phase-in substance in quantities of one tonne or more per year, including without limitation intermediates, shall submit all the following information to the Agency:

(a) the name of the substance as specified in Section 2 of Annex VI, including its EINECS and CAS number or, if not available, any other identity codes;

▼C1

(b) his name and address and the name of the contact person and, where appropriate, the name and address of the person representing him in accordance with Article 4 as specified in Section 1 of Annex VI;

(c) the envisaged deadline for the registration and the tonnage band;

(d) the name(s) of substance(s) as specified in Section 2 of Annex VI, including their EINECS and CAS number or, if not available, any other identity codes, for which the available information is relevant for the application of Sections 1.3 and 1.5 of Annex XI.

2.   The information referred to in paragraph 1 shall be submitted within a time period starting on 1 June 2008 and ending on 1 December 2008.

3.   Registrants who do not submit the information required under paragraph 1 shall not be able to rely on Article 23.

4.   The Agency shall by 1 January 2009 publish on its website a list of the substances referred to in paragraph 1(a) and (d). That list shall comprise only the names of the substances, including their EINECS and CAS number if available and other identity codes, and the first envisaged registration deadline.

5.   After the publication of the list a downstream user of a substance not appearing on the list may notify the Agency of his interest in the substance, his contact details and the details of his current supplier. The Agency shall publish on its website the name of the substance and on request provide contact details of the downstream user to a potential registrant.

6.   Potential registrants who manufacture or import for the first time a phase-in substance in quantities of one tonne or more per year or use for the first time a phase-in substance in the context of production of articles or import for the first time an article containing a phase-in substance that would require registration, after 1 December 2008, shall be entitled to rely on Article 23 provided that they submit the information referred to in paragraph 1 of this Article to the Agency within six months of first manufacturing, importing or using the substance in quantities of one tonne or more per year and no later than 12 months before the relevant deadline in Article 23.

7.   Manufacturers or importers of phase-in substances in quantities of less than one tonne per year that appear on the list published by the Agency in accordance with paragraph 4 of this Article, as well as downstream users of those substances and third parties holding information on those substances, may submit the information referred to in paragraph 1 of this Article or any other relevant information to the Agency for those substances, with the intention of being part of the substance information exchange forum as referred to in Article 29.

▼C1

Article 29

Substance Information Exchange Forums

1.   All potential registrants, downstream users and third parties who have submitted information to the Agency in accordance with Article 28, or whose information is held by the Agency in accordance with Article 15, for the same phase-in substance, or registrants who have submitted a registration for that phase-in substance before the deadline set out in Article 23(3), shall be participants in a substance information exchange forum (SIEF).

2.   The aim of each SIEF shall be to:

(a) facilitate, for the purposes of registration, the exchange of the information specified in Article 10(a) (vi) and (vii) between potential registrants, thereby avoiding the duplication of studies; and

(b) agree classification and labelling where there is a difference in the classification and labelling of the substance between potential registrants.

3.   SIEF participants shall provide other participants with existing studies, react to requests by other participants for information, collectively identify needs for further studies for the purposes of paragraph 2(a) and arrange for such studies to be carried out. Each SIEF shall be operational until 1 June 2018.

Article 30

Sharing of data involving tests

1.   Before testing is carried out in order to meet the information requirements for the purposes of registration, a SIEF participant shall inquire whether a relevant study is available by communicating within his SIEF. If a relevant study involving tests on vertebrate animals is available within the SIEF, a participant of that SIEF shall request that study. If a relevant study not involving tests on vertebrate animals is available within the SIEF, a SIEF participant may request that study.

Within one month of the request, the owner of the study shall provide proof of its cost to the participant(s) requesting it. The participant(s) and the owner shall make every effort to ensure that the costs of sharing the information are determined in a fair, transparent and non discriminatory way. This may be facilitated by following any cost sharing guidance which is based on those principles and is adopted by the Agency in accordance with Article 77(2)(g). If they cannot reach such an agreement, the cost shall be shared equally. The owner shall give permission to refer to the full study report for the purpose of registration within two weeks of receipt of payment. Registrants are only required to share in the costs of information that they are required to submit to satisfy their registration requirements.

▼C1

2.   If a relevant study involving tests is not available within the SIEF, only one study shall be conducted per information requirement within each SIEF by one of its participants acting on behalf of the others. They shall take all reasonable steps to reach an agreement within a deadline set by the Agency as to who is to carry out the test on behalf of the other participants and to submit a summary or robust study summary to the Agency. If no agreement is reached, the Agency shall specify which registrant or downstream user shall perform the test. All participants of the SIEF who require a study shall contribute to the costs for the elaboration of the study with a share corresponding to the number of participating potential registrants. Those participants that do not carry out the study themselves shall have the right to receive the full study report within two weeks following payment to the participant that carried out the study.

3.   If the owner of a study as referred to in paragraph 1 which involves testing on vertebrate animals refuses to provide either proof of the cost of that study or the study itself to (an) other participant(s), he shall not be able to proceed with registration until he provides the information to the other participants(s). The other participant(s) shall proceed with registration without fulfilling the relevant information requirement, explaining the reason for this in the registration dossier. The study shall not be repeated unless within 12 months of the date of registration of the other participant(s), the owner of this information has not provided it to them and the Agency decides that the test should be repeated by them. However, if a registration containing this information has already been submitted by another registrant, the Agency shall give the other participant(s) permission to refer to the information in his registration dossier(s). The other registrant shall have a claim on the other participant(s) for an equal share of the cost, provided he makes the full study report available to the other participant(s), which shall be enforceable in the national courts.

4.   If the owner of a study as referred to in paragraph 1 which does not involve testing on vertebrate animals refuses to provide either proof of the cost of that study or the study itself to (an)other participant(s), the other SIEF participants shall proceed with registration as if no relevant study was available in the SIEF.

5.   An appeal may be brought, in accordance with Articles 91, 92 and 93, against Agency decisions under paragraphs 2 or 3 of this Article.

6.   The owner of the study who has refused to provide either proof of the cost or the study itself, as referred to in paragraph 3 or 4 of this Article, shall be penalised in accordance with Article 126.

TITLE IV

INFORMATION IN THE SUPPLY CHAIN

Article 31

Requirements for safety data sheets

1.   The supplier of a substance or a ►**M3** mixture ◄ shall provide the recipient of the substance or ►**M3** mixture ◄ with a safety data sheet compiled in accordance with Annex II:

▼M3

(a) where a substance meets the criteria for classification as hazardous in accordance with Regulation (EC) No 1272/2008 or a mixture meets the criteria for classification as dangerous in accordance with Directive 1999/45/EC; or

▼C1

(b) where a substance is persistent, bioaccumulative and toxic or very persistent and very bioaccumulative in accordance with the criteria set out in Annex XIII; or

(c) where a substance is included in the list established in accordance with Article 59(1) for reasons other than those referred to in points (a) and (b).

2. Any actor in the supply chain who is required, under Articles 14 or 37, to carry out a chemical safety assessment for a substance shall ensure that the information in the safety data sheet is consistent with the information in this assessment. If the safety data sheet is developed for a ► M3 mixture ◄ and the actor in the supply chain has prepared a chemical safety assessment for that ► M3 mixture ◄, it is sufficient if the information in the safety data sheet is consistent with the chemical safety report for the ► M3 mixture ◄ instead of with the chemical safety report for each substance in the ► M3 mixture ◄.

3. The supplier shall provide the recipient at his request with a safety data sheet compiled in accordance with Annex II, where a ► M3 mixture ◄ does not meet the criteria for classification as dangerous in accordance with Articles 5, 6 and 7 of Directive 1999/45/EC, but contains:

(a) in an individual concentration of ≥ 1 % by weight for non-gaseous ► M3 mixtures ◄ and ≥ 0,2 % by volume for gaseous ► M3 mixtures ◄ at least one substance posing human health or environmental hazards; or

(b) in an individual concentration of ≥ 0,1 % by weight for non-gaseous ► M3 mixtures ◄ at least one substance that is persistent, bioaccumulative and toxic or very persistent and very bioaccumulative in accordance with the criteria set out in Annex XIII or has been included for reasons other than those referred to in point (a) in the list established in accordance with Article 59(1); or

(c) a substance for which there are Community workplace exposure limits.

▼M3

4. The safety data sheet need not be supplied where substances that are hazardous in accordance with Regulation (EC) No 1272/2008 or mixtures that are dangerous in accordance with Directive 1999/45/EC, offered or sold to the general public, are provided with sufficient information to enable users to take the necessary measures as regards the protection of human health, safety and the environment, unless requested by a downstream user or distributor.

▼C1

5. The safety data sheet shall be supplied in an official language of the Member State(s) where the substance or ► M3 mixture ◄ is placed on the market, unless the Member State(s) concerned provide otherwise.

▼C1

6. The safety data sheet shall be dated and shall contain the following headings:

1. identification of the substance/ ►M3 mixture ◄ and of the company/undertaking;

2. hazards identification;

3. composition/information on ingredients;

4. first-aid measures;

5. fire-fighting measures;

6. accidental release measures;

7. handling and storage;

8. exposure controls/personal protection;

9. physical and chemical properties;

10. stability and reactivity;

11. toxicological information;

12. ecological information;

13. disposal considerations;

14. transport information;

15. regulatory information;

16. other information.

7. Any actor in the supply chain who is required to prepare a chemical safety report according to Articles 14 or 37 shall place the relevant exposure scenarios (including use and exposure categories where appropriate) in an annex to the safety data sheet covering identified uses and including specific conditions resulting from the application of Section 3 of Annex XI.

Any downstream user shall include relevant exposure scenarios, and use other relevant information, from the safety data sheet supplied to him when compiling his own safety data sheet for identified uses.

Any distributor shall pass on relevant exposure scenarios, and use other relevant information, from the safety data sheet supplied to him when compiling his own safety data sheet for uses for which he has passed on information according to Article 37(2).

▼M3

8. A safety data sheet shall be provided free of charge on paper or electronically no later than the date on which the substance or mixture is first supplied.

▼C1

9. Suppliers shall update the safety data sheet without delay on the following occasions:

(a) as soon as new information which may affect the risk management measures, or new information on hazards becomes available;

(b) once an authorisation has been granted or refused;

▼C1

(c) once a restriction has been imposed.

The new, dated version of the information, identified as 'Revision: (date)', shall be provided free of charge on paper or electronically to all former recipients to whom they have supplied the substance or ►M3 mixture ◄ within the preceding 12 months. Any updates following registration shall include the registration number.

▼M3

10. Where substances are classified in accordance with Regulation (EC) No 1272/2008 during the period from its entry into force until 1 December 2010, that classification may be added in the safety data sheet together with the classification in accordance with Directive 67/548/EEC.

From 1 December 2010 until 1 June 2015, the safety data sheets for substances shall contain the classification according to both Directive 67/548/EEC and Regulation (EC) No 1272/2008.

Where mixtures are classified in accordance with Regulation (EC) No 1272/2008 during the period from its entry into force until 1 June 2015, that classification may be added in the safety data sheet, together with the classification in accordance with Directive 1999/45/EC. However, until 1 June 2015, where substances or mixtures are both classified and labelled in accordance with Regulation (EC) No 1272/2008 that classification shall be provided in the safety data sheet, together with the classification in accordance with Directives 67/548/EEC and 1999/45/EC respectively, for the substance, the mixture and its constituents.

▼C1

Article 32

Duty to communicate information down the supply chain for substances on their own or in ►M3 mixtures ◄ for which a safety data sheet is not required

1. Any supplier of a substance on its own or in a ►M3 mixture ◄ who does not have to supply a safety data sheet in accordance with Article 31 shall provide the recipient with the following information:

(a) the registration number(s) referred to in Article 20(3), if available, for any substances for which information is communicated under points (b), (c) or (d) of this paragraph;

(b) if the substance is subject to authorisation and details of any authorisation granted or denied under Title VII in this supply chain;

(c) details of any restriction imposed under Title VIII;

(d) any other available and relevant information about the substance that is necessary to enable appropriate risk management measures to be identified and applied including specific conditions resulting from the application of Section 3 of Annex XI.

2. The information referred to in paragraph 1 shall be communicated free of charge on paper or electronically at the latest at the time of the first delivery of a substance on its own or in a ►M3 mixture ◄ after 1 June 2007.

▼C1

3. Suppliers shall update this information without delay on the following occasions:

(a) as soon as new information which may affect the risk management measures, or new information on hazards becomes available;

(b) once an authorisation has been granted or refused;

(c) once a restriction has been imposed.

In addition, the updated information shall be provided free of charge on paper or electronically to all former recipients to whom they have supplied the substance or ►M3 mixture ◄ within the preceding 12 months. Any updates following registration shall include the registration number.

Article 33

Duty to communicate information on substances in articles

1. Any supplier of an article containing a substance meeting the criteria in Article 57 and identified in accordance with Article 59(1) in a concentration above 0,1 % weight by weight (w/w) shall provide the recipient of the article with sufficient information, available to the supplier, to allow safe use of the article including, as a minimum, the name of that substance.

2. On request by a consumer any supplier of an article containing a substance meeting the criteria in Article 57 and identified in accordance with Article 59(1) in a concentration above 0,1 % weight by weight (w/w) shall provide the consumer with sufficient information, available to the supplier, to allow safe use of the article including, as a minimum, the name of that substance.

The relevant information shall be provided, free of charge, within 45 days of receipt of the request.

Article 34

Duty to communicate information on substances and ►M3 mixtures ◄ up the supply chain

Any actor in the supply chain of a substance or a ►M3 mixture ◄ shall communicate the following information to the next actor or distributor up the supply chain:

(a) new information on hazardous properties, regardless of the uses concerned;

(b) any other information that might call into question the appropriateness of the risk management measures identified in a safety data sheet supplied to him, which shall be communicated only for identified uses.

Distributors shall pass on that information to the next actor or distributor up the supply chain.

Article 35

Access to information for workers

Workers and their representatives shall be granted access by their employer to the information provided in accordance with Articles 31 and 32 in relation to substances or ►M3 mixtures ◄ that they use or may be exposed to in the course of their work.

▼C1

Article 36

Obligation to keep information

1.   Each manufacturer, importer, downstream user and distributor shall assemble and keep available all the information he requires to carry out his duties under this Regulation for a period of at least 10 years after he last manufactured, imported, supplied or used the substance or ►**M3** mixture ◄. That manufacturer, importer, downstream user or distributor shall submit this information or make it available without delay upon request to any competent authority of the Member State in which he is established or to the Agency, without prejudice to Titles II and VI.

2.   In the event of a registrant, downstream user or distributor ceasing activity, or transferring part or all of his operations to a third party, the party responsible for liquidating the registrant, downstream user or distributor's undertaking or assuming responsibility for the placing on the market of the substance or ►**M3** mixture ◄ concerned shall be bound by the obligation in paragraph 1 in place of the registrant, downstream user or distributor.

TITLE V

DOWNSTREAM USERS

Article 37

Downstream user chemical safety assessments and duty to identify, apply and recommend risk reduction measures

1.   A downstream user or distributor may provide information to assist in the preparation of a registration.

2.   Any downstream user shall have the right to make a use, as a minimum the brief general description of use, known in writing (on paper or electronically) to the manufacturer, importer, downstream user or distributor who supplies him with a substance on its own or in a ►**M3** mixture ◄ with the aim of making this an identified use. In making a use known, he shall provide sufficient information to allow the manufacturer, importer or downstream user who has supplied the substance, to prepare an exposure scenario, or if appropriate a use and exposure category, for his use in the manufacturer, importer or downstream user's chemical safety assessment.

Distributors shall pass on such information to the next actor or distributor up the supply chain. Downstream users in receipt of such information may prepare an exposure scenario for the identified use(s), or pass the information to the next actor up the supply chain.

3.   For registered substances, the manufacturer, importer or downstream user shall comply with the obligations laid down in Article 14 either before he next supplies the substance on its own or in a ►**M3** mixture ◄ to the downstream user making the request referred to in paragraph 2 of this Article, provided that the request was made at least one month before the supply, or within one month after the request, whichever is the later.

▼C1

For phase-in substances, the manufacturer, importer or downstream user shall comply with this request and with the obligations laid down in Article 14 before the relevant deadline in Article 23 has expired, provided that the downstream user makes his request at least 12 months before the deadline in question.

Where the manufacturer, importer or downstream user, having assessed the use in accordance with Article 14, is unable to include it as an identified use for reasons of protection of human health or the environment, he shall provide the Agency and the downstream user with the reason(s) for that decision in writing without delay and shall not supply downstream user(s) with the substance without including these reason(s) in the information referred to under Articles 31 or 32. The manufacturer or importer shall include this use in Section 3.7 of Annex VI in his update of the registration in accordance with Article 22(1)(d).

4.   A downstream user of a substance on its own or in a ►M3 mixture ◄ shall prepare a chemical safety report in accordance with Annex XII for any use outside the conditions described in an exposure scenario or if appropriate a use and exposure category communicated to him in a safety data sheet or for any use his supplier advises against.

A downstream user need not prepare such a chemical safety report in any of the following cases:

(a) a safety data sheet is not required to be communicated with the substance or ►M3 mixture ◄ in accordance with Article 31;

(b) a chemical safety report is not required to be completed by his supplier in accordance with Article 14;

(c) the downstream user uses the substance or ►M3 mixture ◄ in a total quantity of less than one tonne per year;

(d) the downstream user implements or recommends an exposure scenario which includes as a minimum the conditions described in the exposure scenario communicated to him in the safety data sheet;

(e) the substance is present in a ►M3 mixture ◄ in a concentration lower than any of the concentrations set out in Article 14(2);

(f) the downstream user is using the substance for the purposes of product and process oriented research and development, provided that the risks to human health and the environment are adequately controlled in accordance with the requirements of legislation for the protection of workers and the environment.

5.   Any downstream user shall identify, apply and where suitable, recommend, appropriate measures to adequately control risks identified in any of the following:

(a) the safety data sheet(s) supplied to him;

(b) his own chemical safety assessment;

(c) any information on risk management measures supplied to him in accordance with Article 32.

▼C1

6. Where a downstream user does not prepare a chemical safety report in accordance with paragraph 4(c), he shall consider the use(s) of the substance and identify and apply any appropriate risk management measures needed to ensure that the risks to human health and the environment are adequately controlled. Where necessary, this information shall be included in any safety data sheet prepared by him.

7. Downstream users shall keep their chemical safety report up to date and available.

8. A chemical safety report prepared in accordance with paragraph 4 of this Article need not include consideration of the risks to human health from the end uses set out in Article 14(5).

Article 38

Obligation for downstream users to report information

1. Before commencing or continuing with a particular use of a substance that has been registered by an actor up the supply chain in accordance with Articles 6 or 18, the downstream user shall report to the Agency the information specified in paragraph 2 of this Article, in the following cases:

(a) the downstream user has to prepare a chemical safety report in accordance with Article 37(4); or

(b) the downstream user is relying on the exemptions in Article 37(4)(c) or (f).

2. The information reported by the downstream user shall include the following:

(a) his identity and contact details as specified in Section 1.1 of Annex VI;

(b) the registration number(s) referred to in Article 20(3), if available;

(c) the identity of the substance(s) as specified in Section 2.1 to 2.3.4 of Annex VI;

(d) the identity of the manufacturer(s) or the importer(s) or other supplier as specified in Section 1.1 of Annex VI;

(e) a brief general description of the use(s), as specified in Section 3.5 of Annex VI, and of the conditions of use(s);

(f) except where the downstream user is relying on the exemption in Article 37(4)(c), a proposal for additional testing on vertebrate animals, where this is considered necessary by the downstream user to complete his chemical safety assessment.

3. The downstream user shall update this information without delay in the event of a change in the information reported in accordance with paragraph 1.

4. A downstream user shall report to the Agency if his classification of a substance is different to that of his supplier.

▼C1

5. Except where a downstream user is relying on the exemption in Article 37(4)(c), reporting in accordance with paragraphs 1 to 4 of this Article shall not be required in respect of a substance, on its own or in a ►M3 mixture ◄, used by the downstream user in quantities of less than one tonne per year for that particular use.

Article 39

Application of downstream user obligations

1. Downstream users shall be required to comply with the requirements of Article 37 at the latest 12 months after receiving a registration number communicated to them by their suppliers in a safety data sheet.

2. Downstream users shall be required to comply with the requirements of Article 38 at the latest six months after receiving a registration number communicated to them by their suppliers in a safety data sheet.

TITLE VI

EVALUATION

CHAPTER 1

Dossier evaluation

Article 40

Examination of testing proposals

▼M3

1. The Agency shall examine any testing proposal set out in a registration or a downstream user report for provision of the information specified in Annexes IX and X for a substance. Priority shall be given to registrations of substances which have or may have PBT, vPvB, sensitising and/or carcinogenic, mutagenic or toxic for reproduction (CMR) properties, or substances above 100 tonnes per year with uses resulting in widespread and diffuse exposure, provided they fulfil the criteria for any of the following hazard classes or categories set out in Annex I of Regulation (EC) No 1272/2008:

(a) hazard classes 2.1 to 2.4, 2.6 and 2.7, 2.8 types A and B, 2.9, 2.10, 2.12, 2.13 categories 1 and 2, 2.14 categories 1 and 2, 2.15 types A to F;

(b) hazard classes 3.1 to 3.6, 3.7 adverse effects on sexual function and fertility or on development, 3.8 effects other than narcotic effects, 3.9 and 3.10;

(c) hazard class 4.1;

(d) hazard class 5.1.

▼C1

2.   Information relating to testing proposals involving tests on vertebrate animals shall be published on the Agency website. The Agency shall publish on its website the name of the substance, the hazard end-point for which vertebrate testing is proposed, and the date by which any third party information is required. It shall invite third parties to submit, using the format provided by the Agency, scientifically valid information and studies that address the relevant substance and hazard end-point, addressed by the testing proposal, within 45 days of the date of publication. All such scientifically valid information and studies received shall be taken into account by the Agency in preparing its decision in accordance with paragraph 3.

3.   On the basis of the examination under paragraph 1, the Agency shall draft one of the following decisions and that decision shall be taken in accordance with the procedure laid down in Articles 50 and 51:

(a) a decision requiring the registrant(s) or downstream user(s) concerned to carry out the proposed test and setting a deadline for submission of the study summary, or the robust study summary if required by Annex I;

(b) a decision in accordance with point (a), but modifying the conditions under which the test is to be carried out;

(c) a decision in accordance with points (a), (b) or (d) but requiring registrant(s) or downstream user(s) to carry out one or more additional tests in cases of non-compliance of the testing proposal with Annexes IX, X and XI;

(d) a decision rejecting the testing proposal;

(e) a decision in accordance with points (a), (b) or (c), if several registrants or downstream users of the same substance have submitted proposals for the same test, giving them the opportunity to reach an agreement on who will perform the test on behalf of all of them and to inform the Agency accordingly within 90 days. If the Agency is not informed of such agreement within such 90 days, it shall designate one of the registrants or downstream users, as appropriate, to perform the test on behalf of all of them.

4.   The registrant or downstream user shall submit the information required to the Agency by the deadline set.

Article 41

Compliance check of registrations

1.   The Agency may examine any registration in order to verify any of the following:

(a) that the information in the technical dossier(s) submitted pursuant to Article 10 complies with the requirements of Articles 10, 12 and 13 and with Annexes III and VI to X;

(b) that the adaptations of the standard information requirements and the related justifications submitted in the technical dossier(s) comply with the rules governing such adaptations set out in Annexes VII to X and with the general rules set out in Annex XI;

▼C1

(c) that any required chemical safety assessment and chemical safety report comply with the requirements of Annex I and that the proposed risk management measures are adequate;

(d) that any explanation(s) submitted in accordance with Article 11(3) or Article 19(2) have an objective basis.

2. The list of dossiers being checked for compliance by the Agency shall be made available to Member States competent authorities.

3. On the basis of an examination made pursuant to paragraph 1, the Agency may, within 12 months of the start of the compliance check, prepare a draft decision requiring the registrant(s) to submit any information needed to bring the registration(s) into compliance with the relevant information requirements and specifying adequate time limits for the submission of further information. Such a decision shall be taken in accordance with the procedure laid down in Articles 50 and 51.

4. The registrant shall submit the information required to the Agency by the deadline set.

5. To ensure that registration dossiers comply with this Regulation, the Agency shall select a percentage of those dossiers, no lower than 5 % of the total received by the Agency for each tonnage band, for compliance checking. The Agency shall give priority, but not exclusively, to dossiers meeting at least one of the following criteria:

(a) the dossier contains information in Article 10(a)(iv), (vi) and/or (vii) submitted separately as per Article 11(3); or

(b) the dossier is for a substance manufactured or imported in quantities of one tonne or more per year and does not meet the requirements of Annex VII applying under either Article 12(1)(a) or (b), as the case may be; or

(c) the dossier is for a substance listed in the Community rolling action plan referred to in Article 44(2).

6. Any third party may electronically submit information to the Agency relating to substances that appear on the list referred to in Article 28(4). The Agency shall consider this information together with the information submitted according to Article 124 when checking and selecting dossiers.

7. The Commission may, after consulting with the Agency, take a decision to vary the percentage of dossiers selected and amend or include further criteria in paragraph 5 in accordance with the procedure referred to in Article 133(4).

Article 42

Check of information submitted and follow-up to dossier evaluation

1. The Agency shall examine any information submitted in consequence of a decision taken under Articles 40 or 41, and draft any appropriate decisions in accordance with these Articles, if necessary.

▼C1

2.   Once the dossier evaluation is completed, the Agency shall notify the Commission and the competent authorities of the Member States of the information obtained and any conclusions made. The competent authorities shall use the information obtained from this evaluation for the purposes of Article 45(5), Article 59(3) and Article 69(4). The Agency shall use the information obtained from this evaluation for the purposes of Article 44.

Article 43

Procedure and time periods for examination of testing proposals

1.   In the case of non phase-in substances, the Agency shall prepare a draft decision in accordance with Article 40(3) within 180 days of receiving a registration or downstream user report containing a testing proposal.

2.   In the case of phase-in substances, the Agency shall prepare the draft decisions in accordance with Article 40(3):

(a) by 1 December 2012 for all registrations received by 1 December 2010 containing proposals for testing in order to fulfil the information requirements in Annexes IX and X;

(b) by 1 June 2016 for all registrations received by 1 June 2013 containing proposals for testing in order to fulfil the information requirements in Annex IX only;

(c) by 1 June 2022 for any registrations containing testing proposals received by 1 June 2018.

3.   The list of registration dossiers being evaluated under Article 40 shall be made available to Member States.

CHAPTER 2

Substance evaluation

Article 44

Criteria for substance evaluation

1.   In order to ensure a harmonised approach, the Agency shall in cooperation with the Member States develop criteria for prioritising substances with a view to further evaluation. Prioritisation shall be on a risk-based approach. The criteria shall consider:

(a) hazard information, for instance structural similarity of the substance with known substances of concern or with substances which are persistent and liable to bio-accumulate, suggesting that the substance or one or more of its transformation products has properties of concern or is persistent and liable to bio-accumulate;

(b) exposure information;

▼C1

(c) tonnage, including aggregated tonnage from the registrations submitted by several registrants.

2.   The Agency shall use the criteria in paragraph 1 for the purpose of compiling a draft Community rolling action plan which shall cover a period of three years and shall specify substances to be evaluated each year. Substances shall be included if there are grounds for considering (either on the basis of a dossier evaluation carried out by the Agency or on the basis of any other appropriate source, including information in the registration dossier) that a given substance constitutes a risk to human health or the environment. The Agency shall submit the first draft rolling action plan to the Member States by 1 December 2011. The Agency shall submit draft annual updates to the rolling action plan to the Member States by 28 February each year.

The Agency shall adopt the final Community rolling action plan on the basis of an opinion from the Member State Committee set up under Article 76(1)(e) (hereinafter referred to as the Member State Committee) and shall publish the plan on its website, identifying the Member State who will carry out the evaluation of the substances listed therein as determined according to Article 45.

Article 45

Competent authority

1.   The Agency shall be responsible for coordinating the substance evaluation process and ensuring that substances on the Community rolling action plan are evaluated. In doing so, the Agency shall rely on the competent authorities of Member States. In carrying out an evaluation of a substance, the competent authorities may appoint another body to act on their behalf.

2.   A Member State may choose (a) substance(s) from the draft Community rolling action plan, with the aim of becoming a competent authority for the purposes of Articles 46, 47 and 48. In the event of a substance from the draft Community rolling action plan not being chosen by any Member State, the Agency shall ensure that the substance is evaluated.

3.   In cases where two or more Member States have expressed an interest in evaluating the same substance and they cannot agree who should be the competent authority, the competent authority for the purposes of Articles 46, 47 and 48 shall be determined in accordance with the following procedure.

The Agency shall refer the matter to the Member State Committee, in order to agree which authority shall be the competent authority, taking into account the Member State in which the manufacturer(s) or importer(s) is located, the respective proportions of total Community gross domestic product, the number of substances already being evaluated by a Member State and the expertise available.

If, within 60 days of the referral, the Member State Committee reaches unanimous agreement, the Member States concerned shall adopt substances for evaluation accordingly.

▼C1

If the Member State Committee fails to reach a unanimous agreement, the Agency shall submit the conflicting opinions to the Commission, which shall decide which authority shall be the competent authority, in accordance with the procedure referred to in Article 133(3), and the Member States concerned shall adopt substances for evaluation accordingly.

4.   The competent authority identified in accordance with paragraphs 2 and 3 shall evaluate the allocated substances in accordance with this Chapter.

5.   A Member State may notify the Agency at any time of a substance not on the Community rolling action plan, whenever it is in possession of information which suggests that the substance is a priority for evaluation. The Agency shall decide whether to add this substance to the Community rolling action plan on the basis of an opinion from the Member State Committee. If the substance is added to the Community rolling action plan, the proposing Member State, or another Member State who agrees, shall evaluate that substance.

Article 46

Requests for further information and check of information submitted

1.   If the competent authority considers that further information is required, including, if appropriate, information not required in Annexes VII to X, it shall prepare a draft decision, stating reasons, requiring the registrant(s) to submit the further information and setting a deadline for its submission. A draft decision shall be prepared within 12 months of the publication of the Community rolling action plan on the Agency's website for substances to be evaluated that year. The decision shall be taken in accordance with the procedure laid down in Articles 50 and 52.

2.   The registrant shall submit the information required to the Agency by the deadline set.

3.   The competent authority shall examine any information submitted, and shall draft any appropriate decisions in accordance with this Article, if necessary, within 12 months of the information being submitted.

4.   The competent authority shall finish its evaluation activities within 12 months of the start of the evaluation of the substance or within 12 months of the information being submitted under paragraph 2, and notify the Agency accordingly. If this deadline is exceeded, the evaluation shall be deemed to be finished.

Article 47

Coherence with other activities

1.   An evaluation of a substance shall be based on all relevant information submitted on that particular substance and on any previous evaluation under this Title. Where information on intrinsic properties of a substance has been generated by reference to structurally related substance(s), the evaluation may also cover these related substances. In cases where a decision on an evaluation has been previously taken in accordance with Article 51 or Article 52, any draft decision requiring further information under Article 46 may be justified only by a change of circumstances or acquired knowledge.

▼C1

2. In order to ensure a harmonised approach to requests for further information, the Agency shall monitor draft decisions under Article 46 and shall develop criteria and priorities. Where appropriate, implementing measures shall be adopted in accordance with the procedure referred to in Article 133(3).

Article 48

Follow-up to substance evaluation

Once the substance evaluation has been completed, the competent authority shall consider how to use the information obtained from this evaluation for the purposes of Article 59(3), Article 69(4) and Article 115(1). The competent authority shall inform the Agency of its conclusions as to whether or how to use the information obtained. The Agency shall in turn inform the Commission, the registrant and the competent authorities of the other Member States.

CHAPTER 3

Evaluation of intermediates

Article 49

Further information on on-site isolated intermediates

For on-site isolated intermediates that are used in strictly controlled conditions, neither dossier nor substance evaluation shall apply. However, where the competent authority of the Member State in whose territory the site is located considers that a risk to human health or the environment, equivalent to the level of concern arising from the use of substances meeting the criteria in Article 57, arises from the use of an on-site isolated intermediate and that risk is not properly controlled, it may:

(a) require the registrant to submit further information directly related to the risk identified. This request shall be accompanied by a written justification;

(b) examine any information submitted and, if necessary, recommend any appropriate risk reduction measures to address the risks identified in relation to the site in question.

The procedure provided for in the first paragraph may be undertaken only by the competent authority referred to therein. The competent authority shall inform the Agency of the results of such an evaluation, which shall then inform the competent authorities of the other Member States and make the results available to them.

▼C1

CHAPTER 4

Common provisions

Article 50

Registrants' and downstream users' rights

1. The Agency shall notify any draft decision under Articles 40, 41 or 46 to the registrant(s) or downstream user(s) concerned, informing them of their right to comment within 30 days of receipt. If the concerned registrant(s) or downstream user(s) wish to comment, they shall provide their comments to the Agency. The Agency in turn shall inform the competent authority of the submission of the comments without delay. The competent authority (for decisions taken under Article 46) and the Agency (for decisions taken under Articles 40 and 41) shall take any comments received into account and may amend the draft decision accordingly.

2. If a registrant has ceased the manufacture or import of the substance, or the production or import of an article, or the downstream user the use, he shall inform the Agency of this fact with the consequence that the registered volume in his registration, if appropriate, shall be put to zero and no further information may be requested with respect to that substance, unless the registrant notifies the restart of the manufacture or import of the substance or the production or import of the article, or the downstream user notifies the restart of the use. The Agency shall inform the competent authority of the Member State in which the registrant or downstream user is located.

3. The registrant may cease the manufacture or import of the substance or the production or import of the article, or the downstream user the use, upon receipt of the draft decision. In such cases, the registrant, or downstream user, shall inform the Agency of this fact with the consequence that his registration, or report, shall no longer be valid, and no further information may be requested with respect to that substance, unless he submits a new registration or report. The Agency shall inform the competent authority of the Member State in which the registrant or downstream user is located.

4. Notwithstanding paragraphs 2 and 3, further information may be required in accordance with Article 46 in either or both of the following cases:

(a) where the competent authority prepares a dossier in accordance with Annex XV concluding that there is a potential long-term risk to human health or the environment justifying the need for further information;

(b) where the exposure to the substance manufactured or imported by the registrant(s), or to the substance in the article produced or imported by the registrant(s), or to the substance used by the downstream user(s) contributes significantly to that risk.

The procedure in Articles 69 to 73 shall apply *mutatis mutandis*.

▼C1

Article 51

Adoption of decisions under dossier evaluation

1.   The Agency shall notify its draft decision in accordance with Articles 40 or 41, together with the comments of the registrant, to the competent authorities of the Member States.

2.   Within 30 days of circulation, the Member States may propose amendments to the draft decision to the Agency.

3.   If the Agency does not receive any proposals, it shall take the decision in the version notified under paragraph 1.

4.   If the Agency receives a proposal for amendment, it may modify the draft decision. The Agency shall refer a draft decision, together with any amendments proposed, to the Member State Committee within 15 days of the end of the 30-day period referred to in paragraph 2.

5.   The Agency shall forthwith communicate any proposal for amendment to any registrants or downstream users concerned and allow them to comment within 30 days. The Member State Committee shall take any comments received into account.

6.   If, within 60 days of the referral, the Member State Committee reaches a unanimous agreement on the draft decision, the Agency shall take the decision accordingly.

7.   If the Member State Committee fails to reach unanimous agreement, the Commission shall prepare a draft decision to be taken in accordance with the procedure referred to in Article 133(3).

8.   An appeal may be brought, in accordance with Articles 91, 92 and 93, against Agency decisions under paragraphs 3 and 6 of this Article.

Article 52

Adoption of decisions under substance evaluation

1.   The competent authority shall circulate its draft decision in accordance with Article 46, together with any comments by the registrant or downstream user, to the Agency and to the competent authorities of the other Member States.

2.   The provisions of Article 51(2) to (8) shall apply *mutatis mutandis*.

Article 53

Cost sharing for tests without an agreement between registrants and/or downstream users

1.   Where registrants or downstream users are required to perform a test as a result of a decision taken under this Title, those registrants or downstream users shall make every effort to reach an agreement as to who is to carry it out on behalf of the other registrants or downstream users and to inform the Agency accordingly within 90 days. If the Agency is not informed of such agreement within such 90 days, it shall designate one of the registrants or downstream users to perform the test on behalf of all of them.

▼C1

2. If a registrant or downstream user performs a test on behalf of others, they shall all share the cost of that study equally.

3. In the case referred to in paragraph 1, the registrant or downstream user who performs the test shall provide each of the others concerned with a copy of the full study report.

4. The person performing and submitting the study shall have a claim against the others accordingly. Any person concerned shall be able to make a claim in order to prohibit another person from manufacturing, importing or placing the substance on the market if that other person either fails to pay his share of the cost or to provide security for that amount or fails to hand over a copy of the full study report of the study performed. All claims shall be enforceable in the national courts. Any person may choose to submit their claims for remuneration to an arbitration board and accept the arbitration order.

Article 54

Publication of information on evaluation

By 28 February of each year, the Agency shall publish on its website a report on the progress made over the previous calendar year towards discharging the obligations incumbent upon it in relation to evaluation. This report shall include, in particular, recommendations to potential registrants in order to improve the quality of future registrations.

TITLE VII

AUTHORISATION

CHAPTER 1

Authorisation requirement

Article 55

Aim of authorisation and considerations for substitution

The aim of this Title is to ensure the good functioning of the internal market while assuring that the risks from substances of very high concern are properly controlled and that these substances are progressively replaced by suitable alternative substances or technologies where these are economically and technically viable. To this end all manufacturers, importers and downstream users applying for authorisations shall analyse the availability of alternatives and consider their risks, and the technical and economic feasibility of substitution.

Article 56

General provisions

1. A manufacturer, importer or downstream user shall not place a substance on the market for a use or use it himself if that substance is included in Annex XIV, unless:

(a) the use(s) of that substance on its own or in a ►M3 mixture ◄ or the incorporation of the substance into an article for which the substance is placed on the market or for which he uses the substance himself has been authorised in accordance with Articles 60 to 64; or

▼C1

(b) the use(s) of that substance on its own or in a ►M3 mixture ◄ or the incorporation of the substance into an article for which the substance is placed on the market or for which he uses the substance himself has been exempted from the authorisation requirement in Annex XIV itself in accordance with Article 58(2); or

(c) the date referred to in Article 58(1)(c)(i) has not been reached; or

(d) the date referred to in Article 58(1)(c)(i) has been reached and he made an application 18 months before that date but a decision on the application for authorisation has not yet been taken; or

(e) in cases where the substance is placed on the market, authorisation for that use has been granted to his immediate downstream user.

2. A downstream user may use a substance meeting the criteria set out in paragraph 1 provided that the use is in accordance with the conditions of an authorisation granted to an actor up his supply chain for that use.

3. Paragraphs 1 and 2 shall not apply to the use of substances in scientific research and development. Annex XIV shall specify if paragraphs 1 and 2 apply to product and process orientated research and development as well as the maximum quantity exempted.

4. Paragraphs 1 and 2 shall not apply to the following uses of substances:

(a) uses in plant protection products within the scope of Directive 91/414/EEC;

(b) uses in biocidal products within the scope of Directive 98/8/EC;

(c) use as motor fuels covered by Directive 98/70/EC of the European Parliament and of the Council of 13 October 1998 relating to the quality of petrol and diesel fuels (¹);

(d) uses as fuel in mobile or fixed combustion plants of mineral oil products and use as fuels in closed systems.

5. In the case of substances that are subject to authorisation only because they meet the criteria in Article 57(a), (b) or (c) or because they are identified in accordance with Article 57(f) only because of hazards to human health, paragraphs 1 and 2 of this Article shall not apply to the following uses:

(a) uses in cosmetic products within the scope of Directive 76/768/EEC;

(b) uses in food contact materials within the scope of Regulation (EC) No 1935/2004.

6. Paragraphs 1 and 2 shall not apply to the use of substances when they are present in ►M3 mixtures ◄:

(a) for substances referred to in Article 57(d), (e) and (f), below a concentration limit of 0,1 % weight by weight (w/w);

(¹) OJ L 350, 28.12.1998, p. 58. Directive as amended by Regulation (EC) No 1882/2003.

▼M3

(b) for all other substances, below the lowest of the concentration limits specified in Directive 1999/45/EC or in Part 3 of Annex VI to Regulation (EC) No 1272/2008 which result in the classification of the mixture as dangerous.

▼C1

Article 57

Substances to be included in Annex XIV

The following substances may be included in Annex XIV in accordance with the procedure laid down in Article 58:

▼M3

(a) substances meeting the criteria for classification in the hazard class carcinogenicity category 1A or 1B in accordance with section 3.6 of Annex I to Regulation (EC) No 1272/2008;

(b) substances meeting the criteria for classification in the hazard class germ cell mutagenicity category 1A or 1B in accordance with section 3.5 of Annex I to Regulation (EC) No 1272/2008;

(c) substances meeting the criteria for classification in the hazard class reproductive toxicity category 1A or 1B, adverse effects on sexual function and fertility or on development in accordance with section 3.7 of Annex I to Regulation(EC) No 1272/2008;

▼C1

(d) substances which are persistent, bioaccumulative and toxic in accordance with the criteria set out in Annex XIII of this Regulation;

(e) substances which are very persistent and very bioaccumulative in accordance with the criteria set out in Annex XIII of this Regulation;

(f) substances — such as those having endocrine disrupting properties or those having persistent, bioaccumulative and toxic properties or very persistent and very bioaccumulative properties, which do not fulfil the criteria of points (d) or (e) — for which there is scientific evidence of probable serious effects to human health or the environment which give rise to an equivalent level of concern to those of other substances listed in points (a) to (e) and which are identified on a case-by-case basis in accordance with the procedure set out in Article 59.

Article 58

Inclusion of substances in Annex XIV

1.   Whenever a decision is taken to include in Annex XIV substances referred to in Article 57, such a decision shall be taken in accordance with the procedure referred to in Article 133(4). It shall specify for each substance:

(a) the identity of the substance as specified in Section 2 of Annex VI;

(b) the intrinsic property (properties) of the substance referred to in Article 57;

▼C1

(c) transitional arrangements:

(i) the date(s) from which the placing on the market and the use of the substance shall be prohibited unless an authorisation is granted (hereinafter referred to as the sunset date) which should take into account, where appropriate, the production cycle specified for that use;

(ii) a date or dates at least 18 months before the sunset date(s) by which applications must be received if the applicant wishes to continue to use the substance or place it on the market for certain uses after the sunset date(s); these continued uses shall be allowed after the sunset date until a decision on the application for authorisation is taken;

(d) review periods for certain uses, if appropriate;

(e) uses or categories of uses exempted from the authorisation requirement, if any, and conditions for such exemptions, if any.

2. Uses or categories of uses may be exempted from the authorisation requirement provided that, on the basis of the existing specific Community legislation imposing minimum requirements relating to the protection of human health or the environment for the use of the substance, the risk is properly controlled. In the establishment of such exemptions, account shall be taken, in particular, of the proportionality of risk to human health and the environment related to the nature of the substance, such as where the risk is modified by the physical form.

3. Prior to a decision to include substances in Annex XIV, the Agency shall, taking into account the opinion of the Member State Committee, recommend priority substances to be included specifying for each substance the items set out in paragraph 1. Priority shall normally be given to substances with:

(a) PBT or vPvB properties; or

(b) wide dispersive use; or

(c) high volumes.

The number of substances included in Annex XIV and the dates specified under paragraph 1 shall also take account of the Agency's capacity to handle applications in the time provided for. The Agency shall make its first recommendation of priority substances to be included in Annex XIV by 1 June 2009. The Agency shall make further recommendations at least every second year with a view to including further substances in Annex XIV.

4. Before the Agency sends its recommendation to the Commission it shall make it publicly available on its website, clearly indicating the date of publication, taking into account Articles 118 and 119 on access to information. The Agency shall invite all interested parties to submit comments within three months of the date of publication, in particular on uses which should be exempt from the authorisation requirement.

The Agency shall update its recommendation, taking into account the comments received.

▼C1

5. Subject to paragraph 6, after inclusion of a substance in Annex XIV, this substance shall not be subjected to new restrictions under the procedure outlined in Title VIII covering the risks to human health or the environment from the use of the substance on its own, in a ►M3 mixture ◄ or incorporation of a substance in an article arising from the intrinsic properties specified in Annex XIV.

6. A substance listed in Annex XIV may be subjected to new restrictions under the procedure outlined in Title VIII covering the risks to human health or the environment from the presence of the substance in (an) article(s).

7. Substances for which all uses have been prohibited under Title VIII or by other Community legislation shall not be included in Annex XIV or shall be removed from it.

8. Substances which as a result of new information no longer meet the criteria of Article 57 shall be removed from Annex XIV in accordance with the procedure referred to in Article 133(4).

Article 59

Identification of substances referred to in Article 57

1. The procedure set out in paragraphs 2 to 10 of this Article shall apply for the purpose of identifying substances meeting the criteria referred to in Article 57 and establishing a candidate list for eventual inclusion in Annex XIV. The Agency shall indicate, within this list, the substances that are on its work programme according to Article 83(3)(e).

2. The Commission may ask the Agency to prepare a dossier in accordance with relevant Sections of Annex XV for substances which in its opinion meet the criteria set out in Article 57. ►M3 The dossier may be limited, if appropriate, to a reference to an entry in Part 3 of Annex VI to Regulation (EC) No 1272/2008. ◄ The Agency shall make this dossier available to the Member States.

3. Any Member State may prepare a dossier in accordance with Annex XV for substances which in its opinion meet the criteria set out in Article 57 and forward it to the Agency. ►M3 The dossier may be limited, if appropriate, to a reference to an entry in Part 3 of Annex VI to Regulation (EC) No 1272/2008. ◄ The Agency shall make this dossier available within 30 days of receipt to the other Member States.

4. The Agency shall publish on its website a notice that an Annex XV dossier has been prepared for a substance. The Agency shall invite all interested parties to submit comments within a specified deadline to the Agency.

5. Within 60 days of circulation, the other Member States or the Agency may comment on the identification of the substance in relation to the criteria in Article 57 in the dossier to the Agency.

6. If the Agency does not receive or make any comments, it shall include this substance on the list referred to in paragraph 1. The Agency may include this substance in its recommendations under Article 58(3).

▼C1

7.   When comments are made or received, the Agency shall refer the dossier to the Member State Committee within 15 days of the end of the 60-day period referred to in paragraph 5.

8.   If, within 30 days of the referral, the Member State Committee reaches a unanimous agreement on the identification, the Agency shall include the substance in the list referred to in paragraph 1. The Agency may include that substance in its recommendations under Article 58(3).

9.   If the Member State Committee fails to reach a unanimous agreement, the Commission shall prepare a draft proposal on the identification of the substance within three months of receipt of the opinion of the Member State Committee. A final decision on the identification of the substance shall be taken in accordance with the procedure referred to in Article 133(3).

10.   The Agency shall publish and update the list referred to in paragraph 1 on its website without delay after a decision on inclusion of a substance has been taken.

CHAPTER 2

Granting of authorisations

Article 60

Granting of authorisations

1.   The Commission shall be responsible for taking decisions on applications for authorisations in accordance with this Title.

2.   Without prejudice to paragraph 3, an authorisation shall be granted if the risk to human health or the environment from the use of a substance arising from the intrinsic properties specified in Annex XIV is adequately controlled in accordance with Section 6.4 of Annex I and as documented in the applicant's chemical safety report, taking into account the opinion of the Committee for Risk Assessment referred to in Article 64(4)(a). When granting the authorisation, and in any conditions imposed therein, the Commission shall take into account all discharges, emissions and losses, including risks arising from diffuse or dispersive uses, known at the time of the decision.

The Commission shall not consider the risks to human health arising from the use of a substance in a medical device regulated by Council Directive 90/385/EEC of 20 June 1990 on the approximation of the laws of the Member States relating to active implantable medical devices ([1]), Council Directive 93/42/EEC of 14 June 1993 concerning medical devices ([2]) or Directive 98/79/EC of the European Parliament and of the Council of 27 October 1998 on *in vitro* diagnostic medical devices ([3]).

([1]) OJ L 189, 20.7.1990, p. 17. Directive as last amended by Regulation (EC) No 1882/2003.
([2]) OJ L 169, 12.7.1993, p. 1. Directive as last amended by Regulation (EC) No 1882/2003.
([3]) OJ L 331, 7.12.1998, p. 1. Directive as last amended by Regulation (EC) No 1882/2003.

3. Paragraph 2 shall not apply to:

(a) substances meeting the criteria in Article 57(a), (b), (c) or (f) for which it is not possible to determine a threshold in accordance with Section 6.4 of Annex I;

(b) substances meeting the criteria in Article 57(d) or (e);

(c) substances identified under Article 57(f) having persistent, bioaccumulative and toxic properties or very persistent and very bioaccumulative properties.

4. If an authorisation cannot be granted under paragraph 2 or for substances listed in paragraph 3, an authorisation may only be granted if it is shown that socio-economic benefits outweigh the risk to human health or the environment arising from the use of the substance and if there are no suitable alternative substances or technologies. This decision shall be taken after consideration of all of the following elements and taking into account the opinions of the Committee for Risk Assessment and the Committee for Socio-economic Analysis referred to in Article 64(4)(a) and (b):

(a) the risk posed by the uses of the substance, including the appropriateness and effectiveness of the risk management measures proposed;

(b) the socio-economic benefits arising from its use and the socio-economic implications of a refusal to authorise as demonstrated by the applicant or other interested parties;

(c) the analysis of the alternatives submitted by the applicant under Article 62(4)(e) or any substitution plan submitted by the applicant under Article 62(4)(f), and any third party contributions submitted under Article 64(2);

(d) available information on the risks to human health or the environment of any alternative substances or technologies.

5. When assessing whether suitable alternative substances or technologies are available, all relevant aspects shall be taken into account by the Commission, including:

(a) whether the transfer to alternatives would result in reduced overall risks to human health and the environment, taking into account the appropriateness and effectiveness of risk management measures;

(b) the technical and economic feasibility of alternatives for the applicant.

6. A use shall not be authorised if this would constitute a relaxation of a restriction set out in Annex XVII.

7. An authorisation shall be granted only if the application is made in conformity with the requirements of Article 62.

8. Authorisations shall be subject to a time-limited review without prejudice to any decision on a future review period and shall normally be subject to conditions, including monitoring. The duration of the time-limited review for any authorisation shall be determined on a case-by-case basis taking into account all relevant information including the elements listed in paragraph 4(a) to (d), as appropriate.

▼C1

9.   The authorisation shall specify:

(a) the person(s) to whom the authorisation is granted;

(b) the identity of the substance(s);

(c) the use(s) for which the authorisation is granted;

(d) any conditions under which the authorisation is granted;

(e) the time-limited review period;

(f) any monitoring arrangement.

10.   Notwithstanding any conditions of an authorisation, the holder shall ensure that the exposure is reduced to as low a level as is technically and practically possible.

Article 61

Review of authorisations

1.   Authorisations granted in accordance with Article 60 shall be regarded as valid until the Commission decides to amend or withdraw the authorisation in the context of a review, provided that the holder of the authorisation submits a review report at least 18 months before the expiry of the time-limited review period. Rather than re-submitting all elements of the original application for the current authorisation, the holder of an authorisation may submit only the number of the current authorisation, subject to the second, third and fourth subparagraphs.

A holder of an authorisation granted in accordance with Article 60 shall submit an update of the analysis of alternatives referred to in Article 62(4)(e), including information about any relevant research and development activities by the applicant, if appropriate, and any substitution plan submitted under Article 62(4)(f). If the update of the analysis of alternatives shows that there is a suitable alternative available taking into account the elements in Article 60(5), he shall submit a substitution plan, including a timetable for proposed actions by the applicant. If the holder cannot demonstrate that the risk is adequately controlled, he shall also submit an update of the socio-economic analysis contained in the original application.

If he can now demonstrate that the risk is adequately controlled, he shall submit an update of the chemical safety report.

If any other elements of the original application have changed, he shall also submit updates of these element(s).

When any updated information is submitted in accordance with this paragraph, any decision to amend or withdraw the authorisation in the context of the review shall be taken in accordance with the procedure referred to in Article 64 applied *mutatis mutandis*.

2.   Authorisations may be reviewed at any time if:

(a) the circumstances of the original authorisation have changed so as to affect the risk to human health or the environment, or the socio-economic impact; or

(b) new information on possible substitutes becomes available.

▼C1

The Commission shall set a reasonable deadline by which the holder(s) of the authorisation may submit further information necessary for the review and indicate by when it will take a decision in accordance with Article 64.

3.   In its review decision the Commission may, if circumstances have changed and taking into account the principle of proportionality, amend or withdraw the authorisation, if under the changed circumstances it would not have been granted or if suitable alternatives in accordance with Article 60(5) become available. In the latter case the Commission shall require the holder of the authorisation to present a substitution plan if he has not already done so as part of his application or update.

In cases where there is a serious and immediate risk for human health or the environment, the Commission may suspend the authorisation pending the review, taking into account the principle of proportionality.

4.   If an environmental quality standard referred to in Directive 96/61/EC is not met, the authorisations granted for the use of the substance concerned may be reviewed.

5.   If the environmental objectives as referred to in Article 4(1) of Directive 2000/60/EC are not met, the authorisations granted for the use of the substance concerned in the relevant river basin may be reviewed.

6.   If a use of a substance is subsequently prohibited or otherwise restricted in Regulation (EC) No 850/2004 of the European Parliament and of the Council of 29 April 2004 on persistent organic pollutants (¹), the Commission shall withdraw the authorisation for that use.

Article 62

Applications for authorisations

1.   An application for an authorisation shall be made to the Agency.

2.   Applications for authorisation may be made by the manufacturer(s), importer(s) and/or downstream user(s) of the substance. Applications may be made by one or several persons.

3.   Applications may be made for one or several substances, that meet the definition of a group of substances in Section 1.5 of Annex XI, and for one or several uses. Applications may be made for the applicant's own use(s) and/or for uses for which he intends to place the substance on the market.

4.   An application for authorisation shall include the following information:

(a) the identity of the substance(s), as referred to in Section 2 of Annex VI;

(b) the name and contact details of the person or persons making the application;

(c) a request for authorisation, specifying for which use(s) the authorisation is sought and covering the use of the substance in ►**M3** mixtures ◄ and/or the incorporation of the substance in articles, where this is relevant;

(¹) OJ L 158, 30.4.2004, p. 7, corrected in OJ L 229, 29.6.2004, p. 5. Regulation as amended by Council Regulation (EC) No 1195/2006 (OJ L 217, 8.8.2006, p. 1).

▼C1

(d) unless already submitted as part of the registration, a chemical safety report in accordance with Annex I covering the risks to human health and/or the environment from the use of the substance(s) arising from the intrinsic properties specified in Annex XIV;

(e) an analysis of the alternatives considering their risks and the technical and economic feasibility of substitution and including, if appropriate information about any relevant research and development activities by the applicant;

(f) where the analysis referred to in point (e) shows that suitable alternatives are available, taking into account the elements in Article 60(5), a substitution plan including a timetable for proposed actions by the applicant.

5. The application may include:

(a) a socio-economic analysis conducted in accordance with Annex XVI;

(b) a justification for not considering risks to human health and the environment arising either from:

(i) emissions of a substance from an installation for which a permit was granted in accordance with Directive 96/61/EC; or

(ii) discharges of a substance from a point source governed by the requirement for prior regulation referred to in Article 11(3)(g) of Directive 2000/60/EC and legislation adopted under Article 16 of that Directive.

6. The application shall not include the risks to human health arising from the use of a substance in a medical device regulated by Directives 90/385/EEC, 93/42/EEC or 98/79/EC.

7. An application for an authorisation shall be accompanied by the fee required in accordance with Title IX.

Article 63

Subsequent applications for authorisation

1. If an application has been made for a use of a substance, a subsequent applicant may refer to the appropriate parts of the previous application submitted in accordance with Article 62(4)(d), (e) and (f) and (5)(a), provided that the subsequent applicant has permission from the previous applicant to refer to these parts of the application.

2. If an authorisation has been granted for a use of a substance, a subsequent applicant may refer to the appropriate parts of the previous application submitted in accordance with Article 62(4)(d), (e) and (f) and (5)(a), provided that the subsequent applicant has permission from the holder of the authorisation to refer to these parts of the application.

3. Before referring to any previous application in accordance with paragraphs 1 and 2, the subsequent applicant shall update the information of the original application as necessary.

Article 64

Procedure for authorisation decisions

1.   The Agency shall acknowledge the date of receipt of the application. The Agency's Committees for Risk Assessment and Socio-economic Analysis shall give their draft opinions within ten months of the date of receipt of the application.

2.   The Agency shall make available on its web-site broad information on uses, taking into account Articles 118 and 119 on access to information, for which applications have been received and for reviews of authorisations, with a deadline by which information on alternative substances or technologies may be submitted by interested third parties.

3.   In preparing its opinion, each Committee referred to in paragraph 1 shall first check that the application includes all the information specified in Article 62 that is relevant to its remit. If necessary, the Committees shall, in consultation with each other, make a joint request to the applicant for additional information to bring the application into conformity with the requirements of Article 62. The Committee for Socio-economic Analysis may, if it deems it necessary, require the applicant or request third parties to submit, within a specified time period, additional information on possible alternative substances or technologies. Each Committee shall also take into account any information submitted by third parties.

4.   The draft opinions shall include the following elements:

(a) Committee for Risk Assessment: an assessment of the risk to human health and/or the environment arising from the use(s) of the substance, including the appropriateness and effectiveness of the risk management measures as described in the application and, if relevant, an assessment of the risks arising from possible alternatives;

(b) Committee for Socio-economic Analysis: an assessment of the socio-economic factors and the availability, suitability and technical feasibility of alternatives associated with the use(s) of the substance as described in the application, when an application is made in accordance with Article 62 and of any third party contributions submitted under paragraph 2 of this Article.

5.   The Agency shall send these draft opinions to the applicant by the end of the deadline set out in paragraph 1. Within one month of receipt of the draft opinion, the applicant may provide written notice that he wishes to comment. The draft opinion shall be deemed to have been received seven days after the Agency has sent it.

If the applicant does not wish to comment, the Agency shall send these opinions to the Commission, the Member States and the applicant, within 15 days of the end of the period within which the applicant may comment or within 15 days of receipt of notice from the applicant that he does not intend to comment.

If the applicant wishes to comment, he shall send his written argumentation to the Agency within two months of the receipt of the draft opinion. The Committees shall consider the comments and adopt their final opinions within two months of receipt of the written argumentation, taking this argumentation into account where appropriate. Within a further 15 days the Agency shall send the opinions, with the written argumentation attached, to the Commission, the Member States and the applicant.

▼C1

6. The Agency shall determine in accordance with Articles 118 and 119 which parts of its opinions and parts of any attachments thereto should be made publicly available on its website.

7. In cases covered by Article 63(1), the Agency shall treat the applications together, provided the deadlines for the first application can be met.

8. The Commission shall prepare a draft authorisation decision within three months of receipt of the opinions from the Agency. A final decision granting or refusing the authorisation shall be taken in accordance with the procedure referred to in Article 133(3).

9. Summaries of the Commission decisions, including the authorisation number and the reasons for the decision, in particular where suitable alternatives exist, shall be published in the Official Journal of the European Union and shall be made publicly available in a database established and kept up to date by the Agency.

10. In cases covered by Article 63(2), the deadline set out in paragraph 1 of this Article shall be shortened to five months.

CHAPTER 3

Authorisations in the supply chain

Article 65

Obligation of holders of authorisations

Holders of an authorisation, as well as downstream users referred to in Article 56(2) including the substances in a ►**M3** mixture ◄, shall include the authorisation number on the label before they place the substance or a ►**M3** mixture ◄ containing the substance on the market for an authorised use without prejudice to ►**M3** Directive 67/548/EEC and Regulation (EC) No 1272/2008 ◄ and Directive 1999/45/EC. This shall be done without delay once the authorisation number has been made publicly available in accordance with Article 64(9).

Article 66

Downstream users

1. Downstream users using a substance in accordance with Article 56(2) shall notify the Agency within three months of the first supply of the substance.

2. The Agency shall establish and keep up to date a register of downstream users who have made a notification in accordance with paragraph 1. The Agency shall grant access to this register to the competent authorities of the Member States.

▼C1

RESTRICTIONS ON THE MANUFACTURING, PLACING ON THE MARKET AND USE OF CERTAIN DANGEROUS SUBSTANCES, ►M3 MIXTURES ◄ AND ARTICLES

CHAPTER 1

General issues

Article 67

General provisions

1.   A substance on its own, in a ►M3 mixture ◄ or in an article, for which Annex XVII contains a restriction shall not be manufactured, placed on the market or used unless it complies with the conditions of that restriction. This shall not apply to the manufacture, placing on the market or use of a substance in scientific research and development. Annex XVII shall specify if the restriction shall not apply to product and process orientated research and development, as well as the maximum quantity exempted.

2.   Paragraph 1 shall not apply to the use of substances in cosmetic products, as defined by Directive 76/768/EEC, with regard to restrictions addressing the risks to human health within the scope of that Directive.

3.   Until 1 June 2013, a Member State may maintain any existing and more stringent restrictions in relation to Annex XVII on the manufacture, placing on the market or use of a substance, provided that those restrictions have been notified according to the Treaty. The Commission shall compile and publish an inventory of these restrictions by 1 June 2009.

CHAPTER 2

Restrictions process

Article 68

Introducing new and amending current restrictions

1.   When there is an unacceptable risk to human health or the environment, arising from the manufacture, use or placing on the market of substances, which needs to be addressed on a Community-wide basis, Annex XVII shall be amended in accordance with the procedure referred to in Article 133(4) by adopting new restrictions, or amending current restrictions in Annex XVII, for the manufacture, use or placing on the market of substances on their own, in ►M3 mixtures ◄ or in articles, pursuant to the procedure set out in Articles 69 to 73. Any such decision shall take into account the socio-economic impact of the restriction, including the availability of alternatives.

The first subparagraph shall not apply to the use of a substance as an on-site isolated intermediate.

▼M3

2.   For a substance on its own, in a mixture or in an article which meets the criteria for classification in the hazard classes carcinogenicity, germ cell mutagenicity or reproductive toxicity, category 1A or 1B, and could be used by consumers and for which restrictions to consumer use are proposed by the Commission, Annex XVII shall be amended in accordance with the procedure referred to in Article 133(4). Articles 69 to 73 shall not apply.

▼C1

Article 69

Preparation of a proposal

1.   If the Commission considers that the manufacture, placing on the market or use of a substance on its own, in a ►M3 mixture ◄ or in an article poses a risk to human health or the environment that is not adequately controlled and needs to be addressed, it shall ask the Agency to prepare a dossier which conforms to the requirements of Annex XV.

2.   After the date referred to in Article 58(1)(c)(i) for a substance listed in Annex XIV, the Agency shall consider whether the use of that substance in articles poses a risk to human health or the environment that is not adequately controlled. If the Agency considers that the risk is not adequately controlled, it shall prepare a dossier which conforms to the requirements of Annex XV.

3.   Within 12 months of the receipt of the request from the Commission in paragraph 1 and if this dossier demonstrates that action on a Community-wide basis is necessary, beyond any measures already in place, the Agency shall suggest restrictions, in order to initiate the restrictions process.

4.   If a Member State considers that the manufacture, placing on the market or use of a substance on its own, in a ►M3 mixture ◄ or in an article poses a risk to human health or the environment that is not adequately controlled and needs to be addressed it shall notify the Agency that it proposes to prepare a dossier which conforms to the requirements of the relevant sections of Annex XV. If the substance is not on the list maintained by the Agency referred to in paragraph 5 of this Article, the Member State shall prepare a dossier which conforms to the requirements of Annex XV within 12 months of the notification to the Agency. If this dossier demonstrates that action on a Community-wide basis is necessary, beyond any measures already in place, the Member State shall submit it to the Agency in the format outlined in Annex XV, in order to initiate the restrictions process.

The Agency or Member States shall refer to any dossier, chemical safety report or risk assessment submitted to the Agency or Member State under this Regulation. The Agency or Member States shall also refer to any relevant risk assessment submitted for the purposes of other Community Regulations or Directives. To this end other bodies, such as agencies, established under Community law and carrying out a similar task shall provide information to the Agency or Member State concerned on request.

▼C1

The Committee for Risk Assessment and the Committee for Socio-economic Analysis shall check whether the dossier submitted conforms to the requirements of Annex XV. Within 30 days of receipt, the respective Committee shall inform the Agency or the Member State suggesting restrictions, as to whether the dossier conforms. If the dossier does not conform, the reasons shall be given to the Agency or the Member State in writing within 45 days of receipt. The Agency or the Member State shall bring the dossier into conformity within 60 days of the date of receipt of the reasons from the Committees, otherwise the procedure under this Chapter shall be terminated. The Agency shall publish without delay the intention of the Commission or of a Member State to instigate a restriction procedure for a substance and shall inform those who submitted a registration for that substance.

5. The Agency shall maintain a list of substances for which a dossier conforming to the requirements of Annex XV is planned or underway by either the Agency or a Member State for the purposes of a proposed restriction. If a substance is on the list, no other such dossier shall be prepared. If it is proposed by either a Member State or the Agency that an existing restriction listed in Annex XVII should be re-examined a decision on whether to do so shall be taken in accordance with the procedure referred to in Article 133(2) based on evidence presented by the Member State or the Agency.

6. Without prejudice to Articles 118 and 119, the Agency shall make publicly available on its website all dossiers conforming with Annex XV including the restrictions suggested pursuant to paragraphs 3 and 4 of this Article without delay, clearly indicating the date of publication. The Agency shall invite all interested parties to submit individually or jointly within six months of the date of publication:

(a) comments on dossiers and the suggested restrictions;

(b) a socio-economic analysis, or information which can contribute to one, of the suggested restrictions, examining the advantages and drawbacks of the proposed restrictions. It shall conform to the requirements in Annex XVI.

Article 70

Agency opinion: Committee for Risk Assessment

Within nine months of the date of publication referred to in Article 69(6), the Committee for Risk Assessment shall formulate an opinion as to whether the suggested restrictions are appropriate in reducing the risk to human health and/or the environment, based on its consideration of the relevant parts of the dossier. This opinion shall take account of the Member State dossier or of the dossier prepared by the Agency at the request of the Commission, and the views of interested parties referred to in Article 69(6)(a).

▼C1

Article 71

Agency opinion: Committee for Socio-economic Analysis

1. Within 12 months of the date of publication referred to in Article 69(6), the Committee for Socio-economic Analysis shall formulate an opinion on the suggested restrictions, based on its consideration of the relevant parts of the dossier and the socio-economic impact. It shall prepare a draft opinion on the suggested restrictions and on the related socio-economic impact, taking account of the analyses or information according to Article 69(6)(b), if there are any. The Agency shall publish the draft opinion on its website without delay. The Agency shall invite interested parties to give their comments on the draft opinion no later than 60 days from the publication of that draft opinion.

2. The Committee for Socio-economic Analysis shall without delay adopt its opinion, taking into account where appropriate further comments received by the deadline set. This opinion shall take account of the comments and socio-economic analyses of interested parties submitted under Article 69(6)(b) and under paragraph 1 of this Article.

3. Where the opinion of the Committee for Risk Assessment diverges significantly from the restrictions suggested, the Agency may postpone the deadline for the opinion of the Committee for Socio-economic Analysis by a maximum of 90 days.

Article 72

Submission of an opinion to the Commission

1. The Agency shall submit to the Commission without delay the opinions of the Committees for Risk Assessment and Socio-economic Analysis on restrictions suggested for substances on their own, in ►M3 mixtures ◄ or in articles. If one or both of the Committees do not formulate an opinion by the deadline set in Article 70 and Article 71(1) the Agency shall inform the Commission accordingly, stating the reasons.

2. Without prejudice to Articles 118 and 119 the Agency shall publish the opinions of the two Committees on its website without delay.

3. The Agency shall provide the Commission and/or Member State on request with all documents and evidence submitted to or considered by it.

Article 73

Commission decision

1. If the conditions laid down in Article 68 are fulfilled, the Commission shall prepare a draft amendment to Annex XVII, within three months of receipt of the opinion of the Committee for Socio-economic Analysis or by the end of the deadline established under Article 71 if that Committee does not form an opinion, whichever is the earlier.

Where the draft amendment diverges from the original proposal or if it does not take the opinions from the Agency into account, the Commission shall annex a detailed explanation of the reasons for the differences.

▼C1

2.   A final decision shall be taken in accordance with the procedure referred to in Article 133(4). The Commission shall send the draft amendment to the Member States at least 45 days before voting.

TITLE IX

FEES AND CHARGES

Article 74

Fees and charges

1.   The fees that are required according to Article 6(4), Article 7(1) and (5), Article 9(2), Article 11(4), Article 17(2), Article 18(2), Article 19(3), Article 22(5), Article 62(7) and Article 92(3) shall be specified in a Commission Regulation adopted in accordance with the procedure referred to in Article 133(3) by 1 June 2008.

2.   A fee need not be paid for a registration of a substance in a quantity of between 1 and 10 tonnes where the registration dossier contains the full information in Annex VII.

3.   The structure and amount of the fees referred to in paragraph 1 shall take account of the work required by this Regulation to be carried out by the Agency and the competent authority and shall be fixed at such a level as to ensure that the revenue derived from them when combined with other sources of the Agency's revenue pursuant to Article 96(1) is sufficient to cover the cost of the services delivered. The fees set for registration shall take into account the work that may be done pursuant to Title VI.

In the case of Article 6(4), Article 7(1) and (5), Article 9(2), Article 11(4), Article 17(2) and Article 18(2), the structure and amount of fees shall take account of the tonnage range of the substance being registered.

In all cases, a reduced fee shall be set for SMEs.

In the case of Article 11(4), the structure and amount of fees shall take into account whether information has been submitted jointly or separately.

In the case of a request made under Article 10(a)(xi), the structure and amount of fees shall take into account the work required by the Agency in assessing the justification.

4.   The Regulation referred to in paragraph 1 shall specify the circumstances under which a proportion of the fees will be transferred to the relevant Member State competent authority.

▼C1

5. The Agency may collect charges for other services it provides.

TITLE X

AGENCY

Article 75

Establishment and review

1. A European Chemicals Agency is established for the purposes of managing and in some cases carrying out the technical, scientific and administrative aspects of this Regulation and to ensure consistency at Community level in relation to these aspects.

2. The Agency shall be subject to a review by 1 June 2012.

Article 76

Composition

1. The Agency shall comprise:

(a) a Management Board, which shall exercise the responsibilities set out in Article 78;

(b) an Executive Director, who shall exercise the responsibilities set out in Article 83;

(c) a Committee for Risk Assessment, which shall be responsible for preparing the opinion of the Agency on evaluations, applications for authorisation, proposals for restrictions and proposals for classification and labelling under ►M3 Title V of Regulation (EC) No 1272/2008 ◄ and any other questions that arise from the operation of this Regulation relating to risks to human health or the environment;

(d) a Committee for Socio-economic Analysis, which shall be responsible for preparing the opinion of the Agency on applications for authorisation, proposals for restrictions, and any other questions that arise from the operation of this Regulation relating to the socio-economic impact of possible legislative action on substances;

(e) a Member State Committee, which shall be responsible for resolving potential divergences of opinions on draft decisions proposed by the Agency or the Member States under Title VI and proposals for identification of substances of very high concern to be subjected to the authorisation procedure under Title VII;

(f) a Forum for Exchange of Information on Enforcement (hereinafter referred to as the Forum) which shall coordinate a network of Member States authorities responsible for enforcement of this Regulation;

(g) a Secretariat, which shall work under the leadership of the Executive Director and provide technical, scientific and administrative support for the Committees and the Forum and ensure appropriate coordination between them. It shall also undertake the work required of the Agency under the procedures for pre-registration, registration and evaluation as well as preparation of guidance, database maintenance and information provision;

▼C1

(h) a Board of Appeal, which shall decide on appeals against decisions taken by the Agency.

2.   The Committees referred to in points (c), (d) and (e) of paragraph 1 (hereinafter referred to as the Committees) and the Forum may each establish working groups. For this purpose they shall adopt, in accordance with their rules of procedure, precise arrangements for delegating certain tasks to these working groups.

3.   The Committees and the Forum may, if they consider it appropriate, seek advice on important questions of a general scientific or ethical nature from appropriate sources of expertise.

Article 77

Tasks

1.   The Agency shall provide the Member States and the institutions of the Community with the best possible scientific and technical advice on questions relating to chemicals which fall within its remit and which are referred to it in accordance with the provisions of this Regulation.

2.   The Secretariat shall undertake the following tasks:

(a) performing the tasks allotted to it under Title II; including facilitating the efficient registration of imported substances, in a way consistent with the Community's international trading obligations towards third countries;

(b) performing the tasks allotted to it under Title III;

(c) performing the tasks allotted to it under Title VI;

(d) performing the tasks allotted to it under Title VIII;

▶**M3** (e) establishing and maintaining database(s) with information on all registered substances, the classification and labelling inventory and the harmonised classification and labelling list established in accordance with Regulation (EC) No 1272/2008. ◀ It shall make the information identified in Article 119(1) and (2) in the database(s) publicly available, free of charge, over the Internet, except where a request made under Article 10(a)(xi) is considered justified. The Agency shall make other information in the databases available on request in accordance with Article 118;

(f) making publicly available information as to which substances are being, and have been evaluated within 90 days of receipt of the information at the Agency, in accordance with Article 119(1);

(g) providing technical and scientific guidance and tools where appropriate for the operation of this Regulation in particular to assist the development of chemical safety reports (in accordance with Article 14, Article 31(1) and Article 37(4)) and application of Article 10(a)(viii), Article 11(3) and Article 19(2) by industry and especially by SMEs; and technical and scientific guidance for the application of Article 7 by producers and importers of articles;

▼C1

(h) providing technical and scientific guidance on the operation of this Regulation for Member State competent authorities and providing support to the helpdesks established by Member States under Title XIII;

(i) providing guidance to stakeholders including Member State competent authorities on communication to the public of information on the risks and safe use of substances, on their own, in ►M3 mixtures ◄ or in articles;

(j) providing advice and assistance to manufacturers and importers registering a substance in accordance with Article 12(1);

(k) preparing explanatory information on this Regulation for other stakeholders;

(l) at the Commission's request, providing technical and scientific support for steps to improve cooperation between the Community, its Member States, international organisations and third countries on scientific and technical issues relating to the safety of substances, as well as active participation in technical assistance and capacity building activities on sound management of chemicals in developing countries;

(m) keeping a Manual of Decisions and Opinions based on conclusions from the Member State Committee regarding interpretation and implementation of this Regulation;

(n) notification of decisions taken by the Agency;

(o) provision of formats for submission of information to the Agency.

3. The Committees shall undertake the following tasks:

(a) performing the tasks allotted to them under ►M3 Titles VI to X ◄;

(b) at the Executive Director's request, providing technical and scientific support for steps to improve cooperation between the Community, its Member States, international organisations and third countries on scientific and technical issues relating to the safety of substances, as well as active participation in technical assistance and capacity building activities on sound management of chemicals in developing countries;

(c) at the Executive Director's request, drawing up an opinion on any other aspects concerning the safety of substances on their own, in ►M3 mixtures ◄ or in articles.

4. The Forum shall undertake the following tasks:

(a) spreading good practice and highlighting problems at Community level;

(b) proposing, coordinating and evaluating harmonised enforcement projects and joint inspections;

(c) coordinating exchange of inspectors;

(d) identifying enforcement strategies, as well as best practice in enforcement;

(e) developing working methods and tools of use to local inspectors;

▼C1

(f) developing an electronic information exchange procedure;

(g) liaising with industry, taking particular account of the specific needs of SMEs, and other stakeholders, including relevant international organisations, as necessary;

(h) examining proposals for restrictions with a view to advising on enforceability.

Article 78

Powers of the Management Board

The Management Board shall appoint the Executive Director pursuant to Article 84 and an accounting officer in accordance with Article 43 of Regulation (EC, Euratom) No 2343/2002.

It shall adopt:

(a) by 30 April each year, the general report of the Agency for the previous year;

(b) by 31 October each year the work programme of the Agency for the coming year;

(c) the final budget of the Agency pursuant to Article 96 before the beginning of the financial year, adjusting it, where necessary, according to the Community contribution and any other revenue of the Agency;

(d) a multiannual work programme, which shall be regularly revised.

It shall adopt the internal rules and procedures of the Agency. These rules shall be made public.

It shall perform its duties in relation to the Agency's budget pursuant to Articles 96, 97 and 103.

It shall exercise disciplinary authority over the Executive Director.

It shall adopt its rules of procedure.

It shall appoint the Chairman, the members and alternates of the Board of Appeal in accordance with Article 89.

It shall appoint the members of the Agency committees as set out in Article 85.

It shall forward annually any information relevant to the outcome of the evaluation procedures in accordance with Article 96(6).

Article 79

Composition of the Management Board

1. The Management Board shall be composed of one representative from each Member State and a maximum of six representatives appointed by the Commission, including three individuals from interested parties without voting rights and in addition two independent persons appointed by the European Parliament.

Each Member State shall nominate a member to the Management Board. The members thus nominated shall be appointed by the Council.

▼C1

2.   Members shall be appointed on the basis of their relevant experience and expertise in the field of chemical safety or the regulation of chemicals whilst ensuring there is relevant expertise amongst the board members in the fields of general, financial and legal matters.

3.   The duration of the term of office shall be four years. The term of office may be renewed once. However, for the first mandate, the Commission shall identify half of its appointees, and the Council shall identify 12 of its appointees, for whom this period shall be six years.

Article 80

Chairmanship of the Management Board

1.   The Management Board shall elect a Chairman and a Deputy-Chairman from among the members with voting rights. The Deputy-Chairman shall automatically take the place of the Chairman if he is prevented from attending to his duties.

2.   The terms of office of the Chairman and the Deputy-Chairman shall be two years and shall expire when they cease to be members of the Management Board. The term of office shall be renewable once.

Article 81

Meetings of the Management Board

1.   The meetings of the Management Board shall be convened by invitation of its Chairman or at the request of at least one third of the Board members.

2.   The Executive Director shall take part in the meetings of the Management Board, without voting rights.

3.   The Chairmen of the Committees and the Chairman of the Forum, as referred to in Article 76(1)(c) to (f), are entitled to attend the meetings of the Management Board without voting rights.

Article 82

Voting of the Management Board

The Management Board shall adopt rules of procedure for voting, including the conditions for a member to vote on behalf of another member. The Management Board shall act by a two-thirds majority of all members with the right to vote.

Article 83

Duties and powers of the Executive Director

1.   The Agency shall be managed by its Executive Director, who shall perform his duties in the interests of the Community, and independently of any specific interests.

2.   The Executive Director shall be the legal representative of the Agency. He shall be responsible for:

(a) the day-to-day administration of the Agency;

(b) managing all the Agency resources necessary for carrying out its tasks;

▼C1

(c) ensuring that the time-limits laid down in Community legislation for the adoption of opinions by the Agency are complied with;

(d) ensuring appropriate and timely coordination between the Committees and the Forum;

(e) concluding and managing necessary contracts with service providers;

(f) the preparation of the statement of revenue and expenditure and the implementation of the budget of the Agency pursuant to Articles 96 and 97;

(g) all staff matters;

(h) providing the secretariat for the Management Board;

(i) preparing draft opinions of the Management Board concerning the proposed rules of procedure of the Committees and of the Forum;

(j) making arrangements, upon request from the Management Board, for the execution of any further function(s) (within the remit of Article 77) allotted to the Agency by delegation from the Commission;

(k) establishing and maintaining a regular dialogue with the European Parliament;

(l) determining the terms and conditions for use of software packages;

(m) rectifying a decision made by the Agency following an appeal and after consulting the Chairman of the Board of Appeal.

3. Each year, the Executive Director shall submit the following to the Management Board for approval:

(a) a draft report covering the activities of the Agency in the previous year, including information about the number of registration dossiers received, the number of substances evaluated, the number of applications for authorisation received, the number of proposals for restriction received by the Agency and opined upon, the time taken for completion of the associated procedures, and the substances authorised, dossiers rejected, substances restricted; complaints received and the action taken; an overview of the activities of the Forum;

(b) a draft work-programme for the coming year;

(c) the draft annual accounts;

(d) the draft forecast budget for the coming year;

(e) a draft multiannual work programme.

The Executive Director shall, following approval by the Management Board, forward the work programme for the coming year and the multi-annual work programme to the Member States, the European Parliament, the Council and the Commission, and shall have them published.

▼C1

The Executive Director shall, following approval by the Management Board, forward the Agency's general report to the Member States, the European Parliament, the Council, the Commission, the European Economic and Social Committee and the Court of Auditors, and shall have it published.

Article 84

Appointment of the Executive Director

1.   The Executive Director of the Agency shall be appointed by the Management Board on the basis of a list of candidates proposed by the Commission following a call for expressions of interest published in the *Official Journal of the European Union* and in other periodicals or on Internet sites.

The Executive Director shall be appointed on the grounds of merit and documented administrative and management skills, as well as his relevant experience in the fields of chemical safety or regulation. The Management Board shall take its decision by a two-thirds majority of all members with a right to vote.

Power to dismiss the Executive Director shall lie with the Management Board, in accordance with the same procedure.

Before being appointed, the candidate selected by the Management Board shall be invited as soon as possible to make a statement before the European Parliament and to answer questions from Members of Parliament.

2.   The term of the office of the Executive Director shall be five years. It may be prolonged by the Management Board once for another period of up to five years.

Article 85

Establishment of the Committees

1.   Each Member State may nominate candidates to membership of the Committee for Risk Assessment. The Executive Director shall establish a list of the nominees, which shall be published on the Agency's website, without prejudice to Article 88(1). The Management Board shall appoint the members of the Committee from this list, including at least one member but not more than two from the nominees of each Member State that has nominated candidates. Members shall be appointed for their role and experience in performing the tasks specified in Article 77(3).

2.   Each Member State may nominate candidates to membership of the Committee for Socio-economic Analysis. The Executive Director shall establish a list of the nominees, which shall be published on the Agency's website, without prejudice to Article 88(1). The Management Board shall appoint the members of the Committee from this list, including at least one member but not more than two from the nominees of each Member State that has nominated candidates. Members shall be appointed for their role and experience in performing the tasks specified in Article 77(3).

3.   Each Member State shall appoint one member to the Member State Committee.

▼C1

4. The Committees shall aim to have a broad range of relevant expertise among their members. To this end each Committee may co-opt a maximum of five additional members chosen on the basis of their specific competence.

Members of the Committees shall be appointed for a term of three years which shall be renewable.

The members of the Management Board may not be members of the Committees.

The members of each Committee may be accompanied by advisers on scientific, technical or regulatory matters.

The Executive Director or his representative and representatives of the Commission shall be entitled to attend all the meetings of the Committees and working groups convened by the Agency or its committees as observers. Stakeholders may also be invited to attend meetings as observers, as appropriate, at the request of the Committee members, or the Management Board.

5. The members of each Committee appointed following nomination by a Member State shall ensure that there is appropriate coordination between the tasks of the Agency and the work of their Member State competent authority.

6. The members of the Committees shall be supported by the scientific and technical resources available to the Member States. To this end, Member States shall provide adequate scientific and technical resources to the members of the Committees that they have nominated. Each Member State competent authority shall facilitate the activities of the Committees and their working groups.

7. The Member States shall refrain from giving the members of the Committee for Risk Assessment or of the Committee for Socio-Economic Analysis, or their scientific and technical advisers and experts, any instruction which is incompatible with the individual tasks of those persons or with the tasks, responsibilities and independence of the Agency.

8. When preparing an opinion, each Committee shall use its best endeavours to reach a consensus. If such a consensus cannot be reached, the opinion shall consist of the position of the majority of members, including their grounds. The minority position(s), including their grounds, shall also be published.

9. Each Committee shall draft a proposal for its own rules of procedure, to be approved by the Management Board, within six months of the Committees first being appointed.

These rules shall in particular lay down the procedures for replacing members, the procedures for delegating certain tasks to working groups, the creation of working groups and the establishment of a procedure for the urgent adoption of opinions. The Chairman of each Committee shall be an employee of the Agency.

Article 86

Establishment of the Forum

1. Each Member State shall appoint, for a three-year term, which shall be renewable, one member to the Forum. Members shall be chosen for their role and experience in enforcement of chemicals legislation and shall maintain relevant contacts with the Member State competent authorities.

▼C1

The Forum shall aim to have a broad range of relevant expertise among its members. To this end the Forum may co-opt a maximum of five additional members chosen on the basis of their specific competence. These members shall be appointed for a term of three years, which shall be renewable. Members of the Management Board may not be members of the Forum.

The members of the Forum may be accompanied by scientific and technical advisers.

The Executive Director of the Agency or his representative and representatives of the Commission shall be entitled to attend all the meetings of the Forum and its working groups. Stakeholders may also be invited to attend meetings as observers, as appropriate, at the request of Forum members, or the Management Board.

2. The members of the Forum appointed by a Member State shall ensure that there is appropriate coordination between the tasks of the Forum and the work of their Member State competent authority.

3. The members of the Forum shall be supported by the scientific and technical resources available to the competent authorities of the Member States. Each Member State competent authority shall facilitate the activities of the Forum and its working groups. The Member States shall refrain from giving the Forum members, or their scientific and technical advisers and experts any instruction which is incompatible with the individual tasks of those persons or with the tasks and responsibilities of the Forum.

4. The Forum shall draft a proposal for its own rules of procedure, to be adopted by the Management Board, within six months of the Forum first being appointed.

These rules shall in particular lay down the procedures for appointing and replacing the Chairman, replacing members and the procedures for delegating certain tasks to working groups.

Article 87

Rapporteurs of Committees and use of experts

1. Where, in accordance with Article 77, a Committee is required to provide an opinion or consider whether a Member State dossier conforms with the requirements of Annex XV, it shall appoint one of its members as a rapporteur. The Committee concerned may appoint a second member to act as co-rapporteur. For each case, rapporteurs and co-rapporteurs shall undertake to act in the interests of the Community and shall make a declaration of commitment to fulfil their duties and a declaration of interests in writing. A member of a Committee shall not be appointed rapporteur for a particular case if he indicates any interest that might be prejudicial to the independent consideration of that case. The Committee concerned may replace the rapporteur or co-rapporteur by another one of its members at any time, if, for example, they are unable to fulfil their duties within the prescribed time limits, or if a potentially prejudicial interest comes to light.

2. Member States shall transmit to the Agency the names of experts with proven experience in the tasks required by Article 77, who would be available to serve on working groups of the Committees, together with an indication of their qualifications and specific areas of expertise.

▼C1

The Agency shall keep an up-to-date list of experts. The list shall include the experts referred to in the first subparagraph and other experts identified directly by the Secretariat.

3. The provision of services by Committee members or any expert serving on a working group of the Committees or Forum, or performing any other task for the Agency shall be governed by a written contract between the Agency and the person concerned, or where appropriate between the Agency and the employer of the person concerned.

The person concerned, or his employer, shall be remunerated by the Agency in accordance with a scale of fees to be included in the financial arrangements established by the Management Board. Where the person concerned fails to fulfil his duties, the Executive Director has the right to terminate or suspend the contract or withhold remuneration.

4. The provision of services for which there are several potential providers may require a call for an expression of interest:

(a) if the scientific and technical context allows; and

(b) if it is compatible with the duties of the Agency, in particular the need to provide a high level of protection of human health and the environment.

The Management Board shall adopt the appropriate procedures on a proposal from the Executive Director.

5. The Agency may use the services of experts for the discharge of other specific tasks for which it is responsible.

Article 88

Qualification and interests

1. The membership of the Committees and of the Forum shall be made public. Individual members may request that their names not be made public if they believe that such publication could place them at risk. The Executive Director shall decide whether to agree to such requests. When each appointment is published, the professional qualifications of each member shall be specified.

2. Members of the Management Board, the Executive Director and members of the Committees and of the Forum shall make a declaration of commitment to fulfil their duties and a declaration of interests which could be considered to be prejudicial to their independence. These declarations shall be made annually in writing and, without prejudice to paragraph 1, be entered in a register held by the Agency which is accessible to the public, on request, at the Agency's offices.

3. At each of their meetings, members of the Management Board, the Executive Director, members of the Committees and of the Forum and any experts participating in the meeting shall declare any interests which could be considered to be prejudicial to their independence with respect to any points on the agenda. Anyone declaring such interests shall not participate in any voting on the relevant agenda point.

▼C1

Article 89

Establishment of the Board of Appeal

1.   The Board of Appeal shall consist of a Chairman and two other members.

2.   The Chairman and the two members shall have alternates who shall represent them in their absence.

3.   The Chairman, the other members and the alternates shall be appointed by the Management Board on the basis of a list of candidates proposed by the Commission following a call for expressions of interest published in the *Official Journal of the European Union* and in other periodicals or on Internet sites. They shall be appointed on the basis of their relevant experience and expertise in the field of chemical safety, natural sciences or regulatory and judicial procedures from a list of qualified candidates adopted by the Commission.

The Management Board may appoint additional members and their alternates, on recommendation by the Executive Director, following the same procedure, if this is necessary to ensure that the appeals can be processed at a satisfactory rate.

4.   The qualifications required for the members of the Board of Appeal shall be determined by the Commission in accordance with the procedure referred to in Article 133(3).

5.   The Chairman and the members shall have equal voting rights.

Article 90

Members of the Board of Appeal

1.   The term of office of the members of the Board of Appeal, including the Chairman and the alternates shall be five years. It may be prolonged once.

2.   The members of the Board of Appeal shall be independent. In making their decisions they shall not be bound by any instructions.

3.   The members of the Board of Appeal may not perform any other duties in the Agency.

4.   The members of the Board of Appeal may not be removed either from office or from the list during their respective terms, unless there are serious grounds for such removal and the Commission, after obtaining the opinion of the Management Board, takes a decision to this effect.

5.   Members of the Board of Appeal may not take part in any appeal proceedings if they have any personal interest therein, or if they have previously been involved as representatives of one of the parties to the proceedings, or if they participated in the decision under appeal.

6.   If a member of the Board of Appeal considers for reasons mentioned in paragraph 5 that he must not take part in a specific appeal proceedings, he shall inform the Board of Appeal accordingly. Members of the Board may be objected to by any party to the appeal proceedings on any of the grounds mentioned in paragraph 5, or if suspected of partiality. No objection may be based on the nationality of members.

▼C1

7. The Board of Appeal shall decide as to the action to be taken in the cases specified in paragraphs 5 and 6 without the participation of the member concerned. For the purposes of taking this decision, the member concerned shall be replaced on the Board of Appeal by an alternate.

Article 91

Decisions subject to appeal

1. An appeal may be brought against decisions of the Agency taken pursuant to Article 9, Article 20, Article 27(6), Article 30(2) and (3) and Article 51.

2. An appeal lodged pursuant to paragraph 1 shall have suspensive effect.

Article 92

Persons entitled to appeal, time-limits, fees and form

1. Any natural or legal person may appeal against a decision addressed to that person, or against a decision which, although addressed to another person, is of direct and individual concern to the former.

2. The appeal, together with the statements of the grounds thereof, shall be filed in writing to the Agency within three months of the notification of the decision to the person concerned, or in the absence thereof, of the day on which it became known to the latter, unless otherwise provided in this Regulation.

3. A fee may be payable by persons bringing an appeal against an Agency decision, in accordance with Title IX.

Article 93

Examination and decisions on appeal

1. If, after consultation with the Chairman of the Board of Appeal, the Executive Director considers the appeal to be admissible and well founded he may rectify the decision within 30 days of the appeal being filed in accordance with Article 92(2).

2. In cases other than those referred to in paragraph 1 of this Article, the Chairman of the Board of Appeal shall examine whether the appeal is admissible within 30 days of the appeal being filed in accordance with Article 92(2). In the affirmative, the appeal shall be remitted to the Board of Appeal for examination of the grounds. Parties to the appeal proceedings shall be entitled to make an oral presentation during the procedure.

3. The Board of Appeal may exercise any power which lies within the competence of the Agency or remit the case to the competent body of the Agency for further action.

4. The procedures for the Board of Appeal shall be determined by the Commission in accordance with the procedure referred to in Article 133(3).

▼C1

Article 94

Actions before the Court of First Instance and the Court of Justice

1. An action may be brought before the Court of First Instance or the Court of Justice, in accordance with Article 230 of the Treaty, contesting a decision taken by the Board of Appeal or, in cases where no right of appeal lies before the Board, by the Agency.

2. Should the Agency fail to take a decision, proceedings for failure to act may be brought before the Court of First Instance or the Court of Justice in accordance with Article 232 of the Treaty.

3. The Agency shall be required to take the necessary measures to comply with the judgment of the Court of First Instance or the Court of Justice.

Article 95

Conflicts of opinion with other bodies

1. The Agency shall take care to ensure early identification of potential sources of conflict between its opinions and those of other bodies established under Community law, including Community Agencies, carrying out a similar task in relation to issues of common concern.

2. Where the Agency identifies a potential source of conflict, it shall contact the body concerned in order to ensure that any relevant scientific or technical information is shared and to identify the scientific or technical points which are potentially contentious.

3. Where there is a fundamental conflict over scientific or technical points and the body concerned is a Community Agency or a scientific committee, the Agency and the body concerned shall work together either to solve the conflict or to submit a joint document to the Commission clarifying the scientific and/or technical points of conflict.

Article 96

The budget of the Agency

1. The revenues of the Agency shall consist of:

(a) a subsidy from the Community, entered in the general budget of the European Communities (Commission Section);

(b) the fees paid by undertakings;

(c) any voluntary contribution from the Member States.

2. The expenditure of the Agency shall include the staff, administrative, infrastructure and operational expenses.

3. By 15 February of each year at the latest, the Executive Director shall draw up a preliminary draft budget covering the operational expenditure and the programme of work anticipated for the following financial year, and shall forward this preliminary draft to the Management Board together with an establishment plan accompanied by a provisional list of posts.

4. Revenue and expenditure shall be in balance.

▼C1

5. Each year the Management Board, on the basis of a draft drawn up by the Executive Director, shall produce an estimate of revenue and expenditure for the Agency for the following financial year. This estimate, which shall include a draft establishment plan, shall be forwarded by the Management Board to the Commission by 31 March at the latest.

6. The estimate shall be forwarded by the Commission to the European Parliament and the Council (hereinafter referred to as the budgetary authority) together with the preliminary draft budget of the European Communities.

7. On the basis of the estimate, the Commission shall enter in the preliminary draft budget of the European Communities the estimates it considers necessary for the establishment plan and the amount of the subsidy to be charged to the general budget, which it shall place before the budgetary authority in accordance with Article 272 of the Treaty.

8. The budgetary authority shall authorise the appropriations for the subsidy to the Agency.

The budgetary authority shall adopt the establishment plan for the Agency.

9. The budget of the Agency shall be adopted by the Management Board. It shall become final following final adoption of the general budget of the European Communities. Where appropriate, it shall be adjusted accordingly.

10. Any modification to the budget, including the establishment plan, shall follow the procedure referred to above.

11. The Management Board shall, without delay, notify the budgetary authority of its intention to implement any project which may have significant financial implications for the funding of its budget, in particular any projects relating to property such as the rental or purchase of buildings. It shall inform the Commission thereof.

Where a branch of the budgetary authority has notified its intention to deliver an opinion, it shall forward its opinion to the Management Board within a period of six weeks from the date of notification of the project.

Article 97

Implementation of the budget of the Agency

1. The Executive Director shall perform the duties of authorising officer and shall implement the Agency's budget.

2. Monitoring of the commitment and payment of all the Agency's expenditure and of the establishment and recovery of all the Agency's revenue shall be carried out by the Accounting Officer of the Agency.

3. By 1 March at the latest following each financial year, the Agency's accounting officer shall communicate the provisional accounts to the Commission's accounting officer together with a report on the budgetary and financial management for that financial year. The Commission's accounting officer shall consolidate the provisional accounts of the institutions and decentralised bodies in accordance with Article 128 of Council Regulation (EC, Euratom) No 1605/2002 of 25 June 2002 on the Financial Regulation applicable to the general budget of the European Communities (¹).

(¹) OJ L 248, 16.9.2002, p. 1. Regulation as amended by Regulation (EC, Euratom) No 1995/2006 (OJ L 390, 30.12.2006, p. 1).

▼C1

4.   By 31 March at the latest following each financial year, the Commission's accounting officer shall forward the Agency's provisional accounts to the Court of Auditors, together with a report on the budgetary and financial management for that financial year. The report on the budgetary and financial management for that financial year shall also be forwarded to the European Parliament and the Council.

5.   On receipt of the Court of Auditors' observations on the Agency's provisional accounts, pursuant to Article 129 of Regulation (EC, Euratom) No 1605/2002, the Executive Director shall draw up the Agency's final accounts under his own responsibility and forward them to the Management Board for an opinion.

6.   The Management Board shall deliver an opinion on the Agency's final accounts.

7.   By 1 July of the following year at the latest, the Executive Director shall send the final accounts, together with the opinion of the Management Board, to the European Parliament, the Council, the Commission and the Court of Auditors.

8.   The final accounts shall be published.

9.   The Executive Director shall send the Court of Auditors a reply to its observations by 30 September at the latest. He shall also send this reply to the Management Board.

10.   The European Parliament, upon a recommendation from the Council, shall, before 30 April of year N + 2, give a discharge to the Executive Director in respect of the implementation of the budget for year N.

Article 98

Combating fraud

1.   In order to combat fraud, corruption and other unlawful activities, the provisions of Regulation (EC) No 1073/1999 of the European Parliament and of the Council of 25 May 1999 concerning investigations conducted by the European Anti-Fraud Office (OLAF) (¹) shall apply without restrictions to the Agency.

2.   The Agency shall be bound by the Interinstitutional Agreement of 25 May 1999 between the European Parliament, the Council of the European Union and the Commission of the European Communities concerning internal investigations by the European Anti-Fraud Office (OLAF) (²) and shall issue, without delay, the appropriate provisions applicable to all of its staff.

3.   The decisions concerning funding and the implementing agreements and instruments resulting from them shall explicitly stipulate that the Court of Auditors and OLAF may carry out, if necessary, on-the-spot checks of the recipients of the Agency's funding and the agents responsible for allocating it.

(¹) OJ L 136, 31.5.1999, p. 1.
(²) OJ L 136, 31.5.1999, p. 15.

▼C1

Article 99

Financial rules

The financial rules applicable to the Agency shall be adopted by the Management Board after the Commission has been consulted. They may not depart from Regulation (EC, Euratom) No 2343/2002 unless specifically necessary for the Agency's operation and with the Commission's prior consent.

Article 100

Legal personality of the Agency

1.   The Agency shall be a body of the Community and shall have legal personality. In each Member State it shall enjoy the most extensive legal capacity accorded to legal persons under their laws. In particular it may acquire and dispose of movable and immovable property and may be a party to legal proceedings.

2.   The Agency shall be represented by its Executive Director.

Article 101

Liability of the Agency

1.   The contractual liability of the Agency shall be governed by the law applicable to the contract in question. The Court of Justice shall have jurisdiction pursuant to any arbitration clause contained in a contract concluded by the Agency.

2.   In the case of non-contractual liability, the Agency shall, in accordance with the general principles common to the laws of the Member States, make good any damage caused by it or by its servants in the performance of their duties.

The Court of Justice shall have jurisdiction in any dispute relating to compensation for such damages.

3.   The personal financial and disciplinary liability of its servants towards the Agency shall be governed by the relevant rules applying to the staff of the Agency.

Article 102

Privileges and immunities of the Agency

The Protocol on the Privileges and Immunities of the European Communities shall apply to the Agency.

Article 103

Staff rules and regulations

1.   The staff of the Agency shall be subject to the Regulations and Rules applicable to officials and other servants of the European Communities. In respect of its staff, the Agency shall exercise the powers which have been devolved to the appointing authority.

2.   The Management Board shall, in agreement with the Commission, adopt the necessary implementing provisions.

▼C1

3. The Agency's staff shall consist of officials assigned or seconded by the Commission or Member States on a temporary basis and of other servants recruited by the Agency as necessary to carry out its tasks. The Agency shall recruit its personnel on the basis of a staffing plan to be included in the multiannual work programme referred to in Article 78(d).

Article 104

Languages

1. Regulation No 1 of 15 April 1958 determining the languages to be used in the European Economic Community (¹) shall apply to the Agency.

2. The translation services required for the functioning of the Agency shall be provided by the Translation Centre of the bodies of the European Union.

Article 105

Duty of confidentiality

Members of the Management Board, members of the Committees and of the Forum, experts and officials and other servants of the Agency, shall be required, even after their duties have ceased, not to disclose information of the kind covered by the duty of professional secrecy.

Article 106

Participation of third countries

The Management Board may, in agreement with the relevant Committee or the Forum, invite representatives of third countries to participate in the work of the Agency.

Article 107

Participation of international organisations

The Management Board may, in agreement with the relevant Committee or the Forum, invite representatives of international organisations with interests in the field of chemicals regulation to participate as observers in the work of the Agency.

Article 108

Contacts with stakeholder organisations

The Management Board shall, in agreement with the Commission, develop appropriate contacts between the Agency and relevant stakeholder organisations.

(¹) OJ 17, 6.10.1958, p. 385/58. Regulation as last amended by Council Regulation (EC) No 920/2005 (OJ L 156, 18.6.2005, p. 3).

▼C1

Article 109

Rules on transparency

To ensure transparency, the Management Board shall, on the basis of a proposal by the Executive Director and in agreement with the Commission, adopt rules to ensure the availability to the public of regulatory, scientific or technical information concerning the safety of substances on their own, in ►__M3__ mixtures ◄ or in articles which is not of a confidential nature.

Article 110

Relations with relevant Community bodies

1.   The Agency shall cooperate with other Community bodies to ensure mutual support in the accomplishment of their respective tasks in particular to avoid duplication of work.

2.   The Executive Director, having consulted the Committee on Risk Assessment and the European Food Safety Authority, shall establish rules of procedure concerning substances for which an opinion has been sought in a food safety context. These rules of procedure shall be adopted by the Management Board, in agreement with the Commission.

This Title shall not otherwise affect the competences vested in the European Food Safety Authority.

3.   This Title shall not affect the competences vested in the European Medicines Agency.

4.   The Executive Director, having consulted the Committee on Risk Assessment, the Committee on Socio-economic Analysis and the Advisory Committee on Safety, Hygiene and Health Protection at Work, shall establish rules of procedure concerning worker protection issues. These rules of procedure shall be adopted by the Management Board, in agreement with the Commission.

This Title shall not affect the competences vested in the Advisory Committee on Safety, Hygiene and Health Protection at Work and the European Agency for Health and Safety at Work.

Article 111

Formats and software for submission of information to the Agency

The Agency shall specify formats and make them available free of charge, and software packages and make them available on its website for any submissions to the Agency. Member States, manufactures, importers, distributors or downstream users shall use these formats and packages in their submissions to the Agency pursuant to this Regulation. In particular, the Agency shall make available software tools to facilitate the submission of all information relating to substances registered in accordance with Article 12(1).

For the purposes of registration, the format of the technical dossier referred to in Article 10(a) shall be IUCLID. The Agency shall coordinate the further development of this format with the Organisation for Economic Cooperation and Development to ensure maximum harmonisation.

▼__M3__

▼C1

TITLE XII

INFORMATION

Article 117

Reporting

1. Every five years, Member States shall submit to the Commission a report on the operation of this Regulation in their respective territories, including sections on evaluation and enforcement as described in Article 127.

The first report shall be submitted by 1 June 2010.

2. Every five years, the Agency shall submit to the Commission a report on the operation of this Regulation. The Agency shall include in its report information on the joint submission of information in accordance with Article 11 and an overview of the explanations given for submitting information separately.

The first report shall be submitted by 1 June 2011.

3. Every three years the Agency, in accordance with the objective of promoting non-animal testing methods, shall submit to the Commission a report on the status of implementation and use of non-animal test methods and testing strategies used to generate information on intrinsic properties and for risk assessment to meet the requirements of this Regulation.

The first report shall be submitted by 1 June 2011.

4. Every five years, the Commission shall publish a general report on:

(a) the experience acquired with the operation of this Regulation, including the information referred to in paragraphs 1, 2 and 3 and;

(b) the amount and distribution of funding made available by the Commission for the development and evaluation of alternative test methods.

The first report shall be published by 1 June 2012.

Article 118

Access to information

1. Regulation (EC) No 1049/2001 shall apply to documents held by the Agency.

2. Disclosure of the following information shall normally be deemed to undermine the protection of the commercial interests of the concerned person:

(a) details of the full composition of a ►__M3__ mixture ◄;

(b) without prejudice to Article 7(6) and Article 64(2), the precise use, function or application of a substance or ►__M3__ mixture ◄, including information about its precise use as an intermediate;

(c) the precise tonnage of the substance or ►__M3__ mixture ◄ manufactured or placed on the market;

▼C1

(d) links between a manufacturer or importer and his distributors or downstream users.

Where urgent action is essential to protect human health, safety or the environment, such as emergency situations, the Agency may disclose the information referred to in this paragraph.

3. The Management Board shall adopt the practical arrangements for implementing Regulation (EC) No 1049/2001, including appeals or remedies necessary for reviewing a partial or full rejection of a confidentiality request, by 1 June 2008.

4. Decisions taken by the Agency pursuant to Article 8 of Regulation (EC) No 1049/2001 may form the subject of a complaint to the Ombudsman or of an action before the Court of Justice, under the conditions laid down in Articles 195 and 230 of the Treaty respectively.

Article 119

Electronic public access

1. The following information held by the Agency on substances whether on their own, in ▶M3 mixtures ◀ or in articles, shall be made publicly available, free of charge, over the Internet in accordance with Article 77(2)(e):

▼M3

(a) without prejudice to paragraph 2(f) and (g) of this Article, the name in the IUPAC nomenclature for substances fulfilling the criteria for any of the following hazard classes or categories set out in Annex I to Regulation (EC) No 1272/2008:

— hazard classes 2.1 to 2.4, 2.6 and 2.7, 2.8 types A and B, 2.9, 2.10, 2.12, 2.13 categories 1 and 2, 2.14 categories 1 and 2, 2.15 types A to F;

— hazard classes 3.1 to 3.6, 3.7 adverse effects on sexual function and fertility or on development, 3.8 effects other than narcotic effects, 3.9 and 3.10;

— hazard class 4.1;

— hazard class 5.1;

▼C1

(b) if applicable, the name of the substance as given in EINECS;

(c) the classification and labelling of the substance;

(d) physicochemical data concerning the substance and on pathways and environmental fate;

(e) the result of each toxicological and ecotoxicological study;

(f) any derived no-effect level (DNEL) or predicted no-effect concentration (PNEC) established in accordance with Annex I;

(g) the guidance on safe use provided in accordance with Sections 4 and 5 of Annex VI;

(h) analytical methods if requested in accordance with Annexes IX or X which make it possible to detect a dangerous substance when discharged into the environment as well as to determine the direct exposure of humans.

▼C1

2. The following information on substances whether on their own, in ►M3 mixtures ◄ or in articles, shall be made publicly available, free of charge, over the Internet in accordance with Article 77(2)(e) except where a party submitting the information submits a justification in accordance with Article 10(a)(xi), accepted as valid by the Agency, as to why such publication is potentially harmful for the commercial interests of the registrant or any other party concerned:

(a) if essential to classification and labelling, the degree of purity of the substance and the identity of impurities and/or additives which are known to be dangerous;

(b) the total tonnage band (i.e. 1 to 10 tonnes, 10 to 100 tonnes, 100 to 1 000 tonnes or over 1 000 tonnes) within which a particular substance has been registered;

(c) the study summaries or robust study summaries of the information referred to in paragraph 1(d) and (e);

(d) information, other than that listed in paragraph 1, contained in the safety data sheet;

(e) the trade name(s) of the substance;

▼M3

(f) subject to Article 24 of Regulation (EC) No 1272/2008, the name in the IUPAC nomenclature for non-phase-in substances referred to in paragraph 1(a) of this Article for a period of six years;

(g) subject to Article 24 of Regulation (EC) No 1272/2008, the name in the IUPAC nomenclature for substances referred to in paragraph 1(a) of this Article that are only used as one or more of the following:

▼C1

(i) as an intermediate;

(ii) in scientific research and development;

(iii) in product and process orientated research and development.

Article 120

Cooperation with third countries and international organisations

Notwithstanding Articles 118 and 119, information received by the Agency under this Regulation may be disclosed to any government or national authority of a third country or an international organisation in accordance with an agreement concluded between the Community and the third party concerned under Regulation (EC) No 304/2003 of the European Parliament and of the Council of 28 January 2003 concerning the export and import of dangerous chemicals (¹) or under Article 181a(3) of the Treaty, provided that both the following conditions are met:

(a) the purpose of the agreement is cooperation on the implementation or management of legislation concerning chemicals covered by this Regulation;

_____

(¹) OJ L 63, 6.3.2003, p. 1. Regulation as last amended by Commission Regulation (EC) No 777/2006 (OJ L 136, 24.5.2006, p. 9).

▼C1

(b) the third party protects the confidential information as mutually agreed.

TITLE XIII

COMPETENT AUTHORITIES

Article 121

Appointment

Member States shall appoint the competent authority or competent authorities responsible for performing the tasks allotted to competent authorities under this Regulation and for cooperating with the Commission and the Agency in the implementation of this Regulation. Member States shall place adequate resources at the disposal of the competent authorities to enable them, in conjunction with any other available resources, to fulfil their tasks under this Regulation in a timely and effective manner.

Article 122

Cooperation between competent authorities

The competent authorities shall cooperate with each other in the performance of their tasks under this Regulation and shall give the competent authorities of other Member States all the necessary and useful support to this end.

Article 123

Communication to the public of information on risks of substances

The competent authorities of the Member States shall inform the general public about the risks arising from substances where this is considered necessary for the protection of human health or the environment. The Agency, in consultation with competent authorities and stakeholders and drawing as appropriate on relevant best practice, shall provide guidance for the communication of information on the risks and safe use of chemical substances, on their own, in ►**M3** mixtures ◄ or in articles, with a view to coordinating Member States in these activities.

Article 124

Other responsibilities

Competent authorities shall submit electronically to the Agency any available information that they hold on substances registered in accordance with Article 12(1) whose dossiers do not contain the full information referred to in Annex VII, in particular whether enforcement or monitoring activities have identified suspicions of risk. The competent authority shall update this information as appropriate.

Member States shall establish national helpdesks to provide advice to manufacturers, importers, downstream users and any other interested parties on their respective responsibilities and obligations under this Regulation, in particular in relation to the registration of substances in accordance with Article 12(1), in addition to the operational guidance documents provided by the Agency under Article 77(2)(g).

▼C1

TITLE XIV

ENFORCEMENT

Article 125

Tasks of the Member States

Member States shall maintain a system of official controls and other activities as appropriate to the circumstances.

Article 126

Penalties for non-compliance

Member States shall lay down the provisions on penalties applicable for infringement of the provisions of this Regulation and shall take all measures necessary to ensure that they are implemented. The penalties provided for must be effective, proportionate and dissuasive. The Member States shall notify those provisions to the Commission no later than 1 December 2008 and shall notify it without delay of any subsequent amendment affecting them.

Article 127

Report

The report referred to in Article 117(1) shall, in relation to enforcement, include the results of the official inspections, the monitoring carried out, the penalties provided for and the other measures taken pursuant to Articles 125 and 126 during the previous reporting period. The common issues to be covered in the reports shall be agreed by the Forum. The Commission shall make these reports available to the Agency and the Forum.

TITLE XV

TRANSITIONAL AND FINAL PROVISIONS

Article 128

Free movement

1.   Subject to paragraph 2, Member States shall not prohibit, restrict or impede the manufacturing, import, placing on the market or use of a substance, on its own, in a ►**M3** mixture ◄ or in an article, falling within the scope of this Regulation, which complies with this Regulation and, where appropriate, with Community acts adopted in implementation of this Regulation.

2.   Nothing in this Regulation shall prevent Member States from maintaining or laying down national rules to protect workers, human health and the environment applying in cases where this Regulation does not harmonise the requirements on manufacture, placing on the market or use.

▼C1

Article 129

Safeguard clause

1.   Where a Member State has justifiable grounds for believing that urgent action is essential to protect human health or the environment in respect of a substance, on its own, in a ►M3 mixture ◄ or in an article, even if satisfying the requirements of this Regulation, it may take appropriate provisional measures. The Member State shall immediately inform the Commission, the Agency and the other Member States thereof, giving reasons for its decision and submitting the scientific or technical information on which the provisional measure is based.

2.   The Commission shall take a decision in accordance with the procedure referred to in Article 133(3) within 60 days of receipt of the information from the Member State. This decision shall either:

(a) authorise the provisional measure for a time period defined in the decision; or

(b) require the Member State to revoke the provisional measure.

3.   If, in the case of a decision as referred to in paragraph 2(a), the provisional measure taken by the Member State consists in a restriction on the placing on the market or use of a substance, the Member State concerned shall initiate a Community restrictions procedure by submitting to the Agency a dossier, in accordance with Annex XV, within three months of the date of the Commission decision.

4.   In the case of a decision as referred to in paragraph 2(a), the Commission shall consider whether this Regulation needs to be adapted.

Article 130

Statement of reasons for decisions

The competent authorities, the Agency and the Commission shall state the reasons for all decisions they take under this Regulation.

Article 131

Amendments to the Annexes

The Annexes may be amended in accordance with the procedure referred to in Article 133(4).

Article 132

Implementing legislation

The measures necessary to put the provisions of this Regulation efficiently into effect shall be adopted in accordance with the procedure referred to in Article 133(3).

Article 133

Committee procedure

1.   The Commission shall be assisted by a Committee.

2.   Where reference is made to this paragraph, Articles 3 and 7 of Decision 1999/468/EC shall apply, having regard to the provisions of Article 8 thereof.

▼C1

3.   Where reference is made to this paragraph, Articles 5 and 7 of Decision 1999/468/EC shall apply, having regard to the provisions of Article 8 thereof.

The period laid down in Article 5(6) of Decision 1999/468/EC shall be set at three months.

4.   Where reference is made to this paragraph, Article 5a(1) to (4), and Article 7 of Decision 1999/468/EC shall apply, having regard to the provisions of Article 8 thereof.

5.   The Committee shall adopt its Rules of Procedure.

Article 134

Preparation of establishment of the Agency

1.   The Commission shall afford the necessary support towards the establishment of the Agency.

2.   For that purpose, until such time as the Executive Director takes up his duties following his appointment by the Management Board of the Agency in accordance with Article 84, the Commission, on behalf of the Agency, and using the budget provided for the latter, may:

(a) appoint personnel, including a person who shall fulfil the administrative functions of the Executive Director on an interim basis; and

(b) conclude other contracts.

Article 135

Transitional measures regarding notified substances

1.   The requests to notifiers to provide further information to the competent authority in accordance with Article 16(2) of Directive 67/548/EEC, shall be considered as decisions adopted in accordance with Article 51 of this Regulation.

2.   The requests to a notifier to provide further information for a substance in accordance with Article 16(1) of Directive 67/548/EEC, shall be considered as decisions adopted in accordance with Article 52 of this Regulation.

Such substance shall be regarded as being included in the Community rolling action plan in accordance with Article 44(2) of this Regulation and shall be regarded as being chosen in accordance with Article 45(2) of this Regulation by the Member State whose competent authority has requested further information in accordance with Article 7(2) and Article 16(1) of Directive 67/548/EEC.

Article 136

Transitional measures regarding existing substances

1.   The requests to manufacturers and importers to submit information to the Commission made by a Commission Regulation in application of Article 10(2) of Regulation (EEC) No 793/93, shall be considered as decisions adopted in accordance with Article 52 of this Regulation.

▼C1

The competent authority for the substance shall be the competent authority from the Member State identified as rapporteur in accordance with Article 10(1) of Regulation (EEC) No 793/93 and shall carry out the tasks of Article 46(3) and Article 48 of this Regulation.

2. The requests to manufacturers and importers to submit information to the Commission made by a Commission Regulation in application of Article 12(2) of Regulation (EEC) No 793/93, shall be considered as decisions adopted in accordance with Article 52 of this Regulation. The Agency shall identify the competent authority for the substance to carry out the tasks of Article 46(3) and Article 48 of this Regulation.

3. A Member State whose rapporteur has not forwarded by 1 June 2008 the risk evaluation and, where appropriate, the strategy for limiting the risks, in accordance with Article 10(3) of Regulation (EEC) No 793/93, shall:

(a) document information on hazard and risk in accordance with Annex XV, Part B of this Regulation;

(b) apply Article 69(4) of this Regulation on the basis of the information referred to in point (a); and

(c) prepare a documentation of how it considers that any other risks identified would need to be addressed by action other than an amendment of Annex XVII of this Regulation.

The information referred to above shall be submitted to the Agency by 1 December 2008.

Article 137

Transitional measures regarding restrictions

1. By 1 June 2010, the Commission shall, if necessary, prepare a draft amendment to Annex XVII in accordance with either of the following:

(a) any risk evaluation and recommended strategy for limiting risks that has been adopted at Community level in accordance with Article 11 of Regulation (EEC) No 793/93 as far as it includes proposals for restrictions in accordance with Title VIII of this Regulation but for which a decision under Directive 76/769/EEC has not yet been taken;

(b) any proposal, which has been submitted to the relevant institutions but has not yet been adopted, concerning the introduction or the amendment of restrictions under Directive 76/769/EEC.

2. Until 1 June 2010, any dossier referred to in Article 129(3) shall be submitted to the Commission. The Commission shall, if necessary, prepare a draft amendment to Annex XVII.

3. Any amendment to the restrictions adopted under Directive 76/769/EEC from 1 June 2007 shall be incorporated in Annex XVII with effect from 1 June 2009.

▼C1

Article 138

Review

1.   By 1 June 2019, the Commission shall carry out a review to assess whether or not to extend the application of the obligation to perform a chemical safety assessment and to document it in a chemical safety report to substances not covered by this obligation because they are not subject to registration or subject to registration but manufactured or imported in quantities of less than 10 tonnes per year. ►**M3** However, for substances meeting the criteria for classification in the hazard classes carcinogenicity, germ cell mutagenicity or reproductive toxicity, category 1A or 1B, in accordance with Regulation (EC) No 1272/2008, the review shall be carried out by 1 June 2014. ◄ When carrying out the review the Commission shall take into account all relevant factors, including:

(a) the costs for manufacturers and importers of drawing up the chemical safety reports;

(b) the distribution of costs between actors in the supply chain and the downstream user;

(c) the benefits for human health and the environment.

On the basis of these reviews, the Commission may, if appropriate, present legislative proposals to extend this obligation.

2.   The Commission may present legislative proposals as soon as a practicable and cost-efficient way of selecting polymers for registration on the basis of sound technical and valid scientific criteria can be established, and after publishing a report on the following:

(a) the risks posed by polymers in comparison with other substances;

(b) the need, if any, to register certain types of polymer, taking account of competitiveness and innovation on the one hand and the protection of human health and the environment on the other.

3.   The report, referred to in Article 117(4), on the experience acquired with the operation of this Regulation shall include a review of the requirements relating to registration of substances manufactured or imported only in quantities starting at one tonne but less than 10 tonnes per year per manufacturer or importer. On the basis of that review, the Commission may present legislative proposals to modify the information requirements for substances manufactured or imported in quantities of one tonne or more up to 10 tonnes per year per manufacturer or importer, taking into account the latest developments, for example in relation to alternative testing and (quantitative) structure-activity relationships ((Q)SARs).

4.   The Commission shall carry out a review of Annexes I, IV and V by 1 June 2008, with a view to proposing amendments, if appropriate, to them in accordance with the procedure referred to in Article 131.

5.   The Commission shall carry out a review of Annex XIII by 1 December 2008, to assess the adequacy of the criteria for identifying substances which are persistent, bioaccumulative and toxic or very persistent and very bioaccumulative, with a view to proposing an amendment to it, if appropriate, in accordance with the procedure referred to in Article 133(4).

▼C1

6.   By 1 June 2012 the Commission shall carry out a review to assess whether or not to amend the scope of this Regulation to avoid overlaps with other relevant Community provisions. On the basis of that review, the Commission may, if appropriate, present a legislative proposal.

7.   By 1 June 2013 the Commission shall carry out a review to assess whether or not, taking into account latest developments in scientific knowledge, to extend the scope of Article 60(3) to substances identified under Article 57(f) as having endocrine disrupting properties. On the basis of that review the Commission may, if appropriate, present legislative proposals.

8.   By 1 June 2019, the Commission shall carry out a review to assess whether or not to extend the scope of Article 33 to cover other dangerous substances, taking into account the practical experience in implementing that Article. On the basis of that review, the Commission may, if appropriate, present legislative proposals to extend that obligation.

9.   In accordance with the objective of promoting non-animal testing and the replacement, reduction or refinement of animal testing required under this Regulation, the Commission shall review the testing requirements of Section 8.7 of Annex VIII by 1 June 2019. On the basis of this review, while ensuring a high level of protection of health and the environment, the Commission may propose an amendment in accordance with the procedure referred to in Article 133(4).

Article 139

Repeals

Directive 91/155/EEC shall be repealed.

Directives 93/105/EC and 2000/21/EC and Regulations (EEC) No 793/93 and (EC) No 1488/94 shall be repealed with effect from 1 June 2008.

Directive 93/67/EEC shall be repealed with effect from 1 August 2008.

Directive 76/769/EEC shall be repealed with effect from 1 June 2009.

References to the repealed acts shall be construed as references to this Regulation.

Article 140

Amendment of Directive 1999/45/EC

Article 14 of Directive 1999/45/EC shall be deleted.

Article 141

Entry into force and application

1.   This Regulation shall enter into force on 1 June 2007.

2.   Titles II, III, V, VI, VII, XI and XII as well as Articles 128 and 136 shall apply from 1 June 2008.

3.   Article 135 shall apply from 1 August 2008.

4.   Title VIII and Annex XVII shall apply from 1 June 2009.

This Regulation shall be binding in its entirety and directly applicable in all Member States.

▼C1

▼C1

ANNEX I

GENERAL PROVISIONS FOR ASSESSING SUBSTANCES AND PREPARING CHEMICAL SAFETY REPORTS

0.   INTRODUCTION

0.1.   The purpose of this Annex is to set out how manufacturers and importers are to assess and document that the risks arising from the substance they manufacture or import are adequately controlled during manufacture and their own use(s) and that others further down the supply chain can adequately control the risks. This Annex shall also apply as necessary to producers and importers of articles required to make a chemical safety assessment as part of a registration.

0.2.   The chemical safety assessment shall be prepared by one or more competent person(s) who have appropriate experience and received appropriate training, including refresher training.

0.3.   The chemical safety assessment of a manufacturer shall address the manufacture of a substance and all the identified uses. The chemical safety assessment of an importer shall address all identified uses. The chemical safety assessment shall consider the use of the substance on its own (including any major impurities and additives), in a ▶M3 mixture ◀ and in an article, as defined by the identified uses. The assessment shall consider all stages of the life-cycle of the substance resulting from the manufacture and identified uses. The chemical safety assessment shall be based on a comparison of the potential adverse effects of a substance with the known or reasonably foreseeable exposure of man and/or the environment to that substance taking into account implemented and recommended risk management measures and operational conditions.

0.4.   Substances whose physicochemical, toxicological and ecotoxicological properties are likely to be similar or follow a regular pattern as a result of structural similarity may be considered as a group, or 'category' of substances. If the manufacturer or importer considers that the chemical safety assessment carried out for one substance is sufficient to assess and document that the risks arising from another substance or from a group or 'category' of substances are adequately controlled then he can use that chemical safety assessment for the other substance or group or 'category' of substances. The manufacturer or importer shall provide a justification for this.

0.5.   The chemical safety assessment shall be based on the information on the substance contained in the technical dossier and on other available and relevant information. Manufacturers or importers submitting a proposal for testing in accordance with Annexes IX and X shall record this under the relevant heading of the chemical safety report. Available information from assessments carried out under other international and national programmes shall be included. Where available and appropriate, an assessment carried out under Community legislation (e.g. risk assessments completed under Regulation (EEC) No 793/93) shall be taken into account in the development of, and reflected in, the chemical safety report. Deviations from such assessments shall be justified.

        Thus the information to be considered includes information related to the hazards of the substance, the exposure arising from the manufacture or import, the identified uses of the substance, operational conditions and risk management measures applied or recommended to downstream users to be taken into account.

▼C1

In accordance with section 3 of Annex XI in some cases, it may not be necessary to generate missing information, because risk management measures and operational conditions which are necessary to control a well-characterised risk may also be sufficient to control other potential risks, which will not therefore need to be characterised precisely.

If the manufacturer or importer considers that further information is necessary for producing his chemical safety report and that this information can only be obtained by performing tests in accordance with Annex IX or X, he shall submit a proposal for a testing strategy, explaining why he considers that additional information is necessary and record this in the chemical safety report under the appropriate heading. While waiting for results of further testing, he shall record in his chemical safety report, and include in the exposure scenario developed, the interim risk management measures that he has put in place and those he recommends to downstream users intended to manage the risks being explored.

▼M10

0.6. Steps of a chemical safety assessment

0.6.1. A chemical safety assessment performed by a manufacturer or an importer for a substance shall include the following steps 1 to 4 in accordance with the respective sections of this Annex:

1. Human health hazard assessment.

2. Human health hazard assessment of physicochemical properties.

3. Environmental hazard assessment.

4. PBT and vPvB assessment.

0.6.2. In the cases referred to in point 0.6.3 the chemical safety assessment shall also include the following steps 5 and 6 in accordance with Sections 5 and 6 of this Annex:

5. Exposure assessment.

5.1. The generation of exposure scenario(s) (or the identification of relevant use and exposure categories, if appropriate).

5.2. Exposure estimation.

6. Risk characterisation.

0.6.3. Where as a result of steps 1 to 4 the manufacturer or importer concludes that the substance fulfils the criteria for any of the following hazard classes or categories set out in Annex I to Regulation (EC) No 1272/2008 or is assessed to be a PBT or vPvB, the chemical safety assessment shall also include steps 5 and 6 in accordance with Sections 5 and 6 of this Annex:

(a) hazard classes 2.1 to 2.4, 2.6 and 2.7, 2.8 types A and B, 2.9, 2.10, 2.12, 2.13 categories 1 and 2, 2.14 categories 1 and 2, and 2.15 types A to F;

(b) hazard classes 3.1 to 3.6, 3.7 adverse effects on sexual function and fertility or on development, 3.8 effects other than narcotic effects, 3.9, and 3.10;

(c) hazard class 4.1;

(d) hazard class 5.1.

▼__M10__

0.6.4. A summary of all the relevant information used in addressing the points above shall be presented under the relevant heading of the Chemical Safety Report (Section 7).

▼__C1__

0.7. The main element of the exposure part of the chemical safety report is the description of the exposure scenario(s) implemented for the manufacturer's production, the manufacturer or importer's own use, and those recommended by the manufacturer or importer to be implemented for the identified use(s).

An exposure scenario is the set of conditions that describe how the substance is manufactured or used during its life-cycle and how the manufacturer or importer controls, or recommends downstream users to control, exposures of humans and the environment. These sets of conditions contain a description of both the risk management measures and operational conditions which the manufacturer or importer has implemented or recommends to be implemented by downstream users.

If the substance is placed on the market, the relevant exposure scenario(s), including the risk management measures and operational conditions shall be included in an annex to the safety data sheet in accordance with Annex II.

0.8. The level of detail required in describing an exposure scenario will vary substantially from case to case, depending on the use of a substance, its hazardous properties and the amount of information available to the manufacturer or importer. Exposure scenarios may describe the appropriate risk management measures for several individual processes or uses of a substance. An exposure scenario may thereby cover a large range of processes or uses. Exposure scenarios covering a wide range of processes or uses may be referred to as Exposure Categories. Further mention of Exposure Scenario in this Annex and Annex II includes Exposure Categories if they are developed.

0.9. Where information is not necessary in accordance with Annex XI, this fact shall be stated under the appropriate heading of the chemical safety report and a reference shall be made to the justification in the technical dossier. The fact that no information is required shall also be stated in the safety data sheet.

0.10. In relation to particular effects, such as ozone depletion, photochemical ozone creation potential, strong odour and tainting, for which the procedures set out in Sections 1 to 6 are impracticable, the risks associated with such effects shall be assessed on a case-by-case basis and the manufacturer or importer shall include a full description and justification of such assessments in the chemical safety report and summarised in the safety data sheet.

0.11. When assessing the risk of the use of one or more substances incorporated into a special ►__M3__ mixture ◄ (for instance alloys), the way the constituent substances are bonded in the chemical matrix shall be taken into account.

0.12. Where the methodology described in this Annex is not appropriate, details of alternative methodology used shall be explained and justified in the chemical safety report.

▼C1

0.13. Part A of the chemical safety report shall include a declaration that the risk management measures outlined in the relevant exposure scenarios for the manufacturer's or importer's own use(s) are implemented by the manufacturer or importer and that those exposure scenarios for the identified uses are communicated to distributors and downstream users in the safety data sheet(s).

1. HUMAN HEALTH HAZARD ASSESSMENT

1.0. **Introduction**

▼M10

1.0.1. The objectives of the human health hazard assessment shall be to determine the classification of a substance in accordance with Regulation (EC) No 1272/2008; and to derive levels of exposure to the substance above which humans should not be exposed. This level of exposure is known as the Derived No-Effect Level (DNEL).

1.0.2. The human health hazard assessment shall consider the toxicokinetic profile (i.e. absorption, metabolism, distribution and elimination) of the substance and the following groups of effects:

(1) acute effects such as acute toxicity, irritation and corrosivity;

(2) sensitisation;

(3) repeated dose toxicity; and

(4) CMR effects (carcinogenity, germ cell mutagenicity and toxicity for reproduction).

Based on all the available information, other effects shall be considered when necessary.

▼C1

1.0.3. The hazard assessment shall comprise the following four steps:

Step 1: Evaluation of non-human information.

Step 2: Evaluation of human information.

Step 3: Classification and Labelling.

Step 4: Derivation of DNELs.

1.0.4. The first three steps shall be undertaken for every effect for which information is available and shall be recorded under the relevant section of the Chemical Safety Report and where required and in accordance with Article 31, summarised in the Safety Data Sheet under headings 2 and 11.

1.0.5. For any effect for which no relevant information is available, the relevant section shall contain the sentence: 'This information is not available'. The justification, including reference to any literature search carried out, shall be included in the technical dossier.

▼C1

1.0.6.　Step 4 of the human health hazard assessment shall be undertaken by integrating the results from the first three steps and shall be included under the relevant heading of the Chemical Safety Report and summarised in the Safety Data Sheet under heading 8.1.

1.1.　**Step 1: Evaluation of non-human information**

1.1.1.　The evaluation of non-human information shall comprise:

— the hazard identification for the effect based on all available non-human information,

— the establishment of the quantitative dose (concentration)-response (effect) relationship.

1.1.2.　When it is not possible to establish the quantitative dose (concentration)-response (effect) relationship, then this should be justified and a semi-quantitative or qualitative analysis shall be included. For instance, for acute effects it is usually not possible to establish the quantitative dose (concentration)-response (effect) relationship on the basis of the results of a test conducted in accordance with test methods laid down in a Commission Regulation as specified in Article 13(3). In such cases it suffices to determine whether and to which degree the substance has an inherent capacity to cause the effect.

▼M10

1.1.3.　All non-human information used to assess a particular effect on humans and to establish the dose (concentration) – response (effect) relationship, shall be briefly presented, if possible in the form of a table or tables, distinguishing between *in vitro*, *in vivo* and other information. The relevant test results (e.g. ATE, LD50, NO(A)EL or LO(A)EL) and test conditions (e.g. test duration, route of administration) and other relevant information shall be presented, in internationally recognised units of measurement for that effect.

▼C1

1.1.4.　If one study is available then a robust study summary should be prepared for that study. If there are several studies addressing the same effect, then, having taken into account possible variables (e.g. conduct, adequacy, relevance of test species, quality of results, etc.), normally the study or studies giving rise to the highest concern shall be used to establish the DNELs and a robust study summary shall be prepared for that study or studies and included as part of the technical dossier. Robust summaries will be required of all key data used in the hazard assessment. If the study or studies giving rise to the highest concern are not used, then this shall be fully justified and included as part of the technical dossier, not only for the study being used but also for all studies demonstrating a higher concern than the study being used. It is important irrespective of whether hazards have been identified or not that the validity of the study be considered.

1.2.　**Step 2: Evaluation of human information**

If no human information is available, this part shall contain the statement: 'No human information is available'. However, if human information is available, it shall be presented, if possible in the form of a table.

▼C1

1.3.   **Step 3: Classification and Labelling**

▼M10

1.3.1.   The appropriate classification developed in accordance with the criteria in Regulation (EC) No 1272/2008 shall be presented and justified. Where applicable, Specific Concentration limits resulting from the application of Article 10 of Regulation (EC) No 1272/2008 and Articles 4 to 7 of Directive 1999/45/EC shall be presented and, if they are not included in Part 3 of Annex VI to Regulation (EC) No 1272/2008, justified.

The assessment should always include a statement as to whether the substance fulfils or does not fulfil the criteria given in Regulation (EC) No 1272/2008 for classification in the hazard class carcinogenicity category 1A or 1B, in the hazard class germ cell mutagenicity category 1A or 1B or in the hazard class reproductive toxicity category 1A or 1B.

1.3.2.   If the information is inadequate to decide whether a substance should be classified for a particular hazard class or category, the registrant shall indicate and justify the action or decision he has taken as a result.

▼C1

1.4.   **Step 4: Identification of DNEL(s)**

1.4.1.   Based on the outcomes of steps 1 and 2, (a) DNEL(s) shall be established for the substance, reflecting the likely route(s), duration and frequency of exposure. ►**M10** For some hazard classes, especially germ cell mutagenicity and carcinogenicity, the available information may not enable a toxicological threshold, and therefore a DNEL, to be established. ◄ If justified by the exposure scenario(s), a single DNEL may be sufficient. However, taking into account the available information and the exposure scenario(s) in Section 9 of the Chemical Safety Report it may be necessary to identify different DNELs for each relevant human population (e.g. workers, consumers and humans liable to exposure indirectly via the environment) and possibly for certain vulnerable sub-populations (e.g. children, pregnant women) and for different routes of exposure. A full justification shall be given specifying, *inter alia*, the choice of the information used, the route of exposure (oral, dermal, inhalation) and the duration and frequency of exposure to the substance for which the DNEL is valid. If more than one route of exposure is likely to occur, then a DNEL shall be established for each route of exposure and for the exposure from all routes combined. When establishing the DNEL, the following factors shall, *inter alia*, be taken into account:

(a) the uncertainty arising, among other factors, from the variability in the experimental information and from intra- and inter-species variation;

(b) the nature and severity of the effect;

(c) the sensitivity of the human (sub-)population to which the quantitative and/or qualitative information on exposure applies.

1.4.2.   If it is not possible to identify a DNEL, then this shall be clearly stated and fully justified.

2.   PHYSICOCHEMICAL HAZARD ASSESSMENT

▼M10

2.1.   The objective of the hazard assessment for physicochemical properties shall be to determine the classification of a substance in accordance with Regulation (EC) No 1272/2008.

▼__M10__

2.2. As a minimum, the potential effects to human health shall be assessed for the following physicochemical properties:

— explosivity,

— flammability,

— oxidising potential.

If the information is inadequate to decide whether a substance should be classified for a particular hazard class or category, the registrant shall indicate and justify the action or decision he has taken as a result.

▼__C1__

2.3. The assessment of each effect shall be presented under the relevant heading of the Chemical Safety Report (Section 7) and where required and in accordance with Article 31, summarised in the Safety Data Sheet under headings 2 and 9.

2.4. For every physicochemical property, the assessment shall entail an evaluation of the inherent capacity of the substance to cause the effect resulting from the manufacture and identified uses.

▼__M10__

2.5. The appropriate classification developed in accordance with the criteria in Regulation (EC) No 1272/2008 shall be presented and justified.

▼__C1__

3. ENVIRONMENTAL HAZARD ASSESSMENT

3.0. **Introduction**

▼__M10__

3.0.1. The objective of the environmental hazard assessment shall be to determine the classification of a substance in accordance with Regulation (EC) No 1272/2008 and to identify the concentration of the substance below which adverse effects in the environmental sphere of concern are not expected to occur. This concentration is known as the Predicted No-Effect Concentration (PNEC).

▼__C1__

3.0.2. The environmental hazard assessment shall consider the potential effects on the environment, comprising the (1) aquatic (including sediment), (2) terrestrial and (3) atmospheric compartments, including the potential effects that may occur (4) via food-chain accumulation. In addition, the potential effects on the (5) microbiological activity of sewage treatment systems shall be considered. The assessment of the effects on each of these five environmental spheres shall be presented under the relevant heading of the Chemical Safety Report (Section 7) and where required and in accordance with Article 31, summarised in the Safety Data Sheet under headings 2 and 12.

3.0.3. For any environmental sphere, for which no effect information is available, the relevant section of the chemical safety report shall contain the sentence: 'This information is not available'. The justification, including reference to any literature research carried out, shall be included in the technical dossier. For any environmental sphere for which information is available, but the manufacturer or importer believes that it is not necessary to conduct the hazard assessment, the manufacturer or importer shall present a justification, with reference to pertinent information, under the relevant heading of the Chemical Safety Report (Section 7) and where required and in accordance with Article 31, summarised in the Safety Data Sheet under heading 12.

▼C1

3.0.4. The hazard assessment shall comprise the following three steps, which shall be clearly identified as such in the Chemical Safety Report:

Step 1:   Evaluation of information.

Step 2:   Classification and Labelling.

Step 3:   Derivation of the PNEC.

3.1.   **Step 1: Evaluation of information**

3.1.1.   The evaluation of all available information shall comprise:

— the hazard identification based on all available information,

— the establishment of the quantitative dose (concentration)-response (effect) relationship.

3.1.2.   When it is not possible to establish the quantitative dose (concentration)-response (effect) relationship, then this should be justified and a semi-quantitative or qualitative analysis shall be included.

3.1.3.   All information used to assess the effects on a specific environmental sphere shall be briefly presented, if possible in the form of a table or tables. The relevant test results (e.g. LC50 or NOEC) and test conditions (e.g. test duration, route of administration) and other relevant information shall be presented, in internationally recognised units of measurement for that effect.

3.1.4.   All information used to assess the environmental fate of the substance shall be briefly presented, if possible in the form of a table or tables. The relevant test results and test conditions and other relevant information shall be presented, in internationally recognised units of measurement for that effect.

3.1.5.   If one study is available then a robust study summary should be prepared for that study. Where there is more than one study addressing the same effect, then the study or studies giving rise to the highest concern shall be used to draw a conclusion and a robust study summary shall be prepared for that study or studies and included as part of the technical dossier. Robust summaries will be required of all key data used in the hazard assessment. If the study or studies giving rise to the highest concern are not used, then this shall be fully justified and included as part of the technical dossier, not only for the study being used but also for all studies reaching a higher concern than the study being used. For substances where all available studies indicate no hazards an overall assessment of the validity of all studies should be performed.

3.2.   **Step 2: Classification and Labelling**

▼M10

3.2.1.   The appropriate classification developed in accordance with the criteria in Regulation (EC) No 1272/2008 shall be presented and justified. Any M-factor resulting from the application of Article 10 of Regulation (EC) No 1272/2008 shall be presented and, if it is not included in Part 3 of Annex VI to Regulation (EC) No 1272/2008, justified.

3.2.2.   If the information is inadequate to decide whether a substance should be classified for a particular hazard class or category, the registrant shall indicate and justify the action or decision he has taken as a result.

▼__C1__

3.3.   **Step 3: Identification of the PNEC**

3.3.1.   Based on the available information, the PNEC for each environmental
         sphere shall be established. The PNEC may be calculated by applying an
         appropriate assessment factor to the effect values (e.g. LC50 or NOEC).
         An assessment factor expresses the difference between effects values
         derived for a limited number of species from laboratory tests and the
         PNEC for the environmental sphere (¹).

3.3.2.   If it is not possible to derive the PNEC, then this shall be clearly stated
         and fully justified.

4.   PBT AND VPVB ASSESSMENT

4.0.   **Introduction**

4.0.1.   The objective of the PBT and vPvB assessment shall be to determine if
         the substance fulfils the criteria given in Annex XIII and if so, to char-
         acterise the potential emissions of the substance. A hazard assessment in
         accordance with Sections 1 and 3 of this Annex addressing all the long-
         term effects and the estimation of the long-term exposure of humans and
         the environment as carried out in accordance with Section 5 (Exposure
         Assessment), step 2 (Exposure Estimation), cannot be carried out with
         sufficient reliability for substances satisfying the PBT and vPvB criteria
         in Annex XIII. Therefore, a separate PBT and vPvB assessment is
         required.

4.0.2.   The PBT and vPvB assessment shall comprise the following two steps,
         which shall be clearly identified as such in Part B, Section 8 of the
         Chemical Safety Report:

         Step 1:   Comparison with the Criteria.

         Step 2:   Emission Characterisation.

         The assessment shall also be summarised in the Safety Data Sheet under
         heading 12.

▼__M10__

4.1.   **Step 1: Comparison with the criteria**

         This part of the PBT and vPvB assessment shall entail the comparison of
         the available information with the criteria given in Section 1 of Annex
         XIII and a statement of whether the substance fulfils or does not fulfil
         the criteria. The assessment shall be conducted in accordance with the
         provisions laid down in the introductory part of Annex XIII as well as
         Sections 2 and 3 of that Annex.

4.2.   **Step 2: Emission Characterisation**

         If the substance fulfils the criteria or it is considered as if it is a PBT or
         vPvB in the registration dossier an emission characterisation shall be
         conducted comprising the relevant parts of the exposure assessment as
         described in Section 5. In particular it shall contain an estimation of the
         amounts of the substance released to the different environmental
         compartments during all activities carried out by the manufacturer or
         importer and all identified uses, and an identification of the likely
         routes by which humans and the environment are exposed to the
         substance.

(¹) In general, the more extensive the data and the longer the duration of the tests, the
    smaller is the degree of uncertainty and the size of the assessment factor. An assessment
    factor of 1 000 is typically applied to the lowest of three short term L(E)C50 values
    derived from species representing different trophic levels and a factor of 10 to the lowest
    of three long-term NOEC values derived from species representing different trophic
    levels.

▼C1

5.   EXPOSURE ASSESSMENT

5.0.   **Introduction**

The objective of the exposure assessment shall be to make a quantitative or qualitative estimate of the dose/concentration of the substance to which humans and the environment are or may be exposed. The assessment shall consider all stages of the life-cycle of the substance resulting from the manufacture and identified uses and shall cover any exposures that may relate to the hazards identified in Sections 1 to 4. The exposure assessment shall entail the following two steps, which shall be clearly identified as such in the Chemical Safety Report:

Step 1: Generation of exposure scenario(s) or the generation of relevant use and exposure categories.

Step 2: Exposure Estimation.

Where required and in accordance with Article 31, the exposure scenario shall also be included in an annex to the Safety Data Sheet.

5.1.   **Step 1: Development of exposure scenarios**

5.1.1.   Exposure scenarios as described in Sections 0.7 and 0.8 shall be generated. Exposure scenarios are the core of the process to carry out a chemical safety assessment. The chemical safety assessment process may be iterative. The first assessment will be based on the required minimum and all available hazard information and on the exposure estimation that corresponds to the initial assumptions about the operating conditions and risk management measures (an initial exposure scenario). If the initial assumptions lead to a risk characterisation indicating that risks to human health and the environment are not adequately controlled, then it is necessary to carry out an iterative process with amendment of one or a number of factors in hazard or exposure assessment with the aim to demonstrate adequate control. The refinement of hazard assessment may require generation of additional hazard information. The refinement of exposure assessment may involve appropriate alteration of the operational conditions or risk management measures in the exposure scenario or more precise exposure estimation. The exposure scenario, resulting from the final iteration (a final exposure scenario), shall be included in the chemical safety report and attached to the safety data sheet in accordance with Article 31.

The final exposure scenario shall be presented under the relevant heading of the chemical safety report, and included in an annex to the safety data sheet, using an appropriate short title giving a brief general description of the use, consistent with those given in Section 3.5 of Annex VI. Exposure scenarios shall cover any manufacture in the Community and all identified uses.

In particular, an exposure scenario includes, where relevant, a description of:

Operational conditions

— the processes involved, including the physical form in which the substance is manufactured, processed and/or used,

— the activities of workers related to the processes and the duration and frequency of their exposure to the substance,

▼<u>C1</u>

— the activities of consumers and the duration and frequency of their exposure to the substance,

— the duration and frequency of emissions of the substance to the different environmental compartments and sewage treatment systems and the dilution in the receiving environmental compartment.

Risk management measures

— the risk management measures to reduce or avoid direct and indirect exposure of humans (including workers and consumers) and the different environmental compartments to the substance,

— the waste management measures to reduce or avoid exposure of humans and the environment to the substance during waste disposal and/or recycling.

5.1.2. Where a manufacturer, importer or downstream user applies for an application for an authorisation for a specific use, exposure scenarios need only be developed for that use and the subsequent life-cycle steps.

5.2. **Step 2: Exposure Estimation**

5.2.1. The exposure shall be estimated for each exposure scenario developed and shall be presented under the relevant heading of the Chemical Safety Report and where required and in accordance with Article 31, summarised in an annex to the safety data sheet. The exposure estimation entails three elements: (1) emission estimation; (2) assessment of chemical fate and pathways; and (3) estimation of exposure levels.

5.2.2. The emission estimation shall consider the emissions during all relevant parts of the life-cycle of the substance resulting from the manufacture and each of the identified uses. The life-cycle stages resulting from the manufacture of the substance cover, where relevant, the waste stage. The life-cycle stages resulting from identified uses cover, where relevant, the service-life of articles and the waste stage. The emission estimation shall be performed under the assumption that the risk management measures and operational conditions described in the exposure scenario have been implemented.

5.2.3. A characterisation of possible degradation, transformation, or reaction processes and an estimation of environmental distribution and fate shall be performed.

5.2.4. An estimation of the exposure levels shall be performed for all human populations (workers, consumers and humans liable to exposure indirectly via the environment) and environmental spheres for which exposure to the substance is known or reasonably foreseeable. Each relevant route of human exposure (inhalation, oral, dermal and combined through all relevant routes and sources of exposure) shall be addressed. Such estimations shall take account of spatial and temporal variations in the exposure pattern. In particular, the exposure estimation shall take account of:

— adequately measured, representative exposure data,

▼C1

— any major impurities and additives in the substance,

— the quantity in which the substance is produced and/or imported,

— the quantity for each identified use,

— implemented or recommended risk management, including the degree of containment,

— duration and frequency of exposure according to the operational conditions,

— the activities of workers related to the processes and the duration and frequency of their exposure to the substance,

— the activities of consumers and the duration and frequency of their exposure to the substance,

— the duration and frequency of emissions of the substance to the different environmental compartments and the dilution in the receiving environmental compartment,

— the physicochemical properties of the substance,

— transformation and/or degradation products,

— the likely routes of exposure of and potential for absorption in humans,

— the likely pathways to the environment and environmental distribution and degradation and/or transformation (see also Section 3 Step 1),

— scale (geographical) of exposure,

— matrix dependent release/migration of the substance.

5.2.5.   Where adequately measured representative exposure data are available, special consideration shall be given to them when conducting the exposure assessment. Appropriate models can be used for the estimation of exposure levels. Relevant monitoring data from substances with analogous use and exposure patterns or analogous properties can also be considered.

6.   RISK CHARACTERISATION

6.1.   The risk characterisation shall be carried out for each exposure scenario and shall be presented under the relevant heading of the Chemical Safety Report.

6.2.   The risk characterisation shall consider the human populations (exposed as workers, consumers or indirectly via the environment and if relevant a combination thereof) and the environmental spheres for which exposure to the substance is known or reasonably foreseeable, under the assumption that the risk management measures described in the exposure scenarios in the Section 5 have been implemented. In addition, the overall environmental risk caused by the substance shall be reviewed by integrating the results for the overall releases, emissions and losses from all sources to all environmental compartments.

6.3.   The risk characterisation consists of:

— a comparison of the exposure of each human population known to be or likely to be exposed with the appropriate DNEL,

— a comparison of the predicted environmental concentrations in each environmental sphere with the PNECs, and

— an assessment of the likelihood and severity of an event occurring due to the physicochemical properties of the substance.

▼C1

6.4. For any exposure scenario, the risk to humans and the environment can be considered to be adequately controlled, throughout the lifecycle of the substance that results from manufacture or identified uses, if:

— the exposure levels estimated in Section 6.2 do not exceed the appropriate DNEL or the PNEC, as determined in Sections 1 and 3, respectively, and,

— the likelihood and severity of an event occurring due to the physicochemical properties of the substance as determined in Section 2 is negligible.

6.5. For those human effects and those environmental spheres for which it was not possible to determine a DNEL or a PNEC, a qualitative assessment of the likelihood that effects are avoided when implementing the exposure scenario shall be carried out.

For substances satisfying the PBT and vPvB criteria, the manufacturer or importer shall use the information as obtained in Section 5, Step 2 when implementing on its site, and recommending for downstream users, risk management measures which minimise exposures and emissions to humans and the environment, throughout the lifecycle of the substance that results from manufacture or identified uses.

7. CHEMICAL SAFETY REPORT FORMAT

The Chemical Safety Report shall include the following headings:

CHEMICAL SAFETY REPORT FORMAT
PART A
1. SUMMARY OF RISK MANAGEMENT MEASURES
2. DECLARATION THAT RISK MANAGEMENT MEASURES ARE IMPLEMENTED
3. DECLARATION THAT RISK MANAGEMENT MEASURES ARE COMMUNICATED
PART B
1. IDENTITY OF THE SUBSTANCE AND PHYSICAL AND CHEMICAL PROPERTIES
2. MANUFACTURE AND USES
2.1. Manufacture
2.2. Identified uses
2.3. Uses advised against
3. CLASSIFICATION AND LABELLING
4. ENVIRONMENTAL FATE PROPERTIES
4.1. Degradation
4.2. Environmental distribution
4.3. Bioaccumulation
4.4. Secondary poisoning

▼C1

CHEMICAL SAFETY REPORT FORMAT

5. HUMAN HEALTH HAZARD ASSESSMENT

    5.1.   Toxicokinetics (absorption, metabolism, distribution and elimination)

    5.2.   Acute toxicity

    5.3.   Irritation

▼M10

▼C1

    5.4.   Corrosivity

    5.5.   Sensitisation

▼M10

▼C1

    5.6.   Repeated dose toxicity

▼M10

    5.7.   Germ cell mutagenicity

▼C1

    5.8.   Carcinogenicity

    5.9.   Toxicity for reproduction

▼M10

▼C1

    5.10. Other effects

    5.11. Derivation of DNEL(s)

6. HUMAN HEALTH HAZARD ASSESSMENT OF PHYSICO-CHEMICAL PROPERTIES

    6.1.   Explosivity

    6.2.   Flammability

    6.3.   Oxidising potential

7. ENVIRONMENTAL HAZARD ASSESSMENT

    7.1.   Aquatic compartment (including sediment)

    7.2.   Terrestrial compartment

    7.3.   Atmospheric compartment

    7.4.   Microbiological activity in sewage treatment systems

8. PBT AND VPVB ASSESSMENT

9. EXPOSURE ASSESSMENT

    9.1.   (Title of exposure scenario 1)

        9.1.1.   Exposure scenario

        9.1.2.   Exposure estimation

▼C1

CHEMICAL SAFETY REPORT FORMAT

9.2.   (Title of exposure scenario 2)

    9.2.1.   Exposure scenario

    9.2.2.   Exposure estimation

    (etc.)

10. RISK CHARACTERISATION

  10.1.   (Title of exposure scenario 1)

    10.1.1.   Human health

      10.1.1.1.   Workers

      10.1.1.2.   Consumers

      10.1.1.3.   Indirect exposure to humans via the environment

    10.1.2.   Environment

      10.1.2.1.   Aquatic compartment (including sediment)

      10.1.2.2.   Terrestrial compartment

      10.1.2.3.   Atmospheric compartment

      10.1.2.4.   Microbiological activity in sewage treatment systems

  10.2.   (Title of exposure scenario 2)

    10.2.1.   Human health

      10.2.1.1.   Workers

      10.2.1.2.   Consumers

      10.2.1.3.   Indirect exposure to humans via the environment

    10.2.2.   Environment

      10.2.2.1.   Aquatic compartment (including sediment)

      10.2.2.2.   Terrestrial compartment

      10.2.2.3.   Atmospheric compartment

      10.2.2.4.   Microbiological activity in sewage treatment systems

    (etc.)

  10.x.   Overall exposure (combined for all relevant emission/release sources)

    10.x.1.   Human health (combined for all exposure routes)

      10.x.1.1.

    10.x.2.   Environment (combined for all emission sources)

      10.x.2.1.

▼__M7__

ANNEX II

REQUIREMENTS FOR THE COMPILATION OF SAFETY DATA
SHEETS

PART A

0.1.   **Introduction**

0.1.1.   This Annex sets out the requirements that the supplier shall fulfil for
the compilation of a safety data sheet that is provided for a substance
or a mixture in accordance with Article 31.

0.1.2.   The information provided in the safety data sheet shall be consistent
with the information in the chemical safety report, where one is
required. Where a chemical safety report has been completed, the
relevant exposure scenario(s) shall be placed in an annex to the
safety data sheet.

0.2.   **General requirements for compiling a safety data sheet**

0.2.1.   The safety data sheet shall enable users to take the necessary
measures relating to protection of human health and safety at the
workplace, and protection of the environment. The writer of the
safety data sheet shall take into account that a safety data sheet
must inform its audience of the hazards of a substance or a
mixture and provide information on the safe storage, handling and
disposal of the substance or the mixture.

0.2.2.   The information provided by safety data sheets shall also meet the
requirements set out in Council Directive 98/24/EC. In particular, the
safety data sheet shall enable employers to determine whether any
hazardous chemical agents are present in the workplace, and to assess
any risk to the health and safety of workers arising from their use.

0.2.3.   The information in the safety data sheet shall be written in a clear and
concise manner. The safety data sheet shall be prepared by a
competent person who shall take into account the specific needs
and knowledge of the user audience, as far as they are known.
Suppliers of substances and mixtures shall ensure that such
competent persons have received appropriate training, including
refresher training.

0.2.4.   The language used in the safety data sheet shall be simple, clear and
precise, avoiding jargon, acronyms and abbreviations. Statements
such as 'may be dangerous', 'no health effects', 'safe under most
conditions of use' or 'harmless' or any other statements indicating
that the substance or mixture is not hazardous or any other statements
that are inconsistent with the classification of that substance or
mixture shall not be used.

0.2.5.   The date of compilation of the safety data sheet shall be given on the
first page. When a safety data sheet has been revised and the new,
revised version is provided to recipients, the changes shall be brought
to the attention of the recipient in Section 16 of the safety data sheet,
unless they have been indicated elsewhere. In that case, the date of
compilation identified as 'Revision: (date)' as well as a version
number, revision number, supersedes date or other indication of
what version is replaced shall appear on the first page.

0.3.   **Safety data sheet format**

0.3.1.   A safety data sheet is not a fixed length document. The length of the
safety data sheet shall be commensurate with the hazard of the
substance or mixture and the information available.

▼__M7__

0.3.2.   All pages of a safety data sheet, including any annexes, shall be numbered and shall bear either an indication of the length of the safety data sheet (such as 'page 1 of 3') or an indication whether there is a page following (such as 'Continued on next page' or 'End of safety data sheet').

0.4.   **Safety data sheet content**

The information required by this Annex shall be included in the safety data sheet, where applicable and available, in the relevant subsections set out in Part B. The safety data sheet shall not contain blank subsections.

0.5.   **Other information requirements**

The inclusion of additional relevant and available information in the relevant subsections may be necessary in some cases in view of the wide range of properties of substances and mixtures.

0.6.   **Units**

The units of measurement as set out in Council Directive 80/181/EEC (^{1}) shall be used.

0.7.   **Special cases**

Safety data sheets shall also be required for the special cases listed in paragraph 1.3 of Annex I to Regulation (EC) No 1272/2008 for which there are labelling derogations.

1.   ***SECTION 1: Identification of the substance/mixture and of the company/undertaking***

This section prescribes how the substance or mixture shall be identified and how the identified relevant uses, the name of the supplier of the substance or mixture and the contact detail information of the supplier of the substance or mixture including an emergency contact shall be provided in the safety data sheet.

1.1.   **Product identifier**

In the case of a substance, the product identifier shall be provided in accordance with Article 18(2) of Regulation (EC) No 1272/2008 and as provided on the label in the official language(s) of the Member State(s) where the substance is placed on the market, unless the Member State(s) concerned provide(s) otherwise.

For substances subject to registration, the product identifier shall be consistent with that provided in the registration and the registration number assigned under Article 20(3) of this Regulation shall also be indicated.

Without affecting the obligations of downstream users laid down in Article 39 of this Regulation, the part of the registration number referring to the individual registrant of a joint submission may be omitted by a supplier who is a distributor or a downstream user provided that:

(a)   this supplier assumes the responsibility to provide the full registration number upon request for enforcement purposes or, if the full registration number is not available to him, to forward the request to his supplier, in line with point (b); and

_____

(^{1}) OJ L 39, 15.2.1980, p. 40.

▼M7

(b) this supplier provides the full registration number to the Member State authority responsible for enforcement (hereinafter referred to as the enforcement authority) within 7 days upon request, received either directly from the enforcement authority or forwarded by his recipient, or, if the full registration number is not available to him, this supplier shall forward the request to his supplier within 7 days upon request and at the same time inform the enforcement authority thereof.

In the case of a mixture, the trade name or designation shall be provided in accordance with Article 10(2.1) of Directive 1999/45/EC.

A single safety data sheet may be provided to cover more than one substance or mixture where the information in that safety data sheet fulfils the requirements of this Annex for each of those substances or mixtures.

Other means of identification

Other names or synonyms by which the substance or mixture is labelled or commonly known, such as alternative names, numbers, company product codes, or other unique identifiers may be provided.

1.2. **Relevant identified uses of the substance or mixture and uses advised against**

At least the identified uses relevant for the recipient(s) of the substance or mixture shall be indicated. This shall be a brief description of what the substance or mixture is intended to do, such as 'flame retardant', 'antioxidant'.

The uses which the supplier advises against and why shall, where applicable, be stated. This need not be an exhaustive list.

Where a chemical safety report is required, the information in this subsection of the safety data sheet shall be consistent with the identified uses in the chemical safety report and the exposure scenarios from the chemical safety report set out in the annex to the safety data sheet.

1.3. **Details of the supplier of the safety data sheet**

The supplier, whether it is the manufacturer, importer, only representative, downstream user or distributor, shall be identified. The full address and telephone number of the supplier shall be given as well as an e-mail address for a competent person responsible for the safety data sheet.

In addition, if the supplier is not located in the Member State where the substance or mixture is placed on the market and he has nominated a responsible person for that Member State, a full address and telephone number for that responsible person shall be given.

For registrants, the information shall be consistent with the information on the identity of the manufacturer or importer provided in the registration.

Where an only representative has been appointed, details of the non-Community manufacturer or formulator may also be provided.

▼M7

1.4.   **Emergency telephone number**

References to emergency information services shall be provided. If an official advisory body exists in the Member State where the substance or mixture is placed on the market (this may be the body responsible for receiving information relating to health referred to in Article 45 of Regulation (EC) No 1272/2008 and Article 17 of Directive 1999/45/EC), its telephone number shall be given and can suffice. If availability of such services is limited for any reasons, such as hours of operation, or if there are limits on specific types of information provided, this shall be clearly stated.

2.   *SECTION 2: Hazards identification*

This section of the safety data sheet shall describe the hazards of the substance or mixture and the appropriate warning information associated with those hazards.

2.1.   **Classification of the substance or mixture**

In the case of a substance, the classification which arises from the application of the classification rules in Regulation (EC) No 1272/2008 shall be given. Where the supplier has notified information regarding the substance to the classification and labelling inventory in accordance with Article 40 of Regulation (EC) No 1272/2008, the classification given in the safety data sheet shall be the same as the classification provided in that notification.

The classification of the substance according to Directive 67/548/EEC shall also be given.

In the case of a mixture, the classification which arises from the application of the classification rules in Directive 1999/45/EC shall be given. If the mixture does not meet the criteria for classification in accordance with Directive 1999/45/EC, this shall be clearly stated. Information on the substances in the mixture is provided under subsection 3.2.

If the classification, including the hazard statements and R phrases, is not written out in full, reference shall be made to Section 16 where the full text of each classification, including each hazard statement and R phrase, shall be given.

The most important adverse physicochemical, human health and environmental effects shall be listed consistent with Sections 9 to 12 of the safety data sheet, in a way as to allow non-experts to identify the hazards of the substance or mixture.

2.2.   **Label elements**

In the case of a substance, based on the classification, at least the following elements appearing on the label in accordance with Regulation (EC) No 1272/2008 shall be provided: hazard pictogram(s), signal word(s), hazard statement(s) and precautionary statement(s). A graphical reproduction of the full hazard pictogram in black and white or a graphical reproduction of the symbol only may be substituted for the colour pictogram provided in Regulation (EC) No 1272/2008.

In the case of a mixture, based on the classification, at least the appropriate symbol(s), indication(s) of danger, risk phrase(s) and safety advice appearing on the label in accordance with Directive 1999/45/EC shall be provided. The symbol may be provided as a graphical reproduction of the symbol in black and white.

▼__M7__

The applicable label elements in accordance with Article 25 and Article 32(6) of Regulation (EC) No 1272/2008, in the case of a substance, or Sections A and B of Annex V to Directive 1999/45/EC, in the case of a mixture, shall be provided.

2.3.   **Other hazards**

Information on whether the substance or mixture meets the criteria for PBT or vPvB in accordance with Annex XIII shall be provided.

Information shall be provided on other hazards which do not result in classification but which may contribute to the overall hazards of the substance or mixture, such as formation of air contaminants during hardening or processing, dustiness, dust explosion hazards, cross-sensitisation, suffocation, freezing, high potency for odour or taste, or environmental effects like hazards to soil-dwelling organisms, or photochemical ozone creation potential.

3.   *SECTION 3: Composition/information on ingredients*

This section of the safety data sheet shall describe the chemical identity of the ingredient(s) of the substance or mixture, including impurities and stabilising additives as set out below. Appropriate and available safety information on surface chemistry shall be indicated.

3.1.   **Substances**

The chemical identity of the main constituent of the substance shall be provided by providing at least the product identifier or one of the other means of identification given in subsection 1.1.

The chemical identity of any impurity, stabilising additive, or individual constituent other than the main constituent, which is itself classified and which contributes to the classification of the substance shall be provided as follows:

(a) the product identifier in accordance with Article 18(2) of Regulation (EC) No 1272/2008;

(b) if the product identifier is not available, one of the other names (usual name, trade name, abbreviation) or identification numbers.

Suppliers of substances may choose to list in addition all constituents including non-classified ones.

This subsection may also be used to provide information on multi-constituent substances.

3.2.   **Mixtures**

The product identifier when available, concentration or concentration ranges and classifications shall be provided for at least all substances referred to in points 3.2.1 or 3.2.2. Suppliers of mixtures may choose to list in addition all substances in the mixture, including substances not meeting the criteria for classification. This information shall enable the recipient to identify readily the hazards of the substances in the mixture. The hazards of the mixture itself shall be given in Section 2.

The concentrations of the substances in a mixture shall be described as either of the following:

(a) exact percentages in descending order by mass or volume, if technically possible;

(b) ranges of percentages in descending order by mass or volume, if technically possible.

▼M7

When using a range of percentages, the health and environmental hazards shall describe the effects of the highest concentration of each ingredient.

If the effects of the mixture as a whole are available, this information shall be included under Section 2.

Where the use of an alternative chemical name has been allowed under Article 15 of Directive 1999/45/EC or under Article 24 of Regulation (EC) No 1272/2008, that name can be used.

3.2.1. For a mixture meeting the criteria for classification in accordance with Directive 1999/45/EC, the following substances shall be indicated, together with their concentration or concentration range in the mixture:

(a) substances presenting a health or environmental hazard within the meaning of Directive 67/548/EEC and substances presenting a health or environmental hazard within the meaning of Regulation (EC) No 1272/2008, provided that information complying with the classification criteria of that Regulation has been made available to the supplier of the mixture, if those substances are present in concentrations equal to or greater than the lowest of any of the following:

(i) the applicable concentrations defined in the table of Article 3(3) of Directive 1999/45/EC;

(ii) the specific concentration limits given in Part 3 of Annex VI to Regulation (EC) No 1272/2008;

(iii) if an M-factor has been given in Part 3 of Annex VI to Regulation (EC) No 1272/2008, the generic cut-off value in Table 1.1 of Annex I to that Regulation, adjusted using the calculation set out in Section 4.1 of Annex I to that Regulation;

(iv) the concentration limits given in Part B of Annex II to Directive 1999/45/EC;

(v) the concentration limits given in Part B of Annex III to Directive 1999/45/EC;

(vi) the concentration limits given in Annex V to Directive 1999/45/EC;

(vii) the specific concentration limits provided to the classification and labelling inventory established under Regulation (EC) No 1272/2008;

(viii) if an M-factor has been provided to the classification and labelling inventory established under Regulation (EC) No 1272/2008, the generic cut-off value in Table 1.1 of Annex I to that Regulation, adjusted using the calculation set out in Section 4.1 of Annex I to that Regulation.

(b) substances for which there are Community workplace exposure limits, which are not already included under point (a);

▼__M7__

(c) substances that are persistent, bioaccumulative and toxic or very persistent and very bioaccumulative in accordance with the criteria set out in Annex XIII, or substances included in the list established in accordance with Article 59(1) for reasons other than the hazards referred to in point (a), if the concentration of an individual substance is equal to or greater than 0,1 %.

3.2.2. For a mixture not meeting the criteria for classification in accordance with Directive 1999/45/EC, substances present in an individual concentration equal to or greater than the following concentrations shall be indicated, together with their concentration or concentration range:

(a) 1 % by weight in non-gaseous mixtures and 0,2 % by volume in gaseous mixtures for

(i) substances which present a health or environmental hazard within the meaning of Directive 67/548/EEC and substances which present a health or environmental hazard within the meaning of Regulation (EC) No 1272/2008, provided that information complying with the classification criteria of that Regulation has been made available to the supplier of the mixture; or

(ii) substances which are assigned Community workplace exposure limits;

(b) 0,1 % by weight for substances which are persistent, bioaccumulative and toxic in accordance with the criteria set out in Annex XIII, very persistent and very bioaccumulative in accordance with the criteria set out in Annex XIII, or included in the list established in accordance with Article 59(1) for reasons other than the hazards referred to in point (a).

3.2.3. For the substances indicated in subsection 3.2, the classification of the substance according to Directive 67/548/EEC, including indication of danger, symbol letter(s) and R phrases, shall be provided. The classification of the substance according to Regulation (EC) No 1272/2008, including the hazard class(es) and category code(s) as provided in Table 1.1 of Annex VI to that Regulation as well as the hazard statements which are assigned in accordance with their physical, human health and environmental hazards, shall also be provided, provided that information complying with the classification criteria of that Regulation has been made available to the supplier of the mixture. The hazard statements and R phrases do not need to be written out in full in this section; their codes shall be sufficient. In cases where they are not written out in full, reference shall be made to Section 16, where the full text of each relevant hazard statement and R phrase shall be listed. If the substance does not meet the classification criteria, the reason for indicating the substance in subsection 3.2 shall be described, such as 'non-classified vPvB substance' or 'substance with a Community workplace exposure limit'.

3.2.4. For the substances indicated in subsection 3.2 the name and, if available, the registration number, as assigned under Article 20(3) of this Regulation shall be given.

▼M7

Without affecting the obligations of downstream users laid down in Article 39 of this Regulation, the part of the registration number referring to the individual registrant of a joint submission may be omitted by the supplier of the mixture provided that:

(a) this supplier assumes the responsibility to provide the full registration number upon request for enforcement purposes, or, if the full registration number is not available to him, to forward the request to his supplier, in line with point (b); and

(b) this supplier provides the full registration number to the Member State authority responsible for enforcement (hereinafter referred to as the enforcement authority) within 7 days upon request, received either directly from the enforcement authority or forwarded by his recipient, or, if the full registration number is not available to him, this supplier shall forward the request to his supplier within 7 days upon request and at the same time inform the enforcement authority thereof.

The EC number, if available, shall be given in accordance with Regulation (EC) No 1272/2008. The CAS number, if available, and IUPAC name, if available, may also be given.

For substances indicated in this subsection by means of an alternative chemical name in accordance with Article 15 of Directive 1999/45/EC or Article 24 of Regulation (EC) No 1272/2008, the registration number, EC number and other precise chemical identifiers are not necessary.

4.   **SECTION 4: First aid measures**

This section of the safety data sheet shall describe the initial care in such a way that it can be understood and given by an untrained responder without the use of sophisticated equipment and without the availability of a wide selection of medications. If medical attention is required, the instructions shall state this, including its urgency.

4.1.   **Description of first aid measures**

4.1.1.   First aid instructions shall be provided by relevant routes of exposure. Subdivisions shall be used to indicate the procedure for each route, such as inhalation, skin, eye and ingestion.

4.1.2.   Advice shall be provided as to whether:

(a) immediate medical attention is required and if delayed effects can be expected after exposure;

(b) movement of the exposed individual from the area to fresh air is recommended;

(c) removal and handling of clothing and shoes from the individual is recommended; and

(d) personal protective equipment for first aid responders is recommended.

4.2.   **Most important symptoms and effects, both acute and delayed**

Briefly summarised information shall be provided on the most important symptoms and effects, both acute and delayed, from exposure.

▼M7

4.3.   **Indication of any immediate medical attention and special treatment needed**

Where appropriate, information shall be provided on clinical testing and medical monitoring for delayed effects, specific details on antidotes (where they are known) and contraindications.

For some substances or mixtures, it may be important to emphasise that special means to provide specific and immediate treatment shall be available at the workplace.

5.   *SECTION 5: Firefighting measures*

This section of the safety data sheet shall describe the requirements for fighting a fire caused by the substance or mixture, or arising in its vicinity.

5.1.   **Extinguishing media**

Suitable extinguishing media:

Information shall be provided on the appropriate extinguishing media.

Unsuitable extinguishing media:

Indications shall be given whether any extinguishing media are inappropriate for a particular situation involving the substance or mixture.

5.2.   **Special hazards arising from the substance or mixture**

Information shall be provided on hazards that may arise from the substance or mixture, like hazardous combustion products that form when the substance or mixture burns, such as 'may produce toxic fumes of carbon monoxide if burning' or 'produces oxides of sulphur and nitrogen on combustion'.

5.3.   **Advice for firefighters**

Advice shall be provided on any protective actions to be taken during firefighting, such as 'keep containers cool with water spray', and on special protective equipment for firefighters, such as boots, overalls, gloves, eye and face protection and breathing apparatus.

6.   *SECTION 6: Accidental release measures*

This section of the safety data sheet shall recommend the appropriate response to spills, leaks, or releases, to prevent or minimise the adverse effects on persons, property and the environment. It shall distinguish between responses to large and small spills, in cases where the spill volume has a significant impact on the hazard. If the procedures for containment and recovery indicate that different practices are required, these shall be indicated in the safety data sheet.

6.1.   **Personal precautions, protective equipment and emergency procedures**

6.1.1. *For non-emergency personnel*

Advice shall be provided related to accidental spills and release of the substance or mixture such as:

(a) the wearing of suitable protective equipment (including personal protective equipment referred to under Section 8 of the safety data sheet) to prevent any contamination of skin, eyes and personal clothing;

▼__M7__

(b) removal of ignition sources, provision of sufficient ventilation, control of dust; and

(c) emergency procedures such as the need to evacuate the danger area or to consult an expert.

6.1.2. *For emergency responders*

Advice shall be provided related to suitable fabric for personal protective clothing (such as 'appropriate: Butylene'; 'not appropriate: PVC').

6.2. **Environmental precautions**

Advice shall be provided on any environmental precautions to be taken related to accidental spills and release of the substance or mixture, such as keeping away from drains, surface and ground water.

6.3. **Methods and material for containment and cleaning up**

6.3.1. Appropriate advice shall be provided on how to contain a spill. Appropriate containment techniques may include any of the following:

(a) bunding, covering of drains;

(b) capping procedures.

6.3.2. Appropriate advice shall be provided on how to clean-up a spill. Appropriate clean-up procedures may include any of the following:

(a) neutralisation techniques;

(b) decontamination techniques;

(c) adsorbent materials;

(d) cleaning techniques;

(e) vacuuming techniques;

(f) equipment required for containment/clean-up (include the use of non-sparking tools and equipment where applicable).

6.3.3. Any other information shall be provided relating to spills and releases, including advice on inappropriate containment or clean-up techniques, such as by indications like 'never use ...'.

6.4. **Reference to other sections**

If appropriate Sections 8 and 13 shall be referred to.

7. *SECTION 7: Handling and storage*

This section of the safety data sheet shall provide advice on safe handling practices. It shall emphasise precautions that are appropriate to the identified uses referred to under subsection 1.2 and to the unique properties of the substance or mixture.

Information in this section of the safety data sheet shall relate to the protection of human health, safety and the environment. It shall assist the employer in devising suitable working procedures and organisational measures according to Article 5 of Directive 98/24/EC and Article 5 of Directive 2004/37/EC of the European Parliament and of the Council.

▼M7

Where a chemical safety report is required, the information in this section of the safety data sheet shall be consistent with the information given for the identified uses in the chemical safety report and the exposure scenarios showing control of risk from the chemical safety report set out in the annex to the safety data sheet.

In addition to information given in this section, relevant information may also be found in Section 8.

7.1.   **Precautions for safe handling**

7.1.1.   Recommendations shall be specified to:

(a) allow safe handling of the substance or mixture, such as containment and measures to prevent fire as well as aerosol and dust generation;

(b) prevent handling of incompatible substances or mixtures; and

(c) reduce the release of the substance or mixture to the environment, such as avoiding spills or keeping away from drains.

7.1.2.   Advice on general occupational hygiene shall be provided, such as:

(a) not to eat, drink and smoke in work areas;

(b) to wash hands after use; and

(c) to remove contaminated clothing and protective equipment before entering eating areas.

7.2.   **Conditions for safe storage, including any incompatibilities**

The advice provided shall be consistent with the physical and chemical properties described in Section 9 of the safety data sheet. If relevant, advice shall be provided on specific storage requirements including:

(a) how to manage risks associated with:

(i) explosive atmospheres;

(ii) corrosive conditions;

(iii) flammability hazards;

(iv) incompatible substances or mixtures;

(v) evaporative conditions; and

(vi) potential ignition sources (including electrical equipment);

(b) how to control the effects of:

(i) weather conditions;

(ii) ambient pressure;

(iii) temperature;

(iv) sunlight;

(v) humidity; and

(vi) vibration;

(c) how to maintain the integrity of the substance or mixture by the use of:

(i) stabilisers; and

(ii) antioxidants;

2006R1907 — EN — 01.06.2012 — 012.001 — 149

▼__M7__

(d) other advice including:

(i) ventilation requirements;

(ii) specific designs for storage rooms or vessels (including retention walls and ventilation);

(iii) quantity limits under storage conditions (if relevant); and

(iv) packaging compatibilities.

7.3.   **Specific end use(s)**

For substances and mixtures designed for specific end use(s), recommendations shall relate to the identified use(s) referred to in subsection 1.2 and be detailed and operational. If an exposure scenario is attached, reference to it may be made or the information as required in subsections 7.1 and 7.2 shall be provided. If an actor in the supply chain has carried out a chemical safety assessment for the mixture, it is sufficient that the safety data sheet and the exposure scenarios are consistent with the chemical safety report for the mixture instead of with the chemical safety reports for each substance in the mixture. If industry or sector specific guidance is available, detailed reference to it (including source and issuing date) may be made.

8.   *SECTION 8: Exposure controls/personal protection*

This section of the safety data sheet shall describe the applicable occupational exposure limits and necessary risk management measures.

Where a chemical safety report is required, the information in this section of the safety data sheet shall be consistent with the information given for the identified uses in the chemical safety report and the exposure scenarios showing control of risk from the chemical safety report set out in the annex to the safety data sheet.

8.1.   **Control parameters**

8.1.1.   Where available, the following national limit values, including the legal basis of each of them, which are currently applicable in the Member State in which the safety data sheet is being provided shall be listed for the substance or for each of the substances in the mixture. When listing occupational exposure limit values, the chemical identity as specified in Section 3 shall be used.

8.1.1.1.   the national occupational exposure limit values that correspond to Community occupational exposure limit values in accordance with Directive 98/24/EC, including any notations as referred to in Article 2(1) of Commission Decision 95/320/EC ([1]);

8.1.1.2.   the national occupational exposure limit values that correspond to Community limit values in accordance with Directive 2004/37/EC, including any notations as referred to in Article 2(1) of Decision 95/320/EC;

8.1.1.3.   any other national occupational exposure limit values;

8.1.1.4.   the national biological limit values that correspond to Community biological limit values in accordance with Directive 98/24/EC, including any notations as referred to in Article 2(1) of Decision 95/320/EC;

([1]) OJ L 188, 9.8.1995, p. 14.

▼__M7__

8.1.1.5. any other national biological limit values.

8.1.2. Information on currently recommended monitoring procedures shall be provided at least for the most relevant substances.

8.1.3. If air contaminants are formed when using the substance or mixture as intended, applicable occupational exposure limit values and/or biological limit values for these shall also be listed.

8.1.4. Where a chemical safety report is required or a DNEL as referred to in Section 1.4 of Annex I or a PNEC as referred to in Section 3.3 of Annex I is available, the relevant DNELs and PNECs for the substance shall be given for the exposure scenarios from the chemical safety report set out in the annex to the safety data sheet.

8.1.5. Where a control banding approach is used to decide on risk management measures in relation to specific uses, sufficient detail shall be given to enable effective management of the risk. The context and limitations of the specific control banding recommendation shall be made clear.

8.2. **Exposure controls**

The information required in the present subsection shall be provided, unless an exposure scenario containing that information is attached to the safety data sheet.

Where the supplier has waived a test under Section 3 of Annex XI, he shall indicate the specific conditions of use relied on to justify the waiving.

Where a substance has been registered as an isolated intermediate (on-site or transported), the supplier shall indicate that this safety data sheet is consistent with the specific conditions relied on to justify the registration in accordance with Article 17 or 18.

8.2.1. *Appropriate engineering controls*

The description of appropriate exposure control measures shall relate to the identified use(s) of the substance or mixture as referred to in subsection 1.2. This information shall be sufficient to enable the employer to carry out an assessment of risk to the safety and health of workers arising from the presence of the substance or mixture in accordance with Articles 4 to 6 of Directive 98/24/EC as well as in accordance with Articles 3 to 5 of Directive 2004/37/EC, where appropriate.

This information shall complement that already given under Section 7.

8.2.2. *Individual protection measures, such as personal protective equipment*

8.2.2.1. The information on use of personal protective equipment shall be consistent with good occupational hygiene practices and in conjunction with other control measures, including engineering controls, ventilation and isolation. Where appropriate, Section 5 shall be referred to for specific fire/chemical personal protective equipment advice.

▼__M7__

8.2.2.2. Taking into account Council Directive 89/686/EEC (¹) and referring to the appropriate CEN standards, detailed specifications shall be given on which equipment will provide adequate and suitable protection, including:

(a) Eye/face protection

The type of eye/face protection equipment required shall be specified based on the hazard of the substance or mixture and potential for contact, such as safety glasses, safety goggles, face-shield.

(b) Skin protection

(i) *Hand protection*

The type of gloves to be worn when handling the substance or mixture shall be clearly specified based on the hazard of the substance or mixture and potential for contact and with regard to the amount and duration of dermal exposure, including:

— the type of material and its thickness,

— the typical or minimum breakthrough times of the glove material.

If necessary any additional hand protection measures shall be indicated.

(ii) *Other*

If it is necessary to protect a part of the body other than the hands, the type and quality of protection equipment required shall be specified, such as gauntlets, boots, bodysuit based on the hazards associated with the substance or mixture and the potential for contact.

If necessary, any additional skin protection measures and specific hygiene measures shall be indicated.

(c) Respiratory protection

For gases, vapours, mist or dust, the type of protective equipment to be used shall be specified based on the hazard and potential for exposure, including air-purifying respirators, specifying the proper purifying element (cartridge or canister), the adequate particulate filters and the adequate masks, or self-contained breathing apparatus.

(d) Thermal hazards

When specifying protective equipment to be worn for materials that represent a thermal hazard, special consideration shall be given to the construction of the personal protective equipment.

8.2.3. *Environmental exposure controls*

The information required by the employer to fulfil his commitments under Community environmental protection legislation shall be specified.

Where a chemical safety report is required, a summary of the risk management measures that adequately control exposure of the environment to the substance shall be given for the exposure scenarios set out in the annex to the safety data sheet.

(¹) OJ L 399, 30.12.1989, p. 18.

▼__M7__

9. **SECTION 9: Physical and chemical properties**

This section of the safety data sheet shall describe the empirical data relating to the substance or mixture, if relevant. The information in this section shall be consistent with the information provided in the registration and/or in the chemical safety report where required, and with the classification of the substance or mixture.

9.1. **Information on basic physical and chemical properties**

The following properties shall be clearly identified including, where appropriate, a reference to the test methods used and specification of appropriate units of measurement and/or reference conditions. If relevant for the interpretation of the numerical value, the method of determination shall also be provided (for example, the method for flash point, the open-cup/closed-cup method):

(a) Appearance:

The physical state (solid (including appropriate and available safety information on granulometry and specific surface area if not already specified elsewhere in this safety data sheet), liquid, gas) and the colour of the substance or mixture as supplied shall be indicated;

(b) Odour:

If odour is perceptible, a brief description of it shall be given;

(c) Odour threshold;

(d) pH:

The pH shall be indicated of the substance or mixture as supplied or of an aqueous solution; in the latter case, the concentration shall be indicated;

(e) Melting point/freezing point;

(f) Initial boiling point and boiling range;

(g) Flash point;

(h) Evaporation rate;

(i) Flammability (solid, gas);

(j) Upper/lower flammability or explosive limits;

(k) Vapour pressure;

(l) Vapour density;

(m) Relative density;

(n) Solubility(ies);

(o) Partition coefficient: n-octanol/water;

(p) Auto-ignition temperature;

(q) Decomposition temperature;

(r) Viscosity;

(s) Explosive properties;

(t) Oxidising properties.

If it is stated that a particular property does not apply or if information on a particular property is not available, the reasons shall be given.

▼__M7__

To enable proper control measures to be taken, all relevant information on the substance or mixture shall be provided. The information in this section shall be consistent with the information provided in a registration where one is required.

In the case of a mixture, the entries shall clearly indicate to which substance in the mixture the data apply, unless it is valid for the whole mixture.

9.2.   **Other information**

Other physical and chemical parameters shall be indicated as necessary, such as miscibility, fat solubility (solvent — oil to be specified), conductivity, or gas group. Appropriate and available safety information on redox potential, radical formation potential and photocatalytic properties shall be indicated.

10.   *SECTION 10: Stability and reactivity*

This section of the safety data sheet shall describe the stability of the substance or mixture and the possibility of hazardous reactions occurring under certain conditions of use and also if released into the environment, including, where appropriate, a reference to the test methods used. If it is stated that a particular property does not apply or if information on a particular property is not available, the reasons shall be given.

10.1.   **Reactivity**

10.1.1.   The reactivity hazards of the substance or mixture shall be described. Specific test data shall be provided for the substance or mixture as a whole, where available. However, the information may also be based on general data for the class or family of substance or mixture if such data adequately represent the anticipated hazard of the substance or mixture.

10.1.2.   If data for mixtures are not available, data on substances in the mixture shall be provided. In determining incompatibility, the substances, containers and contaminants that the substance or mixture might be exposed to during transportation, storage and use shall be considered.

10.2.   **Chemical stability**

It shall be indicated if the substance or mixture is stable or unstable under normal ambient and anticipated storage and handling conditions of temperature and pressure. Any stabilisers which are, or may need to be, used to maintain the chemical stability of the substance or mixture shall be described. The safety significance of any change in the physical appearance of the substance or mixture shall be indicated.

10.3.   **Possibility of hazardous reactions**

If relevant, it shall be stated if the substance or mixture will react or polymerise, releasing excess pressure or heat, or creating other hazardous conditions. The conditions under which the hazardous reactions may occur shall be described.

10.4.   **Conditions to avoid**

Conditions such as temperature, pressure, light, shock, static discharge, vibrations or other physical stresses that might result in a hazardous situation shall be listed and if appropriate a brief description of measures to be taken to manage risks associated with such hazards shall be given.

▼M7

10.5.   **Incompatible materials**

Families of substances or mixtures or specific substances, such as water, air, acids, bases, oxidising agents, with which the substance or mixture could react to produce a hazardous situation (like an explosion, a release of toxic or flammable materials, or a liberation of excessive heat) shall be listed and if appropriate a brief description of measures to be taken to manage risks associated with such hazards shall be given.

10.6.   **Hazardous decomposition products**

Known and reasonably anticipated hazardous decomposition products produced as a result of use, storage, spill and heating shall be listed. Hazardous combustion products shall be included in Section 5 of the safety data sheet.

11.   *SECTION 11: Toxicological information*

This section of the safety data sheet is meant for use primarily by medical professionals, occupational health and safety professionals and toxicologists. A concise but complete and comprehensible description of the various toxicological (health) effects and the available data used to identify those effects shall be provided, including where appropriate information on toxicokinetics, metabolism and distribution. The information in this section shall be consistent with the information provided in the registration and/or in the chemical safety report where required, and with the classification of the substance or mixture.

11.1.   **Information on toxicological effects**

11.1.1.   *Substances*

11.1.1.1.   The relevant hazard classes for which information shall be provided, are:

(a) acute toxicity;

(b) skin corrosion/irritation;

(c) serious eye damage/irritation;

(d) respiratory or skin sensitisation;

(e) germ cell mutagenicity;

(f) carcinogenicity;

(g) reproductive toxicity;

(h) STOT-single exposure;

(i) STOT-repeated exposure;

(j) aspiration hazard.

11.1.1.2.   For substances subject to registration, brief summaries of the information derived from the application of Annexes VII to XI shall be given, including, where appropriate, a reference to the test methods used. For substances subject to registration, the information shall also include the result of the comparison of the available data with the criteria given in Regulation (EC) No 1272/2008 for CMR, categories 1A and 1B, following point 1.3.1 of Annex I to this Regulation.

11.1.2.   *Mixtures*

11.1.2.1.   The relevant effects, for which information shall be provided, are:

(a) acute toxicity;

(b) irritation;

▼M7

(c) corrosivity;

(d) sensitisation;

(e) repeated dose toxicity;

(f) carcinogenicity;

(g) mutagenicity;

(h) toxicity for reproduction.

11.1.2.2. For the health effects of carcinogenicity, mutagenicity and toxicity for reproduction, classification for a given health effect based on the conventional method outlined in Article 6(1)(a) of Directive 1999/45/EC, and relevant information for the substances listed under Section 3 shall be provided.

11.1.2.3. For other health effects, if a mixture has not been tested as a whole for a given health effect, information relevant to that health effect relating to substances listed under Section 3 shall be provided, if relevant.

11.1.3. Information shall be provided for each hazard class, differentiation or effect. If it is stated that the substance or mixture is not classified for a particular hazard class, differentiation or effect, the safety data sheet shall clearly state whether this is due to lack of data, technical impossibility to obtain the data, inconclusive data or data which are conclusive although insufficient for classification; in the latter case the safety data sheet shall specify 'based on available data, the classification criteria are not met'.

11.1.4. The data included in this subsection shall apply to the substance or mixture as placed on the market. If available, the relevant toxicological properties of the hazardous substances in a mixture shall also be provided, such as the LD50, acute toxicity estimates or LC50.

11.1.5. Where there is a substantial amount of test data on the substance or mixture, it may be necessary to summarise results of the critical studies used, for example, by route of exposure.

11.1.6. Where the classification criteria for a particular hazard class are not met, information supporting this conclusion shall be provided.

11.1.7. *Information on likely routes of exposure*

Information shall be provided on likely routes of exposure and the effects of the substance or mixture via each possible route of exposure, that is, through ingestion (swallowing), inhalation or skin/eye exposure. If health effects are not known, this shall be stated.

11.1.8. *Symptoms related to the physical, chemical and toxicological characteristics*

Potential adverse health effects and symptoms associated with exposure to the substance or mixture and its ingredients or known by-products shall be described. Available information shall be provided on the symptoms related to the physical, chemical, and toxicological characteristics of the substance or mixture following exposure. The first symptoms at low exposures through to the consequences of severe exposure shall be described, such as 'headaches and dizziness may occur, proceeding to fainting or unconsciousness; large doses may result in coma and death'.

▼__M7__

11.1.9. *Delayed and immediate effects as well as chronic effects from short and long-term exposure*

Information shall be provided on whether delayed or immediate effects can be expected after short or long-term exposure. Information on acute and chronic health effects relating to human exposure to the substance or mixture shall also be provided. Where human data are not available, animal data shall be summarised and the species clearly identified. It shall be indicated whether toxicological data is based on human or animal data.

11.1.10. *Interactive effects*

Information on interactions shall be included if relevant and available.

11.1.11. *Absence of specific data*

It may not always be possible to obtain information on the hazards of a substance or mixture. In cases where data on the specific substance or mixture are not available, data on similar substances or mixtures, if appropriate, may be used, provided the relevant similar substance or mixture is identified. Where specific data are not used, or where data are not available, this shall be clearly stated.

11.1.12. *Mixture versus substance information*

11.1.12.1. The substances in a mixture may interact with each other in the body resulting in different rates of absorption, metabolism and excretion. As a result, the toxic actions may be altered and the overall toxicity of the mixture may be different from that of the substances in it. This shall be taken into account when providing toxicological information in this section of the safety data sheet.

11.1.12.2. Classification of mixtures as having effects of carcinogenicity, mutagenicity or toxicity for reproduction must be calculated from available information regarding substances in the mixture. For other health effects, it is necessary to consider whether the concentration of each substance is sufficient to contribute to the overall health effects of the mixture. The information on toxic effects shall be presented for each substance, except for the following cases:

(a) if the information is duplicated, it shall be listed only once for the mixture overall, such as when two substances both cause vomiting and diarrhoea;

(b) if it is unlikely that these effects will occur at the concentrations present, such as when a mild irritant is diluted to below a certain concentration in a non-irritant solution;

(c) where information on interactions between substances in a mixture is not available, assumptions shall not be made and instead the health effects of each substance shall be listed separately.

11.1.13. *Other information*

Other relevant information on adverse health effects shall be included even when not required by the classification criteria.

▼__M7__

12.   SECTION 12: Ecological information

This section of the safety data sheet shall describe the information
provided to evaluate the environmental impact of the substance or
mixture where it is released to the environment. Under subsections
12.1 to 12.6 of the safety data sheet a short summary of the data shall
be provided including, where available, relevant test data and clearly
indicating species, media, units, test duration and test conditions. This
information may assist in handling spills, and evaluating waste
treatment practices, control of release, accidental release measures
and transport. If it is stated that a particular property does not
apply or if information on a particular property is not available, the
reasons shall be indicated.

Information on bioaccumulation, persistence and degradability shall
be given, where available and appropriate, for each relevant substance
in the mixture. Information shall also be provided for hazardous
transformation products arising from the degradation of substances
and mixtures.

The information in this section shall be consistent with the information provided in the registration and/or in the chemical safety
report where required, and with the classification of the substance
or mixture.

12.1.   Toxicity

Information on toxicity using data from tests performed on aquatic
and/or terrestrial organisms shall be provided when available. This
shall include relevant available data on aquatic toxicity, both acute
and chronic for fish, crustaceans, algae and other aquatic plants. In
addition, toxicity data on soil micro and macroorganisms and other
environmentally relevant organisms, such as birds, bees and plants,
shall be included when available. Where the substance or mixture has
inhibitory effects on the activity of microorganisms, the possible
impact on sewage treatment plants shall be mentioned.

For substances subject to registration, summaries of the information
derived from the application of Annexes VII to XI shall be included.

12.2.   Persistence and degradability

Persistence and degradability is the potential for the substance or the
appropriate substances in a mixture to degrade in the environment,
either through biodegradation or other processes such as oxidation or
hydrolysis. Test results relevant to assess persistence
and degradability shall be given where available. If degradation
half-lives are quoted it must be indicated whether these half lives
refer to mineralisation or to primary degradation. The potential of
the substance or certain substances in a mixture to degrade in
sewage treatment plants shall also be mentioned.

This information shall be given where available and appropriate, for
each individual substance in the mixture which is required to be listed
in Section 3 of the safety data sheet.

12.3.   Bioaccumulative potential

Bioaccumulative potential is the potential of the substance or certain
substances in a mixture to accumulate in biota and, eventually, to
pass through the food chain. Test results relevant to assess the bioaccumulative potential shall be given. This shall include reference to the
octanol-water partition coefficient (Kow) and bioconcentration
factor (BCF), if available.

▼M7

This information shall be given where available and appropriate, for each individual substance in the mixture which is required to be listed in Section 3 of the safety data sheet.

12.4.   **Mobility in soil**

Mobility in soil is the potential of the substance or the constituents of a mixture, if released to the environment, to move under natural forces to the groundwater or to a distance from the site of release. The potential for mobility in soil shall be given where available. Information on mobility can be determined from relevant mobility data such as adsorption studies or leaching studies, known or predicted distribution to environmental compartments, or surface tension. For example, Koc values can be predicted from octanol/water partition coefficients (Kow). Leaching and mobility can be predicted from models.

This information shall be given where available and appropriate, for each individual substance in the mixture which is required to be listed in Section 3 of the safety data sheet.

Where experimental data is available, that data shall, in general, take precedence over models and predictions.

12.5.   **Results of PBT and vPvB assessment**

Where a chemical safety report is required, the results of the PBT and vPvB assessment as set out in the chemical safety report shall be given.

12.6.   **Other adverse effects**

Information on any other adverse effects on the environment shall be included where available, such as environmental fate (exposure), photochemical ozone creation potential, ozone depletion potential, endocrine disrupting potential and/or global warming potential.

13.   *SECTION 13: Disposal considerations*

This section of the safety data sheet shall describe information for proper waste management of the substance or mixture and/or its container to assist in the determination of safe and environmentally preferred waste management options, consistent with the requirements in accordance with Directive 2008/98/EC of the European Parliament and of the Council (¹) of the Member State in which the safety data sheet is being supplied. Information relevant for the safety of persons conducting waste management activities shall complement the information given in Section 8.

Where a chemical safety report is required and where a waste stage analysis has been performed, the information on the waste management measures shall be consistent with the identified uses in the chemical safety report and the exposure scenarios from the chemical safety report set out in the annex to the safety data sheet.

13.1.   **Waste treatment methods**

(a) Waste treatment containers and methods shall be specified including the appropriate methods of waste treatment of both the substance or mixture and any contaminated packaging (for example, incineration, recycling, landfilling);

_____
(¹) OJ L 312, 22.11.2008, p. 3.

▼__M7__

(b) Physical/chemical properties that may affect waste treatment options shall be specified;

(c) Sewage disposal shall be discouraged;

(d) Where appropriate, any special precautions for any recommended waste treatment option shall be identified.

Any relevant Community provisions relating to waste shall be referred to. In their absence any relevant national or regional provisions in force shall be referred to.

14.   *SECTION 14: Transport information*

This section of the safety data sheet shall provide basic classification information for transporting/shipment of substances or mixtures mentioned under Section 1 by road, rail, sea, inland waterways or air. Where information is not available or relevant this shall be stated.

Where relevant, it shall provide information on the transport classification for each of the UN Model Regulations: European Agreement concerning the International Carriage of Dangerous Goods by Road (ADR)[1], Regulations concerning the International Carriage of Dangerous Goods by Rail (RID)[2], European Agreement concerning the International Carriage of Dangerous Goods by Inland Waterways (ADN)[3], all three of which have been implemented by Directive 2008/68/EC of the European Parliament and of the Council of 24 September 2008 on the inland transport of dangerous goods [4], International Maritime Dangerous Goods (IMDG) Code [5] (sea), and Technical Instructions for the Safe Transport of Dangerous Goods by Air (ICAO) [6] (air).

14.1.   **UN number**

The UN number (i.e. the four-figure identification number of the substance, mixture or article preceded by the letters 'UN') from the UN Model Regulations shall be provided.

14.2.   **UN proper shipping name**

The UN proper shipping name from the UN Model Regulations shall be provided, unless it has appeared as the product identifier in subsection 1.1.

14.3.   **Transport hazard class(es)**

The transport hazard class (and subsidiary risks) assigned to the substances or mixtures according to the predominant hazard that they present in accordance with the UN Model Regulations shall be provided.

14.4.   **Packing group**

The packing group number from the UN Model Regulations shall be provided, if applicable. The packing group number is assigned to certain substances in accordance with their degree of hazard.

---

[1] United Nations, Economic Commission for Europe, version applicable as from 1 January 2009, ISBN-978-92-1-139131-2.

[2] Annex 1 to Appendix B (Uniform Rules concerning the Contract for International Carriage of Goods by Rail) of the Convention concerning International Carriage by Rail, version with effect from 1 January 2009.

[3] Version as revised as of 1 January 2007.

[4] OJ L 260, 30.9.2008, p. 1.

[5] International Maritime Organisation, 2006 edition, ISBN 978-92-8001-4214-3.

[6] IATA, 2007-2008 edition.

▼__M7__

14.5.   **Environmental hazards**

It shall be indicated whether the substance or mixture is environmentally hazardous according to the criteria of the UN Model Regulations (as reflected in the IMDG Code, ADR, RID and ADN) and/or
a marine pollutant according to the IMDG Code. If authorised or
intended for carriage by inland waterways in tank-vessels, it shall
be indicated whether the substance or mixture is environmentally
hazardous in tank-vessels only according to ADN.

14.6.   **Special precautions for user**

Information shall be provided on any special precautions with which
a user should or must comply or be aware of in connection with
transport or conveyance either within or outside his premises.

14.7.   **Transport in bulk according to Annex II of MARPOL 73/78 and
the IBC Code**

This subsection only applies when cargoes are intended to be carried
in bulk according to the following International Maritime
Organisation (IMO) instruments: Annex II of the International
Convention for the Prevention of Pollution from Ships, 1973, as
modified by the Protocol of 1978 relating thereto (MARPOL
73/78) [1] and the International Code for the Construction and
Equipment of Ships carrying Dangerous Chemicals in Bulk (International Bulk Chemical Code) (IBC Code) [2].

The product name shall be provided (if different from that given in
subsection 1.1) as required by the shipment document and in accordance
with the name used in the lists of product names given in chapters 17 or
18 of the IBC Code or the latest edition of the IMO's Marine Environment
Protection Committee (MEPC).2/Circular [3]. Ship type required and
pollution category shall be indicated.

15.   *SECTION 15: Regulatory information*

This section of the safety data sheet shall describe the other regulatory information on the substance or mixture that is not already
provided in the safety data sheet (such as whether the substance or
mixture is subject to Regulation (EC) No 2037/2000 of the European
Parliament and of the Council of 29 June 2000 on substances that
deplete the ozone layer [4], Regulation (EC) No 850/2004 of the
European Parliament and of the Council of 29 April 2004 on
persistent organic pollutants and amending Directive 79/117/EEC [5]
or Regulation (EC) No 689/2008 of the European Parliament and of
the Council of 17 June 2008 concerning the export and import of
dangerous chemicals [6]).

---

[1] MARPOL 73/78 — Consolidated edition 2006, London, IMO 2007, ISBN 978-92-801-
4216-7.
[2] IBC Code, 2007 edition, London, IMO 2007, ISBN 978-92-801-4226-6.
[3] MEPC.2/Circular, Provisional categorisation of liquid substances, version 14, effective
1 January 2009.
[4] OJ L 244, 29.9.2000, p. 1.
[5] OJ L 158, 30.4.2004, p. 7.
[6] OJ L 204, 31.7.2008, p. 1.

▼__M7__

15.1.   **Safety, health and environmental regulations/legislation specific for the substance or mixture**

Information regarding relevant Community safety, health and environmental provisions (for example, Seveso category/named substances in Annex I of Council Directive 96/82/EC (¹)) or national information on the regulatory status of the substance or mixture (including the substances in the mixture), including advice regarding action that should be taken by the recipient as a result of these provisions shall be provided. Where relevant the national laws of the relevant Member States which implement these provisions and any other national measures that may be relevant shall be mentioned.

If the substance or mixture covered by this safety data sheet is the subject of specific provisions in relation to protection of human health or the environment at Community level (such as authorisations given under Title VII or restrictions under Title VIII) these provisions shall be mentioned.

15.2.   **Chemical safety assessment**

It shall be indicated if a chemical safety assessment has been carried out for the substance or the mixture by the supplier.

16.   **SECTION 16: Other information**

This section of the safety data sheet shall describe the information relevant to the compilation of the safety data sheet. It shall incorporate other information that is not included in Sections 1 to 15, including information on revision of the safety data sheet such as:

(a) in case of a revised safety data sheet, a clear indication of where changes have been made to the previous version of the safety data sheet, unless such indication is given elsewhere in the safety data sheet, with an explanation of the changes, if appropriate. A supplier of a substance or mixture shall maintain an explanation of the changes and provide it upon request;

(b) a key or legend to abbreviations and acronyms used in the safety data sheet;

(c) key literature references and sources for data;

(d) in the case of mixtures, an indication of which of the methods of evaluating information referred to in Article 9 of Regulation (EC) No 1272/2008 was used for the purpose of classification;

(e) list of relevant R phrases, hazard statements, safety phrases and/or precautionary statements. Write out the full text of any statements which are not written out in full under Sections 2 to 15;

(f) advice on any training appropriate for workers to ensure protection of human health and the environment.

If in accordance with Article 31(10) a supplier of a mixture chooses to identify and inform about the classification necessary from 1 June 2015 in advance of using it for classification and labelling on the package, he may include this classification in this section.

_____
(¹) OJ L 10, 14.1.1997, p. 13.

▼M7

PART B

The safety data sheet shall include the following 16 headings in accordance with Article 31(6) and in addition the subheadings also listed except Section 3, where only subsection 3.1 or 3.2 need to be included as appropriate:

SECTION 1: Identification of the substance/mixture and of the company/-undertaking

1.1.   Product identifier

1.2.   Relevant identified uses of the substance or mixture and uses advised against

1.3.   Details of the supplier of the safety data sheet

1.4.   Emergency telephone number

SECTION 2: Hazards identification

2.1.   Classification of the substance or mixture

2.2.   Label elements

2.3.   Other hazards

SECTION 3: Composition/information on ingredients

3.1.   Substances

3.2.   Mixtures

SECTION 4: First aid measures

4.1.   Description of first aid measures

4.2.   Most important symptoms and effects, both acute and delayed

4.3.   Indication of any immediate medical attention and special treatment needed

SECTION 5: Firefighting measures

5.1.   Extinguishing media

5.2.   Special hazards arising from the substance or mixture

5.3.   Advice for firefighters

SECTION 6: Accidental release measures

6.1.   Personal precautions, protective equipment and emergency procedures

6.2.   Environmental precautions

6.3.   Methods and material for containment and cleaning up

6.4.   Reference to other sections

SECTION 7: Handling and storage

7.1.   Precautions for safe handling

7.2.   Conditions for safe storage, including any incompatibilities

7.3.   Specific end use(s)

SECTION 8: Exposure controls/personal protection

8.1.   Control parameters

8.2.   Exposure controls

▼M7

SECTION 9:   Physical and chemical properties

9.1.   Information on basic physical and chemical properties

9.2.   Other information

SECTION 10: Stability and reactivity

10.1.   Reactivity

10.2.   Chemical stability

10.3.   Possibility of hazardous reactions

10.4.   Conditions to avoid

10.5.   Incompatible materials

10.6.   Hazardous decomposition products

SECTION 11: Toxicological information

11.1.   Information on toxicological effects

SECTION 12: Ecological information

12.1.   Toxicity

12.2.   Persistence and degradability

12.3.   Bioaccumulative potential

12.4.   Mobility in soil

12.5.   Results of PBT and vPvB assessment

12.6.   Other adverse effects

SECTION 13: Disposal considerations

13.1.   Waste treatment methods

SECTION 14: Transport information

14.1.   UN number

14.2.   UN proper shipping name

14.3.   Transport hazard class(es)

14.4.   Packing group

14.5.   Environmental hazards

14.6.   Special precautions for user

14.7.   Transport in bulk according to Annex II of MARPOL73/78 and the IBC Code

SECTION 15: Regulatory information

15.1.   Safety, health and environmental regulations/legislation specific for the substance or mixture

15.2.   Chemical safety assessment

SECTION 16: Other information

▼C1

ANNEX III

CRITERIA FOR SUBSTANCES REGISTERED IN QUANTITIES BETWEEN 1 AND 10 TONNES

Criteria for substances registered between 1 and 10 tonnes, with reference to Article 12(1)(a) and (b):

▼M3

(a) substances for which it is predicted (i.e. by the application of (Q)SARs or other evidence) that they are likely to meet the criteria for category 1A or 1B classification in the hazard classes carcinogenicity, germ cell mutagenicity or reproductive toxicity or the criteria in Annex XIII;

▼C1

(b) substances:

(i) with dispersive or diffuse use(s) particularly where such substances are used in consumer ►M3 mixtures ◄ or incorporated into consumer articles; and

▼M3

(ii) for which it is predicted (i.e. by application of (Q)SARs or other evidence) that they are likely to meet the classification criteria for any health or environmental hazard classes or differentiations under Regulation (EC) No 1272/2008.

▼M2

EXEMPTIONS FROM THE OBLIGATION TO REGISTER IN ACCORDANCE WITH ARTICLE 2(7)(a)

Einecs No	Name/Group	CAS No
200-061-5	D-glucitol $C_6H_{14}O_6$	50-70-4
200-066-2	Ascorbic acid $C_6H_8O_6$	50-81-7
200-075-1	Glucose $C_6H_{12}O_6$	50-99-7
200-233-3	Fructose $C_6H_{12}O_6$	57-48-7
200-294-2	L-lysine $C_6H_{14}N_2O_2$	56-87-1
200-334-9	Sucrose, pure $C_{12}H_{22}O_{11}$	57-50-1
200-405-4	α-tocopheryl acetate $C_{31}H_{52}O_3$	58-95-7
200-416-4	Galactose $C_6H_{12}O_6$	59-23-4
200-432-1	DL-methionine $C_5H_{11}NO_2S$	59-51-8
200-559-2	Lactose $C_{12}H_{22}O_{11}$	63-42-3
200-711-8	D-mannitol $C_6H_{14}O_6$	69-65-8
201-771-8	L-sorbose $C_6H_{12}O_6$	87-79-6
204-664-4	Glycerol stearate, pure $C_{21}H_{42}O_4$	123-94-4
204-696-9	Carbon dioxide CO_2	124-38-9
205-278-9	Calcium pantothenate, D-form $C_9H_{17}NO_{5.1/2}Ca$	137-08-6
205-756-7	DL-phenylalanine $C_9H_{11}NO_2$	150-30-1
208-407-7	Sodium gluconate $C_6H_{12}O_7.Na$	527-07-1
215-665-4	Sorbitan oleate $C_{24}H_{44}O_6$	1338-43-8
231-098-5	Krypton Kr	7439-90-9
231-110-9	Neon Ne	7440-01-9
231-147-0	Argon Ar	7440-37-1
231-168-5	Helium He	7440-59-7
231-172-7	Xenon Xe	7440-63-3
231-783-9	Nitrogen N_2	7727-37-9
231-791-2	Water, distilled, conductivity or of similar purity H_2O	7732-18-5
232-307-2	Lecithins The complex combination of diglycerides of fatty acids linked to the choline ester of phosphoric acid	8002-43-5
232-436-4	Syrups, hydrolyzed starch A complex combination obtained by the hydrolysis of cornstarch by the action of acids or enzymes. It consists primarily of d-glucose, maltose and maltodextrins	8029-43-4

▼M2

Einecs No	Name/Group	CAS No
232-442-7	Tallow, hydrogenated	8030-12-4
232-675-4	Dextrin	9004-53-9
232-679-6	Starch High-polymeric carbohydrate material usually derived from cereal grains such as corn, wheat and sorghum, and from roots and tubers such as potatoes and tapioca. Includes starch which has been pregelatinised by heating in the presence of water	9005-25-8
232-940-4	Maltodextrin	9050-36-6
238-976-7	Sodium D-gluconate $C_6H_{12}O_7$.xNa	14906-97-9
248-027-9	D-glucitol monostearate $C_{24}H_{48}O_7$	26836-47-5
262-988-1	Fatty acids, coco, Me esters	61788-59-8
265-995-8	Cellulose pulp	65996-61-4
266-948-4	Glycerides, C_{16-18} and C_{18}-unsaturated. This substance is identified by SDA Substance Name: C_{16}-C_{18} and C_{18} unsaturated trialkyl glyceride and SDA Reporting Number: 11-001-00	67701-30-8
268-616-4	Syrups, corn, dehydrated	68131-37-3
269-658-6	Glycerides, tallow mono-, di- and tri-, hydrogenated	68308-54-3
270-312-1	Glycerides, C_{16-18} and C_{18}-unsaturated, mono- and di- This substance is identified by SDA Substance Name: C_{16}-C_{18} and C_{18} unsaturated alkyl and C_{16}-C_{18} and C_{18} unsaturated dialkyl glyceride and SDA Reporting Number: 11-002-00	68424-61-3
288-123-8	Glycerides, C_{10-18}	85665-33-4

▼M2

ANNEX V

EXEMPTIONS FROM THE OBLIGATION TO REGISTER IN ACCORDANCE WITH ARTICLE 2(7)(b)

1. Substances which result from a chemical reaction that occurs incidental to exposure of another substance or article to environmental factors such as air, moisture, microbial organisms or sunlight.

2. Substances which result from a chemical reaction that occurs incidental to storage of another substance, ►**M3** mixture ◄ or article.

3. Substances which result from a chemical reaction occurring upon end use of other substances, ►**M3** mixtures ◄ or articles and which are not themselves manufactured, imported or placed on the market.

4. Substances which are not themselves manufactured, imported or placed on the market and which result from a chemical reaction that occurs when:

    (a) a stabiliser, colorant, flavouring agent, antioxidant, filler, solvent, carrier, surfactant, plasticiser, corrosion inhibitor, antifoamer or defoamer, dispersant, precipitation inhibitor, desiccant, binder, emulsifier, de-emulsifier, dewatering agent, agglomerating agent, adhesion promoter, flow modifier, pH neutraliser, sequesterant, coagulant, flocculant, fire retardant, lubricant, chelating agent, or quality control reagent functions as intended; or

    (b) a substance solely intended to provide a specific physicochemical characteristic functions as intended.

5. By-products, unless they are imported or placed on the market themselves.

6. Hydrates of a substance or hydrated ions, formed by association of a substance with water, provided that the substance has been registered by the manufacturer or importer using this exemption.

7. The following substances which occur in nature, if they are not chemically modified:

    Minerals, ores, ore concentrates, raw and processed natural gas, crude oil, coal.

8. Substances which occur in nature other than those listed under paragraph 7, if they are not chemically modified, unless they meet the criteria for classification as dangerous according to ►**M3** Regulation (EC) No 1272/2008 ◄ or unless they are persistent, bioaccumulative and toxic or very persistent and very bioaccumulative in accordance with the criteria set out in Annex XIII or unless they were identified in accordance with Article 59(1) at least two years previously as substances giving rise to an equivalent level of concern as set out in Article 57(f).

9. The following substances obtained from natural sources, if they are not chemically modified, unless they meet the criteria for classification as dangerous according to Directive 67/548/EEC with the exception of those only classified as flammable [R10], as a skin irritant [R38] or as an eye irritant [R36] or unless they are persistent, bioaccumulative and toxic or very persistent and very bioaccumulative in accordance with the criteria set out in Annex XIII or unless they were identified in accordance with Article 59(1) at least two years previously as substances giving rise to an equivalent level of concern as set out in Article 57(f):

    Vegetable fats, vegetable oils, vegetable waxes; animal fats, animal oils, animal waxes; fatty acids from C_6 to C_{24} and their potassium, sodium, calcium and magnesium salts; glycerol.

▼M2

10. The following substances if they are not chemically modified:

Liquefied petroleum gas, natural gas condensate, process gases and components thereof, coke, cement clinker, magnesia.

11. The following substances unless they meet the criteria for classification as dangerous according to Directive 67/548/EEC and provided that they do not contain constituents meeting the criteria as dangerous in accordance with Directive 67/548/EEC present in concentrations above the lowest of the applicable concentration limits set out in Directive 1999/45/EC or concentration limits set out in Annex I to Directive 67/548/EEC, unless conclusive scientific experimental data show that these constituents are not available throughout the lifecycle of the substance and those data have been ascertained to be adequate and reliable:

Glass, ceramic frits.

12. Compost and biogas.

13. Hydrogen and oxygen.

▼C1

ANNEX VI

INFORMATION REQUIREMENTS REFERRED TO IN ARTICLE 10

GUIDANCE NOTE ON FULFILLING THE REQUIREMENTS OF ANNEXES
VI TO XI

Annexes VI to XI specify the information that shall be submitted for registration and evaluation purposes according to Articles 10, 12, 13, 40, 41 and 46. For the lowest tonnage level, the standard requirements are in Annex VII, and every time a new tonnage level is reached, the requirements of the corresponding Annex have to be added. For each registration the precise information requirements will differ, according to tonnage, use and exposure. The Annexes shall thus be considered as a whole, and in conjunction with the overall requirements of registration, evaluation and the duty of care.

STEP 1 — GATHER AND SHARE EXISTING INFORMATION

The registrant should gather all existing available test data on the substance to be registered, this would include a literature search for relevant information on the substance. Wherever practicable, registrations should be submitted jointly, in accordance with Articles 11 or 19. This will enable test data to be shared, thereby avoiding unnecessary testing and reducing costs. The registrant should also collect all other available and relevant information on the substance regardless whether testing for a given endpoint is required or not at the specific tonnage level. This should include information from alternative sources (e.g. from (Q)SARs, read-across from other substances, *in vivo* and *in vitro* testing, epidemiological data) which may assist in identifying the presence or absence of hazardous properties of the substance and which can in certain cases replace the results of animal tests.

In addition, information on exposure, use and risk management measures in accordance with Article 10 and this Annex should be collected. Considering all this information together, the registrant will be able to determine the need to generate further information.

STEP 2 — CONSIDER INFORMATION NEEDS

The registrant shall identify what information is required for the registration. First, the relevant Annex or Annexes to be followed shall be identified, according to tonnage. These Annexes set out the standard information requirements, but shall be considered in conjunction with Annex XI, which allows variation from the standard approach, where it can be justified. In particular, information on exposure, use and risk management measures shall be considered at this stage in order to determine the information needs for the substance.

STEP 3 — IDENTIFY INFORMATION GAPS

The registrant shall then compare the information needs for the substance with the information already available and identify where there are gaps. It is important at this stage to ensure that the available data is relevant and has sufficient quality to fulfil the requirements.

STEP 4 — GENERATE NEW DATA/PROPOSE TESTING STRATEGY

In some cases it will not be necessary to generate new data. However, where there is an information gap that needs to be filled, new data shall be generated (Annexes VII and VIII), or a testing strategy shall be proposed (Annexes IX and X), depending on the tonnage. New tests on vertebrates shall only be conducted or proposed as a last resort when all other data sources have been exhausted.

▼<u>C1</u>

In some cases, the rules set out in Annexes VII to XI may require certain tests to be undertaken earlier than or in addition to the standard requirements.

NOTES

Note 1: If it is not technically possible, or if it does not appear scientifically necessary to give information, the reasons shall be clearly stated, in accordance with the relevant provisions.

Note 2: The registrant may wish to declare that certain information submitted in the registration dossier is commercially sensitive and its disclosure might harm him commercially. If this is the case, he shall list the items and provide a justification.

INFORMATION REFERRED TO IN ARTICLE 10(a) (i) TO (v)

1.   GENERAL REGISTRANT INFORMATION

1.1.   Registrant

1.1.1. Name, address, telephone number, fax number and e-mail address

1.1.2. Contact person

1.1.3. Location of the registrant's production and own use site(s), as appropriate

1.2.   Joint submission of data

Articles 11 or 19 foresee that parts of the registration may be submitted by a lead registrant on behalf of other registrants.

In this case, the lead registrant shall identify the other registrants specifying:

— their name, address, telephone number, fax number and e-mail address,

— parts of the present registration which apply to other registrants.

Mention the number(s) given in this Annex or Annexes VII to X, as appropriate.

Any other registrant shall identify the lead registrant submitting on his behalf specifying:

— his name, address, telephone number, fax number and e-mail address,

— parts of the registration which are submitted by the lead registrant.

Mention the number(s) given in this Annex or Annexes VII to X, as appropriate.

1.3   Third party appointed under Article 4

1.3.1. Name, address, telephone number, fax number and e-mail address

1.3.2. Contact person

2.   IDENTIFICATION OF THE SUBSTANCE

For each substance, the information given in this section shall be sufficient to enable each substance to be identified. If it is not technically possible or if it does not appear scientifically necessary to give information on one or more of the items below, the reasons shall be clearly stated.

▼<u>C1</u>

2.1.   Name or other identifier of each substance

2.1.1.   Name(s) in the IUPAC nomenclature or other international chemical name(s)

2.1.2.   Other names (usual name, trade name, abbreviation)

2.1.3.   EINECS or ELINCs number (if available and appropriate)

2.1.4.   CAS name and CAS number (if available)

2.1.5.   Other identity code (if available)

2.2.   Information related to molecular and structural formula of each substance

2.2.1.   Molecular and structural formula (including SMILES notation, if available)

2.2.2.   Information on optical activity and typical ratio of (stereo) isomers (if applicable and appropriate)

2.2.3.   Molecular weight or molecular weight range

2.3.   Composition of each substance

2.3.1.   Degree of purity (%)

2.3.2.   Nature of impurities, including isomers and by-products

2.3.3.   Percentage of (significant) main impurities

2.3.4.   Nature and order of magnitude (… ppm, … %) of any additives (e.g. stabilising agents or inhibitors)

2.3.5.   Spectral data (ultra-violet, infra-red, nuclear magnetic resonance or mass spectrum)

2.3.6.   High-pressure liquid chromatogram, gas chromatogram

2.3.7.   Description of the analytical methods or the appropriate bibliographical references for the identification of the substance and, where appropriate, for the identification of impurities and additives. This information shall be sufficient to allow the methods to be reproduced.

3.   INFORMATION ON MANUFACTURE AND USE(S) OF THE SUBSTANCE(S)

3.1.   Overall manufacture, quantities used for production of an article that is subject to registration, and/or imports in tonnes per registrant per year in:

the calendar year of the registration (estimated quantity)

3.2.   In the case of a manufacturer or producer of articles: brief description of the technological process used in manufacture or production of articles.

Precise details of the process, particularly those of a commercially sensitive nature, are not required.

3.3.   An indication of the tonnage used for his own use(s)

3.4.   Form (substance, ►M3 mixture ◄ or article) and/or physical state under which the substance is made available to downstream users. Concentration or concentration range of the substance in ►M3 mixtures ◄ made available to downstream users and quantities of the substance in articles made available to downstream users.

3.5.   Brief general description of the identified use(s)

▼C1

3.6.	Information on waste quantities and composition of waste resulting from manufacture of the substance, the use in articles and identified uses

3.7.	Uses advised against ►M7 (see Section 1 of the safety data sheet) ◄

Where applicable, an indication of the uses which the registrant advises against and why (i.e. non-statutory recommendations by supplier). This need not be an exhaustive list.

4.	CLASSIFICATION AND LABELLING

▼M3

4.1	The hazard classification of the substance(s), resulting from the application of Title I and II of Regulation (EC) No 1272/2008 for all hazard classes and categories in that Regulation,

In addition, for each entry, the reasons why no classification is given for a hazard class or differentiation of a hazard class should be provided (i.e. if data are lacking, inconclusive, or conclusive but not sufficient for classification),

4.2	The resulting hazard label for the substance(s), resulting from the application of Title III of Regulation (EC) No 1272/2008,

4.3	Specific concentration limits, where applicable, resulting from the application of Article 10 of Regulation (EC) No 1272/2008 and Articles 4 to 7 of Directive 1999/45/EC.

▼C1

5.	GUIDANCE ON SAFE USE CONCERNING:

This information shall be consistent with that in the Safety Data Sheet, where such a Safety Data Sheet is required according to Article 31.

5.1.	First-aid measures (Safety Data Sheet heading 4)

5.2.	Fire-fighting measures (Safety Data Sheet heading 5)

5.3.	Accidental release measures (Safety Data Sheet heading 6)

5.4.	Handling and storage (Safety Data Sheet heading 7)

5.5.	Transport information (Safety Data Sheet heading 14)

Where a Chemical Safety Report is not required, the following additional information is required:

5.6.	Exposure controls/personal protection (Safety Data Sheet heading 8)

5.7.	Stability and reactivity (Safety Data Sheet heading 10)

5.8.	Disposal considerations

5.8.1.	Disposal considerations (Safety Data Sheet heading 13)

5.8.2.	Information on recycling and methods of disposal for industry

5.8.3.	Information on recycling and methods of disposal for the public.

▼C1

6. INFORMATION ON EXPOSURE FOR SUBSTANCES REGISTERED IN QUANTITIES BETWEEN 1 AND 10 TONNES PER YEAR PER MANUFATCURER OR IMPORTER

6.1. Main use category:

6.1.1. (a) industrial use; and/or

(b) professional use; and/or

(c) consumer use.

6.1.2. Specification for industrial and professional use:

(a) used in closed system; and/or

(b) use resulting in inclusion into or onto matrix; and/or

(c) non-dispersive use; and/or

(d) dispersive use.

6.2. Significant route(s) of exposure:

6.2.1. Human exposure:

(a) oral; and/or

(b) dermal; and/or

(c) inhalatory.

6.2.2. Environmental exposure:

(a) water; and/or

(b) air; and/or

(c) solid waste; and/or

(d) soil.

6.3. Pattern of exposure:

(a) accidental/infrequent; and/or

(b) occasional; and/or

(c) continuous/frequent.

▼C1

STANDARD INFORMATION REQUIREMENTS FOR SUBSTANCES MANUFACTURED OR IMPORTED IN QUANTITIES OF ONE TONNE OR MORE ([1])

Column 1 of this Annex establishes the standard information required for:

(a) non-phase-in substances manufactured or imported in quantities of 1 to 10 tonnes;

(b) phase-in substances manufactured or imported in quantities of 1 to 10 tonnes and meeting the criteria in Annex III in accordance with Article 12(1)(a) and (b); and

(c) substances manufactured or imported in quantities of 10 tonnes or more.

Any other relevant physicochemical, toxicological and ecotoxicological information that is available shall be provided. For substances not meeting the criteria in Annex III only the physicochemical requirements as set out in section 7 of this Annex are required.

Column 2 of this Annex lists specific rules according to which the required standard information may be omitted, replaced by other information, provided at a different stage or adapted in another way. If the conditions are met under which column 2 of this Annex allows adaptations, the registrant shall clearly state this fact and the reasons for each adaptation under the appropriate headings in the registration dossier.

In addition to these specific rules, a registrant may adapt the required standard information set out in column 1 of this Annex according to the general rules contained in Annex XI with the exception of Section 3 on substance-tailored exposure waiving. In this case as well, he shall clearly state the reasons for any decision to adapt the standard information under the appropriate headings in the registration dossier referring to the appropriate specific rule(s) in column 2 or in Annex XI ([2]).

Before new tests are carried out to determine the properties listed in this Annex, all available *in vitro* data, *in vivo* data, historical human data, data from valid (Q)SARs and data from structurally related substances (read-across approach) shall be assessed first. *In vivo* testing with corrosive substances at concentration/-dose levels causing corrosivity shall be avoided. Prior to testing, further guidance on testing strategies should be consulted in addition to this Annex.

When, for certain endpoints, information is not provided for other reasons than those mentioned in column 2 of this Annex or in Annex XI, this fact and the reasons shall also be clearly stated.

([1]) This Annex shall apply to producers of articles that are required to register in accordance with Article 7 and to other downstream users that are required to carry out tests under this Regulation adapted as necessary.

([2]) Note: conditions for not requiring a specific test that are set out in the appropriate test methods in the Commission Regulation on test methods as specified in Article 13(3) that are not repeated in column 2, also apply.

▼C1

7. INFORMATION ON THE PHYSICOCHEMICAL PROPERTIES OF THE
SUBSTANCE

COLUMN 1 STANDARD INFORMATION REQUIRED	COLUMN 2 SPECIFIC RULES FOR ADAPTATION FROM COLUMN 1	
7.1. State of the substance at 20 °C and 101,3 kPa		
7.2. Melting/freezing point	7.2.	The study does not need to be conducted below a lower limit of - 20 °C.
7.3. Boiling point	7.3.	The study does not need to be conducted: — for gases, or — for solids which either melt above 300 °C or decompose before boiling. In such cases the boiling point under reduced pressure may be estimated or measured, or — for substances which decompose before boiling (e.g. auto-oxidation, rearrangement, degradation, decomposition, etc.).
7.4. Relative density	7.4.	The study does not need to be conducted if: — the substance is only stable in solution in a particular solvent and the solution density is similar to that of the solvent. In such cases, an indication of whether the solution density is higher or lower than the solvent density is sufficient, or — the substance is a gas. In this case, an estimation based on calculation shall be made from its molecular weight and the Ideal Gas Laws.
7.5. Vapour pressure	7.5.	The study does not need to be conducted if the melting point is above 300 °C. If the melting point is between 200 °C and 300 °C, a limit value based on measurement or a recognised calculation method is sufficient.
7.6. Surface tension	7.6.	The study need only be conducted if: — based on structure, surface activity is expected or can be predicted, or — surface activity is a desired property of the material. If the water solubility is below 1 mg/l at 20 °C the test does not need to be conducted.
7.7. Water solubility	7.7.	The study does not need to be conducted if: — the substance is hydrolytically unstable at pH 4, 7 and 9 (half-life less than 12 hours), or — the substance is readily oxidisable in water. If the substance appears 'insoluble' in water, a limit test up to the detection limit of the analytical method shall be performed.
7.8. Partition coefficient n-octanol/water	7.8.	The study does not need to be conducted if the substance is inorganic. If the test cannot be performed (e.g. the substance decomposes, has a high surface activity, reacts violently during the performance of the test or does not dissolve in water or in octanol, or it is not possible to obtain a sufficiently pure substance), a calculated value for log P as well as details of the calculation method shall be provided.

▼C1

COLUMN 1 STANDARD INFORMATION REQUIRED	COLUMN 2 SPECIFIC RULES FOR ADAPTATION FROM COLUMN 1
7.9. Flash-point	7.9. The study does not need to be conducted if: — the substance is inorganic, or — the substance only contains volatile organic components with flash-points above 100 °C for aqueous solutions, or — the estimated flash-point is above 200 °C, or — the flash-point can be accurately predicted by interpolation from existing characterised materials.
7.10. Flammability	7.10. The study does not need to be conducted: — if the substance is a solid which possesses explosive or pyrophoric properties. These properties should always be considered before considering flammability, or — for gases, if the concentration of the flammable gas in a mixture with inert gases is so low that, when mixed with air, the concentration is all time below the lower limit, or — for substances which spontaneously ignite when in contact with air.

7.11. Explosive properties	7.11. The study does not need to be conducted if:
	
	— there are no chemical groups associated with explosive properties present in the molecule, or
	
	— the substance contains chemical groups associated with explosive properties which include oxygen and the calculated oxygen balance is less than -200, or
	
	— the organic substance or a homogenous mixture of organic substances contains chemical groups associated with explosive properties, but the exothermic decomposition energy is less than 500 J/g and the onset of exothermic decomposition is below 500 °C, or
	
	— for mixtures of inorganic oxidising substances (UN Division 5.1) with organic materials, the concentration of the inorganic oxidising substance is:
	
	  — less than 15 %, by mass, if assigned to UN Packaging Group I (high hazard) or II (medium hazard),
	
	  — less than 30 %, by mass, if assigned to UN Packaging Group III (low hazard).
	
	Note: Neither a test for propagation of detonation nor a test for sensitivity to detonative shock is required if the exothermic decomposition energy of organic materials is less than 800 J/g.

7.12. Self-ignition temperature	7.12. The study does not need to be conducted: — if the substance is explosive or ignites spontaneously with air at room temperature, or — for liquids non flammable in air, e.g. no flash point up to 200 °C, or — for gases having no flammable range, or — for solids, if the substance has a melting point $\leq$ 160 °C, or if preliminary results exclude self-heating of the substance up to 400 °C.

▼C1

COLUMN 1 STANDARD INFORMATION REQUIRED	COLUMN 2 SPECIFIC RULES FOR ADAPTATION FROM COLUMN 1
7.13. Oxidising prop- erties	7.13. The study does not need to be conducted if: — the substance is explosive, or — the substance is highly flammable, or — the substance is an organic peroxide, or — the substance is incapable of reacting exothermically with combustible materials, for example on the basis of the chemical structure (e.g. organic substances not containing oxygen or halogen atoms and these elements are not chemically bonded to nitrogen or oxygen, or inorganic substances not containing oxygen or halogen atoms). The full test does not need to be conducted for solids if the preliminary test clearly indicates that the test substance has oxidising properties. Note that as there is no test method to determine the oxidising properties of gaseous mixtures, the evaluation of these properties must be realised by an estimation method based on the comparison of the oxidising potential of gases in a mixture with that of the oxidising potential of oxygen in air.
7.14. Granulometry	7.14. The study does not need to be conducted if the substance is marketed or used in a non solid or granular form.

8. TOXICOLOGICAL INFORMATION

COLUMN 1 STANDARD INFORMATION REQUIRED	COLUMN 2 SPECIFIC RULES FOR ADAPTATION FROM COLUMN 1
8.1. Skin irritation or skin corrosion The assessment of this endpoint shall comprise the following consecutive steps: (1) an assessment of the available human and animal data, (2) an assessment of the acid or alkaline reserve, (3) *in vitro* study for skin corrosion, (4) *in vitro* study for skin irritation.	8.1. Steps 3 and 4 do not need to be conducted if: — the available information indicates that the criteria are met for classification as corrosive to the skin or irritating to eyes, or — the substance is flammable in air at room temperature, or — the substance is classified as very toxic in contact with skin, or — an acute toxicity study by the dermal route does not indicate skin irritation up to the limit dose level (2 000 mg/kg body weight).

▼C1

COLUMN 1 STANDARD INFORMATION REQUIRED	COLUMN 2 SPECIFIC RULES FOR ADAPTATION FROM COLUMN 1
8.2. Eye irritation The assessment of this endpoint shall comprise the following consecutive steps: (1) an assessment of the available human and animal data, (2) an assessment of the acid or alkaline reserve, (3) *in vitro* study for eye irritation.	8.2. Step 3 does not need to be conducted if: — the available information indicates that the criteria are met for classification as corrosive to the skin or irritating to eyes, or — the substance is flammable in air at room temperature;
8.3. Skin sensitisation The assessment of this endpoint shall comprise the following consecutive steps: (1) an assessment of the available human, animal and alternative data, (2) *In vivo* testing.	8.3. Step 2 does not need to be conducted if: — the available information indicates that the substance should be classified for skin sensitisation or corrosivity, or — the substance is a strong acid (pH ≤ 2,0) or base (pH ≥ 11,5), or — the substance is flammable in air at room temperature. The Murine Local Lymph Node Assay (LLNA) is the first-choice method for *in vivo* testing. Only in exceptional circumstances should another test be used. Justification for the use of another test shall be provided.
8.4. Mutagenicity	8.4. Further mutagenicity studies shall be considered in case of a positive result.
8.4.1. *In vitro* gene mutation study in bacteria	
8.5. Acute toxicity	8.5. The study/ies do(es) not generally need to be conducted if: — the substance is classified as corrosive to the skin.
8.5.1. By oral route	The study need not be conducted if a study on acute toxicity by the inhalation route (8.5.2) is available.

9. ECOTOXICOLOGICAL INFORMATION

COLUMN 1 STANDARD INFORMATION REQUIRED	COLUMN 2 SPECIFIC RULES FOR ADAPTATION FROM COLUMN 1
9.1. Aquatic toxicity	

▼C1

COLUMN 1 STANDARD INFORMATION REQUIRED	COLUMN 2 SPECIFIC RULES FOR ADAPTATION FROM COLUMN 1
9.1.1. Short-term toxicity testing on invertebrates (preferred species *Daphnia*) The registrant may consider long-term toxicity testing instead of short-term.	9.1.1. The study does not need to be conducted if: — there are mitigating factors indicating that aquatic toxicity is unlikely to occur, for instance if the substance is highly insoluble in water or the substance is unlikely to cross biological membranes, or — a long-term aquatic toxicity study on invertebrates is available, or — adequate information for environmental classification and labelling is available. The long-term aquatic toxicity study on *Daphnia* (Annex IX, section 9.1.5) shall be considered if the substance is poorly water soluble.
9.1.2. Growth inhibition study aquatic plants (algae preferred)	9.1.2. The study does not need to be conducted if there are mitigating factors indicating that aquatic toxicity is unlikely to occur for instance if the substance is highly insoluble in water or the substance is unlikely to cross biological membranes.
9.2. Degradation	
9.2.1. Biotic	
9.2.1.1. Ready biodegradability	9.2.1.1. The study does not need to be conducted if the substance is inorganic.

Any other relevant physicochemical, toxicological and ecotoxicological information that is available shall be provided.

▼C1

STANDARD INFORMATION REQUIREMENTS FOR SUBSTANCES MANUFACTURED OR IMPORTED IN QUANTITIES OF 10 TONNES OR MORE ([1])

Column 1 of this Annex establishes the standard information required for all substances manufactured or imported in quantities of 10 tonnes or more in accordance with Article 12(1)(c). Accordingly, the information required in column 1 of this Annex is additional to that required in column 1 of Annex VII. Any other relevant physicochemical, toxicological and ecotoxicological information that is available shall be provided. Column 2 of this Annex lists specific rules according to which the required standard information may be omitted, replaced by other information, provided at a different stage or adapted in another way. If the conditions are met under which column 2 of this Annex allows adaptations, the registrant shall clearly state this fact and the reasons for each adaptation under the appropriate headings in the registration dossier.

In addition to these specific rules, a registrant may adapt the required standard information set out in column 1 of this Annex according to the general rules contained in Annex XI. In this case as well, he shall clearly state the reasons for any decision to adapt the standard information under the appropriate headings in the registration dossier referring to the appropriate specific rule(s) in column 2 or in Annex XI ([2]).

Before new tests are carried out to determine the properties listed in this Annex, all available *in vitro* data, *in vivo* data, historical human data, data from valid (Q)SARs and data from structurally related substances (read-across approach) shall be assessed first. *In vivo* testing with corrosive substances at concentration/-dose levels causing corrosivity shall be avoided. Prior to testing, further guidance on testing strategies should be consulted in addition to this Annex.

When, for certain endpoints, information is not provided for other reasons than those mentioned in column 2 of this Annex or in Annex XI, this fact and the reasons shall also be clearly stated.

8. TOXICOLOGICAL INFORMATION

COLUMN 1 STANDARD INFORMATION REQUIRED	COLUMN 2 SPECIFIC RULES FOR ADAPTATION FROM COLUMN 1
8.1. Skin irritation	
8.1.1. *In vivo* skin irritation	8.1.1. The study does not need to be conducted if: — the substance is classified as corrosive to the skin or as a skin irritant, or — the substance is a strong acid (pH ≤ 2,0) or base (pH ≥ 11,5), or — the substance is flammable in air at room temperature, or — the substance is classified as very toxic in contact with skin, or — an acute toxicity study by the dermal route does not indicate skin irritation up to the limit dose level (2 000 mg/kg body weight).

([1]) This Annex shall apply to producers of articles that are required to register in accordance with Article 7 and to other downstream users that are required to carry out tests under this Regulation adapted as necessary.

([2]) Note: conditions for not requiring a specific test that are set out in the appropriate test methods in the Commission Regulation on test methods as specified in Article 13(3) that are not repeated in column 2, also apply.

▼C1

COLUMN 1 STANDARD INFORMATION REQUIRED		COLUMN 2 SPECIFIC RULES FOR ADAPTATION FROM COLUMN 1
8.2.	Eye irritation	
8.2.1.	*In vivo* eye irritation	8.2.1. The study does not need to be conducted if: — the substance is classified as irritating to eyes with risk of serious damage to eyes, or — the substance is classified as corrosive to the skin and provided that the registrant classified the substance as eye irritant, or — the substance is a strong acid (pH ≤ 2,0) or base (pH ≥ 11,5), or — the substance is flammable in air at room temperature.
8.4.	Mutagenicity	
8.4.2.	*In vitro* cytogenicity study in mammalian cells or *in vitro* micronucleus study	8.4.2. The study does not usually need to be conducted — if adequate data from an *in vivo* cytogenicity test are available, or ▶M3 — the substance is known to be carcinogenic category 1A or 1B or germ cell mutagenic category 1A, 1B or 2. ◀
8.4.3.	*In vitro* gene mutation study in mammalian cells, if a negative result in Annex VII, Section 8.4.1. and Annex VIII, Section 8.4.2.	8.4.3. The study does not usually need to be conducted if adequate data from a reliable *in vivo* mammalian gene mutation test are available.
		8.4. Appropriate *in vivo* mutagenicity studies shall be considered in case of a positive result in any of the genotoxicity studies in Annex VII or VIII.
8.5.	Acute toxicity	8.5. The study/ies do(es) not generally need to be conducted if: — the substance is classified as corrosive to the skin. In addition to the oral route (8.5.1), for substances other than gases, the information mentioned under 8.5.2 to 8.5.3 shall be provided for at least one other route. The choice for the second route will depend on the nature of the substance and the likely route of human exposure. If there is only one route of exposure, information for only that route need be provided.
8.5.2.	By inhalation	8.5.2. Testing by the inhalation route is appropriate if exposure of humans via inhalation is likely taking into account the vapour pressure of the substance and/or the possibility of exposure to aerosols, particles or droplets of an inhalable size.
8.5.3.	By dermal route	8.5.3. Testing by the dermal route is appropriate if: (1) inhalation of the substance is unlikely; and (2) skin contact in production and/or use is likely; and (3) the physicochemical and toxicological properties suggest potential for a significant rate of absorption through the skin.

▼C1

COLUMN 1 STANDARD INFORMATION REQUIRED	COLUMN 2 SPECIFIC RULES FOR ADAPTATION FROM COLUMN 1
8.6. Repeated dose toxicity	
8.6.1. Short-term repeated dose toxicity study (28 days), one species, male and female, most appropriate route of administration, having regard to the likely route of human exposure.	8.6.1. The short-term toxicity study (28 days) does not need to be conducted if: — a reliable sub-chronic (90 days) or chronic toxicity study is available, provided that an appropriate species, dosage, solvent and route of administration were used, or — where a substance undergoes immediate disintegration and there are sufficient data on the cleavage products, or — relevant human exposure can be excluded in accordance with Annex XI Section 3. The appropriate route shall be chosen on the following basis: Testing by the dermal route is appropriate if: (1) inhalation of the substance is unlikely; and (2) skin contact in production and/or use is likely; and (3) the physicochemical and toxicological properties suggest potential for a significant rate of absorption through the skin. Testing by the inhalation route is appropriate if exposure of humans via inhalation is likely taking into account the vapour pressure of the substance and/or the possibility of exposure to aerosols, particles or droplets of an inhalable size. The sub-chronic toxicity study (90 days) (Annex IX, Section 8.6.2) shall be proposed by the registrant if: the frequency and duration of human exposure indicates that a longer term study is appropriate; and one of the following conditions is met: — other available data indicate that the substance may have a dangerous property that cannot be detected in a short-term toxicity study, or — appropriately designed toxicokinetic studies reveal accumulation of the substance or its metabolites in certain tissues or organs which would possibly remain undetected in a short-term toxicity study but which are liable to result in adverse effects after prolonged exposure. Further studies shall be proposed by the registrant or may be required by the Agency in accordance with Article 40 or 41 in case of: — failure to identify a NOAEL in the 28 or the 90 days study, unless the reason for the failure to identify a NOAEL is absence of adverse toxic effects, or — toxicity of particular concern (e.g. serious/severe effects), or — indications of an effect for which the available evidence is inadequate for toxicological and/or risk characterisation. In such cases it may also be more appropriate to perform specific toxicological studies that are designed to investigate these effects (e.g. immunotoxicity, neurotoxicity), or

▼C1

COLUMN 1 STANDARD INFORMATION REQUIRED	COLUMN 2 SPECIFIC RULES FOR ADAPTATION FROM COLUMN 1
	— the route of exposure used in the initial repeated dose study was inappropriate in relation to the expected route of human exposure and route-to-route extrapolation cannot be made, or
	— particular concern regarding exposure (e.g. use in consumer products leading to exposure levels which are close to the dose levels at which toxicity to humans may be expected), or
	— effects shown in substances with a clear relationship in molecular structure with the substance being studied, were not detected in the 28 or the 90 days study.
8.7. Reproductive toxicity	
8.7.1. Screening for reproductive/developmental toxicity, one species (OECD 421 or 422), if there is no evidence from available information on structurally related substances, from (Q)SAR estimates or from *in vitro* methods that the substance may be a developmental toxicant	8.7.1. This study does not need to be conducted if: — the substance is known to be a genotoxic carcinogen and appropriate risk management measures are implemented, or — the substance is known to be a germ cell mutagen and appropriate risk management measures are implemented, or — relevant human exposure can be excluded in accordance with Annex XI section 3, or — a pre-natal developmental toxicity study (Annex IX, 8.7.2) or a two-generation reproductive toxicity study (Annex IX, Section 8.7.3) is available. ►**M3** If a substance is known to have an adverse effect on fertility, meeting the criteria for classification as toxic for reproduction category 1A or 1B: May damage fertility (H360F), and the available data are adequate to support a robust risk assessment, then no further testing for fertility will be necessary. However, testing for developmental toxicity must be considered. If a substance is known to cause developmental toxicity, meeting the criteria for classification as toxic for reproduction category 1A or 1B: May damage the unborn child (H360D), and the available data are adequate to support a robust risk assessment, then no further testing for developmental toxicity will be necessary. However, testing for effects on fertility must be considered. ◄ In cases where there are serious concerns about the potential for adverse effects on fertility or development, either a pre-natal developmental toxicity study (Annex IX, Section 8.7.2) or a two-generation reproductive toxicity study (Annex IX, Section 8.7.3) may be proposed by the registrant instead of the screening study.

▼C1

COLUMN 1 STANDARD INFORMATION REQUIRED	COLUMN 2 SPECIFIC RULES FOR ADAPTATION FROM COLUMN 1
8.8. Toxicokinetics	
8.8.1. Assessment of the toxicokinetic behaviour of the substance to the extent that can be derived from the relevant available information	

9. ECOTOXICOLOGICAL INFORMATION

COLUMN 1 STANDARD INFORMATION REQUIRED	COLUMN 2 SPECIFIC RULES FOR ADAPTATION FROM COLUMN 1
9.1.3. Short-term toxicity testing on fish: the registrant may consider long-term toxicity testing instead of short-term.	9.1.3. The study does not need to be conducted if: — there are mitigating factors indicating that aquatic toxicity is unlikely to occur, for instance if the substance is highly insoluble in water or the substance is unlikely to cross biological membranes, or — a long-term aquatic toxicity study on fish is available. Long-term aquatic toxicity testing as described in Annex IX shall be considered if the chemical safety assessment according to Annex I indicates the need to investigate further effects on aquatic organisms. The choice of the appropriate test(s) will depend on the results of the chemical safety assessment. The long-term aquatic toxicity study on fish (Annex IX, Section 9.1.6) shall be considered if the substance is poorly water soluble.
9.1.4. Activated sludge respiration inhibition testing	9.1.4. The study does not need to be conducted if: — there is no emission to a sewage treatment plant, or — there are mitigating factors indicating that microbial toxicity is unlikely to occur, for instance the substance is highly insoluble in water, or — the substance is found to be readily biodegradable and the applied test concentrations are in the range of concentrations that can be expected in the influent of a sewage treatment plant. The study may be replaced by a nitrification inhibition test if available data show that the substance is likely to be an inhibitor of microbial growth or function, in particular nitrifying bacteria.
9.2. Degradation	9.2. Further degradation testing shall be considered if the chemical safety assessment according to Annex I indicates the need to investigate further the degradation of the substance. The choice of the appropriate test(s) will depend on the results of the chemical safety assessment.

▼C1

COLUMN 1 STANDARD INFORMATION REQUIRED	COLUMN 2 SPECIFIC RULES FOR ADAPTATION FROM COLUMN 1
9.2.2. Abiotic	
9.2.2.1. Hydrolysis as a function of pH.	9.2.2.1. The study does not need to be conducted if: — the substance is readily biodegradable, or — the substance is highly insoluble in water.
9.3. Fate and behaviour in the environment	
9.3.1. Adsorption/desorption screening	9.3.1. The study does not need to be conducted if: — based on the physicochemical properties the substance can be expected to have a low potential for adsorption (e.g. the substance has a low octanol water partition coefficient), or — the substance and its relevant degradation products decompose rapidly.

▼C1

ANNEX IX

STANDARD INFORMATION REQUIREMENTS FOR SUBSTANCES MANUFACTURED OR IMPORTED IN QUANTITIES OF 100 TONNES OR MORE (¹)

At the level of this Annex, the registrant must submit a proposal and a time schedule for fulfilling the information requirements of this Annex in accordance with Article 12(1)(d).

Column 1 of this Annex establishes the standard information required for all substances manufactured or imported in quantities of 100 tonnes or more in accordance with Article 12(1)(d). Accordingly, the information required in column 1 of this Annex is additional to that required in column 1 of Annexes VII and VIII. Any other relevant physicochemical, toxicological and ecotoxicological information that is available shall be provided. Column 2 of this Annex lists specific rules according to which the registrant may propose to omit the required standard information, replace it by other information, provide it at a later stage or adapt it in another way. If the conditions are met under which column 2 of this Annex allows an adaptation to be proposed, the registrant shall clearly state this fact and the reasons for proposing each adaptation under the appropriate headings in the registration dossier.

In addition to these specific rules, a registrant may propose to adapt the required standard information set out in column 1 of this Annex according to the general rules contained in Annex XI. In this case as well, he shall clearly state the reasons for any decision to propose adaptations to the standard information under the appropriate headings in the registration dossier referring to the appropriate specific rule(s) in column 2 or in Annex XI (²).

Before new tests are carried out to determine the properties listed in this Annex, all available *in vitro* data, *in vivo* data, historical human data, data from valid (Q)SARs and data from structurally related substances (read-across approach) shall be assessed first. *In vivo* testing with corrosive substances at concentration/-dose levels causing corrosivity shall be avoided. Prior to testing, further guidance on testing strategies should be consulted in addition to this Annex.

When, for certain endpoints, it is proposed not to provide information for other reasons than those mentioned in column 2 of this Annex or in Annex XI, this fact and the reasons shall also be clearly stated.

7. INFORMATION ON THE PHYSICOCHEMICAL PROPERTIES OF THE SUBSTANCE

COLUMN 1 STANDARD INFORMATION REQUIRED	COLUMN 2 SPECIFIC RULES FOR ADAPTATION FROM COLUMN 1
7.15. Stability in organic solvents and identity of relevant degradation products Only required if stability of the substance is considered to be critical.	7.15. The study does not need to be conducted if the substance is inorganic.

(¹) This Annex shall apply to producers of articles that are required to register in accordance with Article 7 and to other downstream users that are required to carry out tests under this Regulation adapted as necessary.

(²) Note: conditions for not requiring a specific test that are set out in the appropriate test methods in the Commission Regulation on test methods as specified in Article 13(3) that are not repeated in column 2, also apply.

▼C1

COLUMN 1 STANDARD INFORMATION REQUIRED	COLUMN 2 SPECIFIC RULES FOR ADAPTATION FROM COLUMN 1
7.16. Dissociation constant	7.16. The study does not need to be conducted if: — the substance is hydrolytically unstable (half-life less than 12 hours) or is readily oxidisable in water, or — it is scientifically not possible to perform the test for instance if the analytical method is not sensitive enough.
7.17. Viscosity	

8.   TOXICOLOGICAL INFORMATION

COLUMN 1 STANDARD INFORMATION REQUIRED	COLUMN 2 SPECIFIC RULES FOR ADAPTATION FROM COLUMN 1
	8.4. If there is a positive result in any of the *in vitro* genotoxicity studies in Annex VII or VIII and there are no results available from an *in vivo* study already, an appropriate *in vivo* somatic cell genotoxicity study shall be proposed by the registrant. If there is a positive result from an *in vivo* somatic cell study available, the potential for germ cell mutagenicity should be considered on the basis of all available data, including toxicokinetic evidence. If no clear conclusions about germ cell mutagenicity can be made, additional investigations shall be considered.
8.6. Repeated dose toxicity	
8.6.1. Short-term repeated dose toxicity study (28 days), one species, male and female, most appropriate route of administration, having regard to the likely route of human exposure, unless already provided as part of Annex VIII requirements or if tests according to Section 8.6.2 of this Annex is proposed. In this case, Section 3 of Annex XI shall not apply.	

▼C1

COLUMN 1 STANDARD INFORMATION REQUIRED	COLUMN 2 SPECIFIC RULES FOR ADAPTATION FROM COLUMN 1
8.6.2. Sub-chronic toxicity study (90-day), one species, rodent, male and female, most appropriate route of administration, having regard to the likely route of human exposure.	8.6.2. The sub-chronic toxicity study (90 days) does not need to be conducted if:

8.6.2. The sub-chronic toxicity study (90 days) does not need to be conducted if:

— a reliable short-term toxicity study (28 days) is available showing severe toxicity effects according to the criteria for classifying the substance as R48, for which the observed NOAEL-28 days, with the application of an appropriate uncertainty factor, allows the extrapolation towards the NOAEL-90 days for the same route of exposure, or

— a reliable chronic toxicity study is available, provided that an appropriate species and route of administration were used, or

— a substance undergoes immediate disintegration and there are sufficient data on the cleavage products (both for systemic effects and effects at the site of uptake), or

— the substance is unreactive, insoluble and not inhalable and there is no evidence of absorption and no evidence of toxicity in a 28-day 'limit test', particularly if such a pattern is coupled with limited human exposure.

The appropriate route shall be chosen on the following basis:

Testing by the dermal route is appropriate if:

(1) skin contact in production and/or use is likely; and

(2) the physicochemical properties suggest a significant rate of absorption through the skin; and

(3) one of the following conditions is met:

— toxicity is observed in the acute dermal toxicity test at lower doses than in the oral toxicity test, or

— systemic effects or other evidence of absorption is observed in skin and/or eye irritation studies, or

— *in vitro* tests indicate significant dermal absorption, or

— significant dermal toxicity or dermal penetration is recognised for structurally-related substances.

Testing by the inhalation route is appropriate if:

— exposure of humans via inhalation is likely taking into account the vapour pressure of the substance and/or the possibility of exposure to aerosols, particles or droplets of an inhalable size.

▼C1

COLUMN 1 STANDARD INFORMATION REQUIRED	COLUMN 2 SPECIFIC RULES FOR ADAPTATION FROM COLUMN 1
	Further studies shall be proposed by the registrant or may be required by the Agency in accordance with Articles 40 or 41 in case of:
	— failure to identify a NOAEL in the 90 days study unless the reason for the failure to identify a NOAEL is absence of adverse toxic effects, or
	— toxicity of particular concern (e.g. serious/severe effects), or
	— indications of an effect for which the available evidence is inadequate for toxicological and/or risk characterisation. In such cases it may also be more appropriate to perform specific toxicological studies that are designed to investigate these effects (e.g. immunotoxicity, neurotoxicity), or
	— particular concern regarding exposure (e.g. use in consumer products leading to exposure levels which are close to the dose levels at which toxicity to humans may be expected).
8.7. Reproductive toxicity	8.7. The studies do not need to be conducted if:
	— the substance is known to be a genotoxic carcinogen and appropriate risk management measures are implemented, or
	— the substance is known to be a germ cell mutagen and appropriate risk management measures are implemented, or
	— the substance is of low toxicological activity (no evidence of toxicity seen in any of the tests available), it can be proven from toxicokinetic data that no systemic absorption occurs via relevant routes of exposure (e.g. plasma/blood concentrations below detection limit using a sensitive method and absence of the substance and of metabolites of the substance in urine, bile or exhaled air) and there is no or no significant human exposure.
	►M3 If a substance is known to have an adverse effect on fertility, meeting the criteria for classification as toxic for reproduction category 1A or 1B: May damage fertility (H360F), and the available data are adequate to support a robust risk assessment, then no further testing for fertility will be necessary. However, testing for developmental toxicity must be considered.
	If a substance is known to cause developmental toxicity, meeting the criteria for classification as toxic for reproduction category 1A or 1B: May damage the unborn child (H360D), and the available data are adequate to support a robust risk assessment, then no further testing for developmental toxicity will be necessary. However, testing for effects on fertility must be considered. ◄

▼C1

COLUMN 1 STANDARD INFORMATION REQUIRED	COLUMN 2 SPECIFIC RULES FOR ADAPTATION FROM COLUMN 1
8.7.2. Pre-natal developmental toxicity study, one species, most appropriate route of administration, having regard to the likely route of human exposure (B.31 of the Commission Regulation on test methods as specified in Article 13(3) or OECD 414).	8.7.2. The study shall be initially performed on one species. A decision on the need to perform a study at this tonnage level or the next on a second species should be based on the outcome of the first test and all other relevant available data.
8.7.3. Two-generation reproductive toxicity study, one species, male and female, most appropriate route of administration, having regard to the likely route of human exposure, if the 28-day or 90-day study indicates adverse effects on reproductive organs or tissues.	8.7.3. The study shall be initially performed on one species. A decision on the need to perform a study at this tonnage level or the next on a second species should be based on the outcome of the first test and all other relevant available date.

9.   ECOTOXICOLOGICAL INFORMATION

COLUMN 1 STANDARD INFORMATION REQUIRED	COLUMN 2 SPECIFIC RULES FOR ADAPTATION FROM COLUMN 1
9.1. Aquatic toxicity	9.1. Long-term toxicity testing shall be proposed by the registrant if the chemical safety assessment according to Annex I indicates the need to investigate further the effects on aquatic organisms. The choice of the appropriate test(s) depends on the results of the chemical safety assessment.
9.1.5. Long-term toxicity testing on invertebrates (preferred species Daphnia), (unless already provided as part of Annex VII requirements)	
9.1.6. Long-term toxicity testing on fish, (unless already provided as part of Annex VIII requirements) The information shall be provided for one of the Sections 9.1.6.1, 9.1.6.2 or 9.1.6.3.	

▼C1

COLUMN 1 STANDARD INFORMATION REQUIRED	COLUMN 2 SPECIFIC RULES FOR ADAPTATION FROM COLUMN 1
9.1.6.1. Fish early-life stage (FELS) toxicity test	
9.1.6.2. Fish short-term toxicity test on embryo and sac-fry stages	
9.1.6.3. Fish, juvenile growth test	
9.2. Degradation	9.2. Further biotic degradation testing shall be proposed by the registrant if the chemical safety assessment according to Annex I indicates the need to investigate further the degradation of the substance and its degradation products. The choice of the appropriate test(s) depends on the results of the chemical safety assessment and may include simulation testing in appropriate media (e.g. water, sediment or soil).
9.2.1. Biotic	
9.2.1.2. Simulation testing on ultimate degradation in surface water	9.2.1.2. The study need not be conducted if: — the substances is highly insoluble in water, or — the substance is readily biodegradable.
9.2.1.3. Soil simulation testing (for substances with a high potential for adsorption to soil)	9.2.1.3. The study need not be conducted: — if the substance is readily biodegradable, or — if direct and indirect exposure of soil is unlikely.
9.2.1.4. Sediment simulation testing (for substances with a high potential for adsorption to sediment)	9.2.1.4. The study need not be conducted: — if the substance is readily biodegradable, or — if direct and indirect exposure of sediment is unlikely.
9.2.3. Identification of degradation products	9.2.3. Unless the substance is readily biodegradable
9.3. Fate and behaviour in the environment	
9.3.2. Bioaccumulation in aquatic species, preferably fish	9.3.2. The study need not be conducted if: — the substance has a low potential for bioaccumulation (for instance a log $K_{ow} \leq 3$) and/or a low potential to cross biological membranes, or — direct and indirect exposure of the aquatic compartment is unlikely.
9.3.3. Further information on adsorption/desorption depending on the results of the study required in Annex VIII	9.3.3. The study need not be conducted if: — based on the physicochemical properties the substance can be expected to have a low potential for adsorption (e.g. the substance has a low octanol water partition coefficient), or — the substance and its degradation products decompose rapidly.

▼C1

COLUMN 1 STANDARD INFORMATION REQUIRED	COLUMN 2 SPECIFIC RULES FOR ADAPTATION FROM COLUMN 1
9.4. Effects on terrestrial organisms	9.4. These studies do not need to be conducted if direct and indirect exposure of the soil compartment is unlikely. In the absence of toxicity data for soil organisms, the equilibrium partitioning method may be applied to assess the hazard to soil organisms. The choice of the appropriate tests depends on the outcome of the chemical safety assessment. In particular for substances that have a high potential to adsorb to soil or that are very persistent, the registrant shall consider long-term toxicity testing instead of short-term.
9.4.1. Short-term toxicity to invertebrates	
9.4.2. Effects on soil micro-organisms	
9.4.3. Short-term toxicity to plants	

10.   METHODS OF DETECTION AND ANALYSIS

Description of the analytical methods shall be provided on request, for the relevant compartments for which studies were performed using the analytical method concerned. If the analytical methods are not available this shall be justified.

▼C1

STANDARD INFORMATION REQUIREMENTS FOR SUBSTANCES MANUFACTURED OR IMPORTED IN QUANTITIES OF 1 000 TONNES OR MORE (¹)

At the level of this Annex, the registrant must submit a proposal and a time schedule for fulfilling the information requirements of this Annex in accordance with Article 12(1)(e).

Column 1 of this Annex establishes the standard information required for all substances manufactured or imported in quantities of 1 000 tonnes or more in accordance with Article 12(1)(e). Accordingly, the information required in column 1 of this Annex is additional to that required in column 1 of Annexes VII, VIII and IX. Any other relevant physicochemical, toxicological and ecotoxicological information that is available shall be provided. Column 2 of this Annex lists specific rules according to which the registrant may propose to omit the required standard information, replace it by other information, provide it at a later stage or adapt it in another way. If the conditions are met under which column 2 of this Annex allows an adaptation to be proposed, the registrant shall clearly state this fact and the reasons for proposing each adaptation under the appropriate headings in the registration dossier.

In addition to these specific rules, a registrant may propose to adapt the required standard information set out in column 1 of this Annex according to the general rules contained in Annex XI. In this case as well, he shall clearly state the reasons for any decision to propose adaptations to the standard information under the appropriate headings in the registration dossier referring to the appropriate specific rule(s) in column 2 or in Annex XI (²).

Before new tests are carried out to determine the properties listed in this Annex, all available *in vitro* data, *in vivo* data, historical human data, data from valid (Q)SARs and data from structurally related substances (read-across approach) shall be assessed first. *In vivo* testing with corrosive substances at concentration/-dose levels causing corrosivity shall be avoided. Prior to testing, further guidance on testing strategies should be consulted in addition to this Annex.

When, for certain endpoints, it is proposed not to provide information for other reasons than those mentioned in column 2 of this Annex or in Annex XI, this fact and the reasons shall also be clearly stated.

(¹) This Annex shall apply to producers of articles that are required to register in accordance with Article 7 and to other downstream users that are required to carry out tests under this Regulation adapted as necessary.
(²) Note: conditions for not requiring a specific test that are set out in the appropriate test methods in the Commission Regulation on test methods as specified in Article 13(3) that are not repeated in column 2, also apply.

▼C1

8.   TOXICOLOGICAL INFORMATION

COLUMN 1 STANDARD INFORMATION REQUIRED	COLUMN 2 SPECIFIC RULES FOR ADAPTATION FROM COLUMN 1
	8.4. If there is a positive result in any of the *in vitro* genotoxicity studies in Annexes VII or VIII, a second *in vivo* somatic cell test may be necessary, depending on the quality and relevance of all the available data. If there is a positive result from an *in vivo* somatic cell study available, the potential for germ cell mutagenicity should be considered on the basis of all available data, including toxicokinetic evidence. If no clear conclusions about germ cell mutagenicity can be made, additional investigations shall be considered.
	8.6.3. A long-term repeated toxicity study (≥ 12 months) may be proposed by the registrant or required by the Agency in accordance with Articles 40 or 41 if the frequency and duration of human exposure indicates that a longer term study is appropriate and one of the following conditions is met: — serious or severe toxicity effects of particular concern were observed in the 28-day or 90-day study for which the available evidence is inadequate for toxicological evaluation or risk characterisation, or — effects shown in substances with a clear relationship in molecular structure with the substance being studied were not detected in the 28-day or 90-day study, or — the substance may have a dangerous property that cannot be detected in a 90-day study.
	8.6.4. Further studies shall be proposed by the registrant or may be required by the Agency in accordance with Articles 40 or 41 in case of: — toxicity of particular concern (e.g. serious/severe effects), or — indications of an effect for which the available evidence is inadequate for toxicological evaluation and/or risk characterisation. In such cases it may also be more appropriate to perform specific toxicological studies that are designed to investigate these effects (e.g. immunotoxicity, neurotoxicity), or — particular concern regarding exposure (e.g. use in consumer products leading to exposure levels which are close to the dose levels at which toxicity is observed).

▼C1

COLUMN 1 STANDARD INFORMATION REQUIRED	COLUMN 2 SPECIFIC RULES FOR ADAPTATION FROM COLUMN 1
8.7. Reproductive toxicity	8.7. The studies need not be conducted if: — the substance is known to be a genotoxic carcinogen and appropriate risk management measures are implemented, or — the substance is known to be a germ cell mutagen and appropriate risk management measures are implemented, or — the substance is of low toxicological activity (no evidence of toxicity seen in any of the tests available), it can be proven from toxicokinetic data that no systemic absorption occurs via relevant routes of exposure (e.g. plasma/blood concentrations below detection limit using a sensitive method and absence of the substance and of metabolites of the substance in urine, bile or exhaled air) and there is no or no significant human exposure. ▶**M3** If a substance is known to have an adverse effect on fertility, meeting the criteria for classification as toxic for reproduction category 1A or 1B: May damage fertility (H360F), and the available data are adequate to support a robust risk assessment, then no further testing for fertility will be necessary. However, testing for developmental toxicity must be considered. If a substance is known to cause developmental toxicity, meeting the criteria for classification as toxic for reproduction category 1A or 1B: May damage the unborn child (H360D), and the available data are adequate to support a robust risk assessment, then no further testing for developmental toxicity will be necessary. However, testing for effects on fertility must be considered. ◀
8.7.2. Developmental toxicity study, one species, most appropriate route of administration, having regard to the likely route of human exposure (OECD 414).	
8.7.3. Two-generation reproductive toxicity study, one species, male and female, most appropriate route of administration, having regard to the likely route of human exposure, unless already provided as part of Annex IX requirements	

▼C1

COLUMN 1 STANDARD INFORMATION REQUIRED	COLUMN 2 SPECIFIC RULES FOR ADAPTATION FROM COLUMN 1
8.9.1. Carcinogenicity study	8.9.1. A carcinogenicity study may be proposed by the registrant or may be required by the Agency in accordance with Articles 40 or 41 if: — the substance has a widespread dispersive use or there is evidence of frequent or long-term human exposure, and ►M3 — the substance is classified as germ cell mutagen category 2 or there is evidence from the repeated dose study(ies) that the substance is able to induce hyperplasia and/or pre-neoplastic lesions. ◄ ►M3 If the substance is classified as germ cell mutagen category 1A or 1B, the default presumption would be that a genotoxic mechanism for carcinogenicity is likely. In these cases, a carcinogenicity test will normally not be required. ◄

9.   ECOTOXICOLOGICAL INFORMATION

COLUMN 1 STANDARD INFORMATION REQUIRED	COLUMN 2 SPECIFIC RULES FOR ADAPTATION FROM COLUMN 1
9.2. Degradation	9.2. Further biotic degradation testing shall be proposed if the chemical safety assessment according to Annex I indicates the need to investigate further the degradation of the substance and its degradation products. The choice of the appropriate test(s) depends on the results of the chemical safety assessment and may include simulation testing in appropriate media (e.g. water, sediment or soil).
9.2.1. Biotic	
9.3. Fate and behaviour in the environment	
9.3.4. Further information on the environmental fate and behaviour of the substance and/or degradation products	9.3.4. Further testing shall be proposed by the registrant or may be required by the Agency in accordance with Articles 40 or 41 if the chemical safety assessment according to Annex I indicates the need to investigate further the fate and behaviour of the substance. The choice of the appropriate test(s) depends on the results of the chemical safety assessment.
9.4. Effects on terrestrial organisms	9.4. Long-term toxicity testing shall be proposed by the registrant if the results of the chemical safety assessment according to Annex I indicates the need to investigate further the effects of the substance and/or degradation products on terrestrial organisms. The choice of the appropriate test(s) depends on the outcome of the chemical safety assessment. These studies do not need to be conducted if direct and indirect exposure of the soil compartment is unlikely.

▼C1

COLUMN 1 STANDARD INFORMATION REQUIRED	COLUMN 2 SPECIFIC RULES FOR ADAPTATION FROM COLUMN 1
9.4.4. Long-term toxicity testing on invertebrates, unless already provided as part of Annex IX requirements.	
9.4.6. Long-term toxicity testing on plants, unless already provided as part of Annex IX requirements.	
9.5.1. Long-term toxicity to sediment organisms	9.5.1. Long-term toxicity testing shall be proposed by the registrant if the results of the chemical safety assessment indicates the need to investigate further the effects of the substance and/or relevant degradation products on sediment organisms. The choice of the appropriate test(s) depends on the results of the chemical safety assessment.
9.6.1. Long-term or reproductive toxicity to birds	9.6.1. Any need for testing should be carefully considered taking into account the large mammalian dataset that is usually available at this tonnage level.

10.   METHODS OF DETECTION AND ANALYSIS

Description of the analytical methods shall be provided on request, for the relevant compartments for which studies were performed using the analytical method concerned. If the analytical methods are not available this shall be justified.

▼C1

ANNEX XI

GENERAL RULES FOR ADAPTATION OF THE STANDARD TESTING REGIME SET OUT IN ANNEXES VII TO X

Annexes VII to X set out the information requirements for all substances manufactured or imported in quantities of:

— one tonne or more in accordance with Article 12(1)(a),

— 10 tonnes or more in accordance with Article 12(1)(c),

— 100 tonnes or more in accordance with Article 12(1)(d), and

— 1 000 tonnes or more in accordance with Article 12(1)(e).

In addition to the specific rules set out in column 2 of Annexes VII to X, a registrant may adapt the standard testing regime in accordance with the general rules set out in Section 1 of this Annex. Under dossier evaluation the Agency may assess these adaptations to the standard testing regime.

1. TESTING DOES NOT APPEAR SCIENTIFICALLY NECESSARY

1.1. **Use of existing data**

1.1.1. *Data on physical-chemical properties from experiments not carried out according to GLP or the test methods referred to in Article 13(3)*

Data shall be considered to be equivalent to data generated by the corresponding test methods referred to in Article 13(3) if the following conditions are met:

(1) adequacy for the purpose of classification and labelling and/or risk assessment;

(2) sufficient documentation is provided to assess the adequacy of the study; and

(3) the data are valid for the endpoint being investigated and the study is performed using an acceptable level of quality assurance.

1.1.2. *Data on human health and environmental properties from experiments not carried out according to GLP or the test methods referred to in Article 13(3)*

Data shall be considered to be equivalent to data generated by the corresponding test methods referred to in Article 13(3) if the following conditions are met:

(1) adequacy for the purpose of classification and labelling and/or risk assessment;

(2) adequate and reliable coverage of the key parameters foreseen to be investigated in the corresponding test methods referred to in Article 13(3);

(3) exposure duration comparable to or longer than the corresponding test methods referred to in Article 13(3) if exposure duration is a relevant parameter; and

(4) adequate and reliable documentation of the study is provided.

1.1.3. *Historical human data*

Historical human data, such as epidemiological studies on exposed populations, accidental or occupational exposure data and clinical studies, shall be considered.

▼C1

The strength of the data for a specific human health effect depends, among other things, on the type of analysis and on the parameters covered and on the magnitude and specificity of the response and consequently the predictability of the effect. Criteria for assessing the adequacy of the data include:

(1) the proper selection and characterisation of the exposed and control groups;

(2) adequate characterisation of exposure;

(3) sufficient length of follow-up for disease occurrence;

(4) valid method for observing an effect;

(5) proper consideration of bias and confounding factors; and

(6) a reasonable statistical reliability to justify the conclusion.

In all cases adequate and reliable documentation shall be provided.

1.2. **Weight of evidence**

There may be sufficient weight of evidence from several independent sources of information leading to the assumption/conclusion that a substance has or has not a particular dangerous property, while the information from each single source alone is regarded insufficient to support this notion.

There may be sufficient weight of evidence from the use of newly developed test methods, not yet included in the test methods referred to in Article 13(3) or from an international test method recognised by the Commission or the Agency as being equivalent, leading to the conclusion that a substance has or has not a particular dangerous property.

Where sufficient weight of evidence for the presence or absence of a particular dangerous property is available:

— further testing on vertebrate animals for that property shall be omitted,

— further testing not involving vertebrate animals may be omitted.

In all cases adequate and reliable documentation shall be provided.

1.3. **Qualitative or Quantitative structure-activity relationship ((Q)SAR)**

Results obtained from valid qualitative or quantitative structure-activity relationship models ((Q)SARs) may indicate the presence or absence of a certain dangerous property. Results of (Q)SARs may be used instead of testing when the following conditions are met:

— results are derived from a (Q)SAR model whose scientific validity has been established,

— the substance falls within the applicability domain of the (Q)SAR model,

— results are adequate for the purpose of classification and labelling and/or risk assessment, and

— adequate and reliable documentation of the applied method is provided.

The Agency in collaboration with the Commission, Member States and interested parties shall develop and provide guidance in assessing which (Q)SARs will meet these conditions and provide examples.

▼C1

1.4. *In vitro* methods

Results obtained from suitable *in vitro* methods may indicate the presence of a certain dangerous property or may be important in relation to a mechanistic understanding, which may be important for the assessment. In this context, 'suitable' means sufficiently well developed according to internationally agreed test development criteria (e.g. the European Centre for the Validation of Alternative Methods (ECVAM)) criteria for the entry of a test into the prevalidation process). Depending on the potential risk, immediate confirmation requiring testing beyond the information foreseen in Annexes VII or VIII or proposed confirmation requiring testing beyond the information foreseen in Annexes IX or X for the respective tonnage level may be necessary.

If the results obtained from the use of such *in vitro* methods do not indicate a certain dangerous property, the relevant test shall nevertheless be carried out at the appropriate tonnage level to confirm the negative result, unless testing is not required in accordance with Annexes VII to X or the other rules in this Annex.

Such confirmation may be waived, if the following conditions are met:

(1) results are derived from an *in vitro* method whose scientific validity has been established by a validation study, according to internationally agreed validation principles;

(2) results are adequate for the purpose of classification and labelling and/or risk assessment; and

(3) adequate and reliable documentation of the applied method is provided.

1.5. **Grouping of substances and read-across approach**

Substances whose physicochemical, toxicological and ecotoxicological properties are likely to be similar or follow a regular pattern as a result of structural similarity may be considered as a group, or 'category' of substances. Application of the group concept requires that physicochemical properties, human health effects and environmental effects or environmental fate may be predicted from data for reference substance(s) within the group by interpolation to other substances in the group (read-across approach). This avoids the need to test every substance for every endpoint. The Agency, after consulting with relevant stakeholders and other interested parties, shall issue guidance on technically and scientifically justified methodology for the grouping of substances sufficiently in advance of the first registration deadline for phase-in substances.

The similarities may be based on:

(1) a common functional group;

(2) the common precursors and/or the likelihood of common breakdown products via physical and biological processes, which result in structurally similar chemicals; or

(3) a constant pattern in the changing of the potency of the properties across the category.

If the group concept is applied, substances shall be classified and labelled on this basis.

▼__C1__

In all cases results should:

— be adequate for the purpose of classification and labelling and/or risk assessment,

— have adequate and reliable coverage of the key parameters addressed in the corresponding test method referred to in Article 13(3),

— cover an exposure duration comparable to or longer than the corresponding test method referred to in Article 13(3) if exposure duration is a relevant parameter, and

— adequate and reliable documentation of the applied method shall be provided.

2. TESTING IS TECHNICALLY NOT POSSIBLE

Testing for a specific endpoint may be omitted, if it is technically not possible to conduct the study as a consequence of the properties of the substance: e.g. very volatile, highly reactive or unstable substances cannot be used, mixing of the substance with water may cause danger of fire or explosion or the radio-labelling of the substance required in certain studies may not be possible. The guidance given in the test methods referred to in Article 13(3), more specifically on the technical limitations of a specific method, shall always be respected.

▼__M4__

3. SUBSTANCE-TAILORED EXPOSURE-DRIVEN TESTING

3.1. Testing in accordance with Sections 8.6 and 8.7 of Annex VIII and in accordance with Annex IX and Annex X may be omitted, based on the exposure scenario(s) developed in the Chemical Safety Report.

3.2. In all cases, adequate justification and documentation shall be provided. The justification shall be based on a thorough and rigorous exposure assessment in accordance with section 5 of Annex I and shall meet any one of the following criteria:

(a) the manufacturer or importer demonstrates and documents that all of the following conditions are fulfilled:

(i) the results of the exposure assessment covering all relevant exposures throughout the life cycle of the substance demonstrate the absence of or no significant exposure in all scenarios of the manufacture and all identified uses as referred to in Annex VI section 3.5;

(ii) a DNEL or a PNEC can be derived from results of available test data for the substance concerned taking full account of the increased uncertainty resulting from the omission of the information requirement, and that DNEL or PNEC is relevant and appropriate both to the information requirement to be omitted and for risk assessment purposes ([1]);

([1]) For the purpose of subparagraph 3.2(a)(ii), without prejudice to column 2 of Section 8.7 of Annexes IX and X, a DNEL derived from a screening test for reproductive/developmental toxicity shall not be considered appropriate to omit a prenatal developmental toxicity study or a two-generation reproductive toxicity study. For the purpose of subparagraph 3.2(a)(ii), without prejudice to column 2 of section 8.6 of Annexes IX and X, a DNEL derived from a 28-day repeated dose toxicity study shall not be considered appropriate to omit a 90-day repeated dose toxicity study.

▼__M4__

      (iii) the comparison of the derived DNEL or PNEC with the results of the exposure assessment shows that exposures are always well below the derived DNEL or PNEC;

    (b) where the substance is not incorporated in an article the manufacturer or importer demonstrates and documents for all relevant scenarios that throughout the life cycle strictly controlled conditions as set out in Article 18(4)(a) to (f) apply;

    (c) where the substance is incorporated in an article in which it is permanently embedded in a matrix or otherwise rigorously contained by technical means, it is demonstrated and documented that all of the following conditions are fulfilled:

      (i) the substance is not released during its life cycle;

      (ii) the likelihood that workers or the general public or the environment are exposed to the substance under normal or reasonably foreseeable conditions of use is negligible; and

      (iii) the substance is handled according to the conditions set out in Article 18(4)(a) to (f) during all manufacturing and production stages including the waste management of the substance during these stages.

3.3.   The specific conditions of use must be communicated through the supply chain in accordance with Article 31 or 32, as the case may be.

▼C1

GENERAL PROVISIONS FOR DOWNSTREAM USERS TO ASSESS SUBSTANCES AND PREPARE CHEMICAL SAFETY REPORTS

INTRODUCTION

The purpose of this Annex is to set out how downstream users are to assess and document that the risks arising from the substance(s) they use are adequately controlled during their use for a use not covered by the Safety Data Sheet supplied to them and that other users further down the supply chain can adequately control the risks. The assessment shall cover the life-cycle of the substance, from its receipt by the downstream user, for his own uses and for his identified uses further down the supply chain. The assessment shall consider the use of the substance on its own, in a ►**M3** mixture ◄ or in an article.

In carrying out the chemical safety assessment and producing the Chemical Safety Report, the downstream user shall take account of information received from the supplier of the chemical in accordance with Article 31 and 32 of this Regulation. Where available and appropriate, an assessment carried out under Community legislation, (e.g. risk assessments completed under Regulation (EEC) No 793/93) shall be taken into account in the chemical safety assessment and be reflected in the Chemical Safety Report. Deviations from such assessments shall be justified. Assessments carried out under other international and national programmes may also be taken into account.

The process which the downstream user goes through in carrying out the chemical safety assessment and in producing his Chemical Safety Report, involves three steps:

STEP 1: DEVELOPMENT OF EXPOSURE SCENARIO(S)

The downstream user shall develop exposure scenarios for uses not covered in a Safety Data Sheet supplied to him in accordance with Section 5 of Annex I.

STEP 2: IF NECESSARY, A REFINEMENT OF THE HAZARD ASSESSMENT BY THE SUPPLIER

If the downstream user considers the hazard and PBT assessments reported in the Safety Data Sheet supplied to him to be appropriate, then no further hazard assessment or PBT and vPvB assessment is necessary. In this case he shall use the relevant information reported by the supplier for the risk characterisation. This shall be stated in the Chemical Safety Report.

If the downstream user considers the assessments reported in the Safety Data Sheet supplied to him to be inappropriate, then he shall carry out the relevant assessments in accordance with Sections 1 to 4 of Annex I as appropriate to him.

In those cases where the downstream user considers that information in addition to that provided by the supplier is necessary for producing his Chemical Safety Report the downstream user shall gather this information. Where this information can only be obtained by testing on vertebrate animals, he shall submit a proposal for a testing strategy to the Agency in accordance with Article 38. He shall explain why he considers that additional information is necessary. While waiting for results of further testing, he shall record in his chemical safety report the risk management measures intended to manage the risks being explored that he has put in place.

▼C1

On completion of any additional testing, the downstream user shall revise the Chemical Safety Report, and his Safety Data Sheet if he is required to prepare one, as appropriate.

STEP 3: RISK CHARACTERISATION

A risk characterisation shall be carried out for each new exposure scenario as prescribed in Section 6 of Annex I. The risk characterisation shall be presented under the relevant heading of the Chemical Safety Report and summarised in the Safety Data Sheet under the relevant heading(s).

When generating an exposure scenario it will be necessary to make initial assumptions about the operating conditions and risk managements measures. If the initial assumptions lead to a risk characterisation indicating inadequate protection of human health and the environment, then it shall be necessary to carry out an iterative process with amendment of one or a number of factors until adequate control can be demonstrated. This may require the generation of additional hazard or exposure information or appropriate alteration of the process, operating conditions or risk management measures. Therefore, iterations may be made between on the one hand developing and revising an (initial) exposure scenario, which includes developing and implementing risk management measures, and on the other hand generating further information to produce the definitive exposure scenario. The purpose of generating further information is to establish a more precise risk characterisation, based on a refined hazard assessment and/or exposure assessment.

The downstream user shall produce a Chemical Safety Report detailing his chemical safety assessment using Part B, Sections 9 and 10, of the format set out in Section 7 of Annex I and the other sections of this format, if appropriate.

Part A of the Chemical Safety Report shall include a declaration that the risk management measures outlined in the relevant exposure scenarios are implemented by the downstream user for his own uses and that the risk management measures outlined in the exposure scenarios for the identified uses are communicated down the supply chain.

ANNEX XIII

CRITERIA FOR THE IDENTIFICATION OF PERSISTENT, BIOACCUMULATIVE AND TOXIC SUBSTANCES, AND VERY PERSISTENT AND VERY BIOACCUMULATIVE SUBSTANCES

This Annex lays down the criteria for the identification of persistent, bioaccumulative and toxic substances (PBT substances), and very persistent and very bioaccumulative substances (vPvB substances) as well as the information that must be considered for the purpose of assessing the P, B, and T properties of a substance.

For the identification of PBT substances and vPvB substances a weight-of-evidence determination using expert judgement shall be applied, by comparing all relevant and available information listed in Section 3.2 with the criteria set out in Section 1. This shall be applied in particular where the criteria set out in Section 1 cannot be applied directly to the available information.

A weight-of-evidence determination means that all available information bearing on the identification of a PBT or a vPvB substance is considered together, such as the results of monitoring and modelling, suitable in vitro tests, relevant animal data, information from the application of the category approach (grouping, read-across), (Q)SAR results, human experience such as occupational data and data from accident databases, epidemiological and clinical studies and well documented case reports and observations. The quality and consistency of the data shall be given appropriate weight. The available results regardless of their individual conclusions shall be assembled together in a single weight-of-evidence determination.

The information used for the purposes of assessment of the PBT/vPvB properties shall be based on data obtained under relevant conditions.

The identification shall also take account of the PBT/vPvB-properties of relevant constituents of a substance and relevant transformation and/or degradation products.

This Annex shall apply to all organic substances, including organo-metals.

1. CRITERIA FOR THE IDENTIFICATION OF PBT AND vPvB SUBSTANCES

1.1. PBT Substances

A substance that fulfils the persistence, bioaccumulation and toxicity criteria of Sections 1.1.1, 1.1.2 and 1.1.3 shall be considered to be a PBT substance.

1.1.1. Persistence

A substance fulfils the persistence criterion (P) in any of the following situations:

(a) the degradation half-life in marine water is higher than 60 days;

(b) the degradation half-life in fresh or estuarine water is higher than 40 days;

(c) the degradation half-life in marine sediment is higher than 180 days;

(d) the degradation half-life in fresh or estuarine water sediment is higher than 120 days;

(e) the degradation half-life in soil is higher than 120 days.

▼M11

1.1.2. Bioaccumulation

A substance fulfils the bioaccumulation criterion (B) when the bioconcentration factor in aquatic species is higher than 2 000.

1.1.3. Toxicity

A substance fulfils the toxicity criterion (T) in any of the following situations:

(a) the long-term no-observed effect concentration (NOEC) or EC10 for marine or freshwater organisms is less than 0,01 mg/l;

(b) the substance meets the criteria for classification as carcinogenic (category 1A or 1B), germ cell mutagenic (category 1A or 1B), or toxic for reproduction (category 1A, 1B, or 2) according to Regulation EC No 1272/2008;

(c) there is other evidence of chronic toxicity, as identified by the substance meeting the criteria for classification: specific target organ toxicity after repeated exposure (STOT RE category 1 or 2) according to Regulation EC No 1272/2008.

1.2. vPvB Substances

A substance that fulfils the persistence and bioaccumulation criteria of Sections 1.2.1 and 1.2.2 shall be considered to be a vPvB substance.

1.2.1. Persistence

A substance fulfils the 'very persistent' criterion (vP) in any of the following situations:

(a) the degradation half-life in marine, fresh or estuarine water is higher than 60 days;

(b) the degradation half-life in marine, fresh or estuarine water sediment is higher than 180 days;

(c) the degradation half-life in soil is higher than 180 days.

1.2.2. Bioaccumulation

A substance fulfils the 'very bioaccumulative' criterion (vB) when the bioconcentration factor in aquatic species is higher than 5 000.

2. SCREENING AND ASSESSMENT OF P, vP, B, vB and T PROPERTIES

2.1. Registration

For the identification of PBT and vPvB substances in the registration dossier, the registrant shall consider the information as described in Annex I and in Section 3 of this Annex.

If the technical dossier contains for one or more endpoints only information as required in Annexes VII and VIII, the registrant shall consider information relevant for screening for P, B, or T properties in accordance with Section 3.1 of this Annex. If the result from the screening tests or other information indicate that the substance may have PBT or vPvB properties, the registrant shall generate relevant additional information as set out in Section 3.2 of this Annex. In case the generation of relevant additional information would require information listed in Annexes IX or X, the registrant shall submit a testing proposal. Where the process and use conditions of the substance meet the conditions as specified in Section 3.2(b) or (c) of Annex XI the additional information may be omitted, and subsequently the substance is considered as if it is a PBT or vPvB in the registration dossier. No additional information needs to be generated for the assessment of PBT/vPvB properties if there is no indication of P or B properties following the result from the screening test or other information.

▼M11

2.2. Authorisation

For dossiers for the purposes of identifying substances referred to in Article 57(d) and Article 57(e), relevant information from the registration dossiers and other available information as described in Section 3 shall be considered.

3. INFORMATION RELEVANT FOR THE SCREENING AND ASSESSMENT OF P, vP, B, vB and T PROPERTIES

3.1. Screening Information

The following information shall be considered for screening for P, vP, B, vB and T properties in the cases referred to in the second paragraph of Section 2.1 and may be considered for screening for P, vP, B, vB and T properties in the context of Section 2.2.

3.1.1. Indication of P and vP properties

(a) Results from tests on ready biodegradation in accordance with Section 9.2.1.1 of Annex VII;

(b) Results from other screening tests (e.g. enhanced ready test, tests on inherent biodegradability);

(c) Results obtained from biodegradation (Q)SAR models in accordance with Section 1.3 of Annex XI;

(d) Other information provided that its suitability and reliability can be reasonably demonstrated.

3.1.2. Indication of B and vB properties

(a) Octanol-water partitioning coefficient experimentally determined in accordance with Section 7.8 of Annex VII or estimated by (Q)SAR models in accordance with Section 1.3 of Annex XI;

(b) Other information provided that its suitability and reliability can be reasonably demonstrated.

3.1.3. Indication of T properties

(a) Short-term aquatic toxicity in accordance with Section 9.1 of Annex VII and Section 9.1.3 of Annex VIII;

(b) Other information provided that its suitability and reliability can be reasonably demonstrated.

3.2. Assessment Information

The following information shall be considered for the assessment of P, vP, B, vB and T properties, using a weight-of-evidence approach.

3.2.1. Assessment of P or vP properties

(a) Results from simulation testing on degradation in surface water;

(b) Results from simulation testing on degradation in soil;

(c) Results from simulation testing on degradation in sediment;

(d) Other information, such as information from field studies or monitoring studies, provided that its suitability and reliability can be reasonably demonstrated.

▼ M11

3.2.2. Assessment of B or vB properties

(a) Results from a bioconcentration or bioaccumulation study in aquatic species;

(b) Other information on the bioaccumulation potential provided that its suitability and reliability can be reasonably demonstrated, such as:

— Results from a bioaccumulation study in terrestrial species;

— Data from scientific analysis of human body fluids or tissues, such as blood, milk, or fat;

— Detection of elevated levels in biota, in particular in endangered species or in vulnerable populations, compared to levels in their surrounding environment;

— Results from a chronic toxicity study on animals;

— Assessment of the toxicokinetic behaviour of the substance;

(c) Information on the ability of the substance to biomagnify in the food chain, where possible expressed by biomagnification factors or trophic magnification factors.

3.2.3. Assessment of T properties

(a) Results from long-term toxicity testing on invertebrates as set out in Section 9.1.5 of Annex IX;

(b) Results from long-term toxicity testing on fish as set out in Section 9.1.6 of Annex IX;

(c) Results from growth inhibition study on aquatic plants as set out in in Section 9.1.2 of Annex VII;

(d) The substance meeting the criteria for classification as carcinogenic in Category 1A or 1B (assigned hazard phrases: H350 or H350i), germ cell mutagenic in Category 1A or 1B (assigned hazard phrase: H340), toxic for reproduction in Category 1A, 1B and/or 2 (assigned hazard phrases: H360, H360F, H360D, H360FD, H360Fd, H360fD, H361, H361f, H361d or H361fd), specific target organ toxic after repeated dose in Category 1 or 2 (assigned hazard phrase: H372 or H373), according to Regulation EC No 1272/2008;

(e) Results from long-term or reproductive toxicity testing with birds as set out in Section 9.6.1 of Annex X;

(f) Other information provided that its suitability and reliability can be reasonably demonstrated.

▼C1

LIST OF SUBSTANCES SUBJECT TO AUTHORISATION

▼M8
▼C4

Entry Nr	Substance	Intrinsic property(ies) referred to in Article 57	Transitional arrangements		Exempted (categories of) uses	Review periods
			Latest application date (^{1})	Sunset date (^{2})		
1.	5-tert-butyl-2,4,6-trinitro-m-xylene **(Musk xylene)** EC No: 201-329-4 CAS No: 81-15-2	vPvB	21 February 2013	21 August 2014	—	—
2.	4,4'-Diaminodiphenyl-methane **(MDA)** EC No: 202-974-4 CAS No: 101-77-9	Carci-nogenic (category 1B)	21 February 2013	21 August 2014	—	—

3.	Hexabromocyclodo-decane
	
	(HBCDD)
	EC No: 221-695-9,
	       247-148-4,
	CAS No: 3194-55-6
	       25637-99-4
	alpha-hexabromocyclo-dodecane
	CAS No: 134237-50-6,
	beta-hexabromocyclodo-decane
	CAS No: 134237-51-7
	gamma-hexabromocyclo-dodecane
	CAS No: 134237-52-8
		PBT	21 February 2014	21 August 2015	—	—

4.	Bis(2-ethylhexyl) phthalate **(DEHP)** EC No: 204-211-0 CAS No: 117-81-7	Toxic for repro-duction (category 1B)	21 August 2013	21 February 2015	Uses in the immediate packaging of medicinal products covered under Regulation (EC) No 726/2004, Directive 2001/82/EC, and/or Directive 2001/83/EC.	

▼C4

Entry Nr	Substance	Intrinsic property(ies) referred to in Article 57	Transitional arrangements		Exempted (categories of) uses	Review periods
			Latest application date (¹)	Sunset date (²)		
5.	Benzyl butyl phthalate (BBP) EC No: 201-622-7 CAS No: 85-68-7	Toxic for repro-duction (category 1B)	21 August 2013	21 February 2015	Uses in the immediate packaging of medicinal products covered under Regulation (EC) No 726/2004, Directive 2001/82/EC, and/or Directive 2001/83/EC.	
6.	Dibutyl phthalate (DBP) EC No: 201-557-4 CAS No: 84-74-2	Toxic for repro-duction (category 1B)	21 August 2013	21 February 2015	Uses in the immediate packaging of medicinal products covered under Regulation (EC) No 726/2004, Directive 2001/82/EC, and/or Directive 2001/83/EC.	

▼M15

Entry Nr	Substance	Intrinsic property(ies)	Transitional arrangements		Exempted	Review
7.	Diisobutyl phthalate (DIBP) EC No: 201-553-2 CAS No: 84-69-5	Toxic for repro-duction (category 1B)	21 August 2013	21 February 2015	—	—
8.	Diarsenic trioxide EC No: 215-481-4 CAS No: 1327-53-3	Carci-nogenic (category 1A)	21 November 2013	21 May 2015	—	—
9.	Diarsenic pentaoxide EC No: 215-116-9 CAS No: 1303-28-2	Carci-nogenic (category 1A)	21 November 2013	21 May 2015	—	—
10.	Lead chromate EC No: 231-846-0 CAS No: 7758-97-6	Carci-nogenic (category 1B) Toxic for repro-duction (category 1A)	21 November 2013	21 May 2015	—	—
11.	Lead sulfochromate yellow (C.I. Pigment Yellow 34) EC No: 215-693-7 CAS No: 1344-37-2	Carci-nogenic (category 1B) Toxic for repro-duction (category 1A)	21 November 2013	21 May 2015	—	—

▼__M15__

Entry Nr	Substance	Intrinsic property(ies) referred to in Article 57	Transitional arrangements		Exempted (categories of) uses	Review periods
			Latest application date (^{1})	Sunset date (^{2})		
12.	Lead chromate molybdate sulphate red (C.I. Pigment Red 104) EC No: 235-759-9 CAS No: 12656-85-8	Carci-nogenic (category 1B) Toxic for repro-duction (category 1A)	21 November 2013	21 May 2015		
13.	Tris (2-chloroethyl) phosphate (TCEP) EC No: 204-118-5 CAS No: 115-96-8	Toxic for repro-duction (category 1B)	21 February 2014	21 August 2015		
14.	2,4-Dinitrotoluene (2,4-DNT) EC No: 204-450-0 CAS No: 121-14-2	Carci-nogenic (category 1B)	21 February 2014	21 August 2015		

▼__C4__

(^{1}) Date referred to in Article 58(1)(c)(ii) of Regulation (EC) No 1907/2006.
(^{2}) Date referred to in Article 58(1)(c)(i) of Regulation (EC) No 1907/2006.

▼C1

ANNEX XV

DOSSIERS

I.   INTRODUCTION AND GENERAL PROVISIONS

This Annex lays down general principles for preparing dossiers to propose and justify:

▼M3

———————

— the identification of CMRs, PBTs, vPvBs, or a substance of equivalent concern in accordance with Article 59,

▼C1

— restrictions of the manufacture, placing on the market or use of a substance within the Community.

The relevant parts of Annex I shall be used for the methodology and format of any dossier according to this Annex.

For all dossiers any relevant information from registration dossiers shall be considered and other available information may be used. For hazard information which has not been previously submitted to the Agency, a robust study summary shall be included in the dossier.

II.   CONTENT OF DOSSIERS

▼M3

———————

▼C1

2.   Dossier for the identification of a substance as a CMR, PBT, vPvB or a substance of equivalent concern according to Article 59

Proposal

The proposal shall include the identity of substance(s) concerned and whether it is proposed to be identified as a CMR according to Article 57(a), (b) or (c), a PBT according to Article 57(d), a vPvB according to Article 57(e), or a substance of equivalent concern according to Article 57(f).

Justification

A comparison of the available information with the criteria in Annex XIII for PBT according to Article 57(d), and vPvBs according to Article 57(e), or an assessment of the hazards and a comparison with Article 57(f), according to the relevant parts of Sections 1 to 4 of Annex I shall be completed. This shall be documented in the format set out in Part B of the Chemical Safety Report in Annex I.

Information on exposures, alternative substances and risks

The available use and exposure information and information on alternative substances and techniques shall be provided.

3.   Dossiers for restrictions proposal

Proposal

The proposal shall include the identity of the substance and the restriction(s) proposed for the manufacture, placing on the market or use(s) and a summary of the justification.

▼C1

Information on hazard and risk

The risks to be addressed with the restriction shall be described based on an assessment of the hazard and risks according to the relevant parts of Annex I and shall be documented in the format set out in Part B of that Annex for the Chemical Safety Report.

Evidence shall be provided that implemented risk management measures (including those identified in registrations under Articles 10 to 14) are not sufficient.

Information on alternatives

Available information on alternative substances and techniques shall be provided, including:

— information on the risks to human health and the environment related to the manufacture or use of the alternatives,

— availability, including the time scale,

— technical and economical feasibility.

Justification for Restrictions at Community Level

Justification shall be provided that:

— action is required on a Community-wide basis,

— a restriction is the most appropriate Community wide measure which shall be assessed using the following criteria:

  (i) effectiveness: the restriction must be targeted to the effects or exposures that cause the risks identified, capable of reducing these risks to an acceptable level within a reasonable period of time and proportional to the risk;

  (ii) practicality: the restriction must be implementable, enforceable and manageable;

  (iii) monitorability: it must be possible to monitor the result of the implementation of the proposed restriction.

Socio-economic assessment

The socio-economic impacts of the proposed restriction may be analysed with reference to Annex XVI. To this end, the net benefits to human health and the environment of the proposed restriction may be compared to its net costs to manufacturers, importers, downstream users, distributors, consumers and society as a whole.

Information on stakeholder consultation

Information on any consultation of stakeholders and how their views have been taken into account shall be included in the dossier.

▼C1

ANNEX XVI

SOCIO-ECONOMIC ANALYSIS

This Annex outlines the information that may be addressed by those submitting a socio-economic analysis (SEA) with an application for authorisation, as specified in Article 62(5)(a), or in connection with a proposed restriction, as specified in Article 69(6)(b).

The Agency shall prepare guidance for the preparation of SEAs. SEAs, or contributions to them, shall be submitted in the format specified by the Agency in accordance with Article 111.

However, the level of detail and scope of the SEA, or contributions to them, shall be the responsibility of the applicant for authorisation, or, in the case of a proposed restriction, the interested party. The information provided can address the socio-economic impacts at any level.

An SEA may include the following elements:

— impact of a granted or refused authorisation on the applicant(s), or, in the case of a proposed restriction, the impact on industry (e.g. manufacturers and importers). The impact on all other actors in the supply chain, downstream users and associated businesses in terms of commercial consequences such as impact on investment, research and development, innovation, one-off and operating costs (e.g. compliance, transitional arrangements, changes to existing processes, reporting and monitoring systems, installation of new technology, etc.) taking into account general trends in the market and technology,

— impacts of a granted or refused authorisation, or a proposed restriction, on consumers. For example, product prices, changes in composition or quality or performance of products, availability of products, consumer choice, as well as effects on human health and the environment to the extent that these affect consumers,

— social implications of a granted or refused authorisation, or a proposed restriction. For example job security and employment,

— availability, suitability, and technical feasibility of alternative substances and/or technologies, and economic consequences thereof, and information on the rates of, and potential for, technological change in the sector(s) concerned. In the case of an application for authorisation, the social and/or economic impacts of using any available alternatives,

— wider implications on trade, competition and economic development (in particular for SMEs and in relation to third countries) of a granted or refused authorisation, or a proposed restriction. This may include consideration of local, regional, national or international aspects,

— in the case of a proposed restriction, proposals for other regulatory or non-regulatory measures that could meet the aim of the proposed restriction (this shall take account of existing legislation). This should include an assessment of the effectiveness and the costs linked to alternative risk management measures,

— in the case of a proposed restriction or refused authorisation, the benefits for human health and the environment as well as the social and economic benefits of the proposed restriction. For example, worker health, environmental performance and the distribution of these benefits, for example, geographically, population groups,

— an SEA may also address any other issue that is considered to be relevant by the applicant(s) or interested party.

Annex XVII

RESTRICTIONS ON THE MANUFACTURE, PLACING ON THE MARKET AND
USE OF CERTAIN DANGEROUS SUBSTANCES, MIXTURES AND ARTICLES

A reprint of the 300 pages comprising Annex was surrendered.

So far Annex XVII was corrected/amended **seven times**.

A survey on the development of Annex XVII can be found at the
Restrictions website of the European Commission

(http://ec.europa.eu/enterprise/sectors/chemicals/reach/restrictions/index_en.htm).